Essential Dads

The publisher and the University of California Press Foundation
gratefully acknowledge the generous support of the
Barbara S. Isgur Endowment Fund in Public Affairs.

Essential Dads

THE INEQUALITIES AND POLITICS
OF FATHERING

Jennifer M. Randles

UNIVERSITY OF CALIFORNIA PRESS

University of California Press
Oakland, California

Library of Congress Cataloging-in-Publication Data
Names: Randles, Jennifer M., author.
Title: Essential dads : the inequalities and politics of fathering /
    Jennifer M. Randles.
Description: Oakland, California : University of California Press,
    [2020] | Includes bibliographical references and index.
Identifiers: LCCN 2020014438 (print) | LCCN 2020014439
    (ebook) | ISBN 9780520335226 (cloth) | ISBN 9780520335233
    (paperback) | ISBN 9780520974388 (epub)
Subjects: LCSH: Fatherhood—United States—Case studies. |
    Fatherhood responsibility movement—United States—Case
    studies. | Parenting—United States—Case studies. | Equality.
Classification: LCC HQ756 .R355 2020 (print) |
    LCC HQ756 (ebook) | DDC 306.874/20973—dc23
LC record available at https://lccn.loc.gov/2020014438
LC ebook record available at https://lccn.loc.gov/2020014439

Manufactured in the United States of America

29 28 27 26 25 24 23 22 21 20
10 9 8 7 6 5 4 3 2 1

For my dad,
Bennie Randles,
who always knew the importance of being there.

Contents

1 Knowing What a Father Is

"I don't want him to grow up like I grew up. I want my son to have everything. I don't want him to be a have-not," explained Christopher.[1] Father to three-year-old Chris Jr., Christopher, a twenty-two-year-old Black man, was feeling unsteady but hopeful when we met. He was searching for a place to live, looking for a job, and planning how to get back together with Chris Jr.'s mother, Monique. "No matter how bad me and his mom disagree, or how bad other things get, I still try to be there for him because you've only got one dad. There are only two ways to keep me from being there for my son, if I'm in jail or dead."

Christopher knew the heartache of the first and had come dangerously close to the second. A former gang member who left school after the eleventh grade, Christopher was raised by his paternal grandmother in one of the poorest neighborhoods in America. When he was born, his parents struggled with homelessness and addiction. With his mother in prison, Christopher's father tried to care for him, but there was not enough money for both milk and diapers. He relinquished custody when Christopher was three months old, becoming less involved as his son grew older. With a sigh of resignation, Christopher praised his grandmother while expressing longing for a close relationship with his father:

She was an amazing parent, stuck it through no matter what. I got the clothes and food I needed. I might not have had the name brands, but I was never hungry. . . . I always said growing up that I will never be like my dad. I want [Chris Jr.] to know what a father is. I want him to be able to say, "My dad was there." I feel like I'm trying to make up for my dad's flaws in my relationship with my son, to make sure he doesn't grow up and question, "What happened to my dad?" I'm here because I want to do better, as a father and a man in general, to get it together, to be able to support my family like a man should. Because that's how I was raised. Grandma didn't teach me to be a slouch.

Incarcerated the year before for selling drugs, Christopher knew he had to find a safer way to make the money needed to support his family, one that did not involve always "looking over my shoulder" and fearing the ultimate separation from his son. He confided to me, "I'm not going to lie. The thought of doing it again has crossed my mind. But every time it does, I just push it back and think of when I had to talk to my son from across the glass on his birthday." Christopher still felt the sorrow of that isolation. "It broke my heart. I'm not an emotional person, but I cried. My son was crying, asking why he couldn't come to the other side. I couldn't answer. I knew right then, no more."

That decision led him to enroll in DADS, a government-funded "responsible fatherhood" program that provided high school completion classes, paid job training, and fathering and relationship skills education. Government promotion of responsible fatherhood, which began with the 1996 U.S. Personal Responsibility and Work Opportunity Reconciliation Act, also known as welfare reform, has targeted economically vulnerable men like Christopher whose social and financial struggles hinder their fathering aspirations. The U.S. government defines responsible fatherhood as "being present in a child's life, actively contributing to a child's healthy development, sharing economic responsibilities, and cooperating with a child's mother in addressing the full range of a child's and family's needs."[2] For fathers like Christopher—poor, homeless, unemployed, without a diploma, and bearing the stigma of a criminal record—this is a tall order. With no home and little money, Christopher could not keep Chris Jr. overnight, and he struggled to remain on good terms with Monique, who limited Christopher's contact with Chris when they fought. Still, Christopher made it a priority to see his son every day and viewed DADS as an opportunity to "get back on [his] feet" after spending Chris Jr.'s third birthday in jail.

When I asked if DADS helped him do that, he was optimistic but ambivalent. The program offered a safe way to earn $400 a month and an opportunity to finish his diploma, as well as peers and teachers who understood his struggles and treated him with respect. He wanted to prove to his grandmother and Monique that he was committed to being a better dad than his own had been and that he was a "real man" who, despite having little money to offer, could role-model hard work, perseverance, and integrity for his son. Christopher described his time in DADS as a way of ensuring that Chris Jr. would have more, especially a father he knew and admired:

> They give you the right mind frame of being able to do things. I felt good about that [DADS] certificate at the end of the day. I might not have a job, but I got up every day, I went to this class, and I attempted to do something better, to be something better. . . . I was doing something with myself instead of just running the street trying to make a couple dollars. I was actually trying to be a productive part of society. . . . We went from being on this block every day to making it to class every day. It became a priority for us, to prove our parenting.

However, as our interview continued, Christopher admitted having doubts about how much his participation in DADS actually changed his life circumstances. "We got a certificate; now what? . . . How far is two hundred dollars going to go in two weeks when you've got to buy food and clothe yourself? Unless you just plan on going out and hustling with it, what do you expect us to do?" With his DADS certificates proudly hung on his son's bedroom wall, Christopher was unsure about what he would do next.

Christopher's experience points to why responsible fatherhood policy and ideas about family and poverty that motivate it are controversial. Many view fathers like Christopher as a social problem to be solved. According to this logic, without a dad's consistent presence in the home—what many call "father absence" or "fatherlessness"—Christopher had failed to learn how to be a good father from a parent of the same gender who modeled responsible work and family behaviors. With goals to prevent poverty and to promote child well-being, programs like DADS aim to teach men about the importance of fathers and how to meet their paternal obligations. Others criticize this logic as misrepresenting the social and economic factors that shaped Christopher's life chances. They argue that a missing paternal presence did not doom him to poverty and incarceration; rather, a society in which poor children of color face racism and other overwhelming obstacles to education and well-paid jobs did.

Nevertheless, echoing narratives of father absence, Christopher acutely felt the lack of a father in his life. Though he had received all the resources and care he needed from his grandmother, Christopher felt like a "have-not" due to not having had a father in his life. Ultimately, despite his appreciation for the "amazing" grandmother who raised him, he still believed that a father is essential. Christopher's deep desire for a close relationship with a man parent is a critical policy concern and the crux of the debate over the social role of fathers. What is at stake in this debate—and more importantly, in actual families like Christopher's—is how fathering both shapes and is shaped by class, race, and gender inequalities and how policy should intervene. Given that these same inequalities influence Chris Jr.'s chances of being a "have-not," these are high stakes.

Sociological research illuminates the aspirations and challenges of marginalized fathers who struggle to be present in their children's lives.[3] Turning away from deficit understandings of fatherhood that emphasize what fathers lack and do not do for their children, this research highlights how social and economic constraints can undermine the best fathering intentions. Many poor men of color defy the stereotype of the "deadbeat dad" who deliberately neglects his parenting responsibilities. Instead, they embrace ideas of good fathering focused on time and care that seem more attainable in the context of their constraints. Responsible fatherhood policy accords with these changing meanings of men's parenting by officially emphasizing both the financial and relational aspects of fathering.[4] Yet how it does so in practice, and especially how men like Christopher make sense of these messages, has fallen outside the purview of much of this research.[5]

Most studies of fatherhood programs have focused on whether they helped fathers meet federal policy goals, such as more frequent father-child contact and increased earnings.[6] Although important, these variables miss the full sociological significance of responsible fatherhood policy and programming. While they address key policy metrics, they do not fully capture why fathers who go through these programs believe they come out with a more nurturing attitude but no better able to provide for or see their children. To fill that gap, *Essential Dads* draws on the stories of Christopher and sixty-three of his fellow DADS participants. Rather than allowing for claims of causality or program impacts, attention to fathers' narratives captures the interpretive aspects of fathering as shaped by men's experiences in a fatherhood program. These stories powerfully illuminate how policy shapes marginalized men's parenting perspectives and experiences in the context of dire economic circumstances and shifting cultural expectations of fatherhood and manhood.

The ideas men brought to and learned from DADS reveal a great deal about U.S. political understandings of how fathering is implicated in inequality, the gendered dynamics of parenting, and the importance of men as parents. From this vantage point, "responsible" fatherhood is a much more complex issue than whether or not a man financially supports and interacts with his children. It requires careful consideration of the social and economic factors shaping men's abilities to be involved in their children's lives and the ideologies that rationalize the necessity of that involvement.

With that goal in mind, this book provides new insights into what many consider one of the most pressing social problems of our time: marginalized fathers' tenuous connections to their children. It does so by answering key questions about this understudied aspect of U.S. social policy. How do men's understandings of paternal responsibility shape their engagement with fatherhood program messages and services? Does responsible fatherhood programming challenge or reinforce gendered, racialized, and classist ideas of parenting? What does this reveal about the potential for policy to create more equitable conditions for fathering? Answering these questions first requires that we understand how "irresponsible" fathering came to be seen as a social problem.

THE POLITICAL HISTORY OF "FATHERLESSNESS"

Responsible fatherhood programs emerged in the United States in the 1970s as a response to a complex set of social, economic, and political changes in family life and welfare policy.[7] Panics over the "decline" of fathering, however, go back much further. Beginning with mothers' pensions in the early twentieth century, U.S. welfare policy framed poverty as the result of family disruption, specifically the loss of a father and breadwinner. Drawing on this man-as-provider family model, cash assistance policies for poor families—consisting almost exclusively of impoverished mothers and their children—were conceptualized as a husband/father substitute.[8]

As the composition of welfare rolls changed throughout the first half of the twentieth century, race and class stereotypes converged to paint white widows as deserving of public support for doing the labor of raising children and Black single mothers as lazy, promiscuous dependents on the state. Prior to the 1940s, white widows were the majority of mothers who received welfare cash aid as compensation for deceased fathers' wages. Those who advocated for mothers' pensions argued that mothers without income because of the father's death, desertion, or unemployment deserved financial assistance from the state in exchange for the valuable public service they provided as guardians and caretakers of children. As never-married and divorced mothers, especially those who were not white, began to comprise a greater share of welfare recipients, many child and welfare policy advocates criticized the state for encouraging father absence by replacing men's expected contributions to their families with public aid.[9] Much of this concern focused on Black unmarried mothers presumed to be raising the next generation of "juvenile delinquents" without fathers who were deemed necessary to teach children mainstream family values and keep them out of poverty.[10]

Many were also concerned about how increasing industrialization reshaped fathers' family responsibilities to focus on breadwinning. Fearful that time spent away from children undermined men's family authority and that home life had become too feminized, academics emphasized that fathers were essential for children's proper gender socialization. Among the first was Sigmund Freud, whose psychoanalytic theory of gender development posited that boys needed to identify with fathers to adequately separate from mothers.[11] This idea that fathers were important as "sex role models" was dominant from the 1940s to the 1960s when experts warned that boys could become overly identified with mothers who had become primarily responsible for childcare.[12] Assuming that insecure forms of masculinity result when boys spend too little time with fathers, these theories set the stage for a highly racialized discourse of "father absence" that attributed social problems to missing Black fathers during the mid-twentieth century.

Also during this midcentury period, American women, including mothers of young children, entered the labor market in record numbers. This challenged the dominant idea of the single-earner, man-headed household, which had never been a reality for most families of color.[13] It also undercut many assumptions embedded in U.S. welfare policy. The 1965 publication of *The Negro Family: The Case for National Action* by Daniel Patrick Moynihan, then assistant secretary of the Department of Labor, ignited further controversy about the consequences of "family breakdown" and the "tangle of pathology" in African American communities.[14] Attempting to draw attention to race-based job discrimination, the report blamed African American men's economic subjugation on centuries of exploitation, fathers' marginal position in Black families, and an emasculating "matriarchal structure" born of slavery.

This narrative linking father absence and welfare dependency and attributing disproportionately higher poverty, crime, and dropout rates among men of color to missing fathers has been part of U.S. political discourse ever since. Just as Moynihan's point about racism in the labor market was lost in favor of a focus on the pathologies of Black parenting, so too has contemporary inequality been characterized primarily as a result of "broken families." This narrow and oversimplified focus on family structure as the root cause of poverty has obscured how inequality stratifies access to opportunity across lines of race, class, and gender, despite family form.

Rising rates of divorce, cohabitation, and single parenthood in the 1960s accelerated in tandem with growing costs of public aid, prompting calls for greater enforcement of private child support. Congress instituted the first major federal child support policy with bipartisan backing in 1974. Lawmakers wanted to ensure that welfare cash aid was going only to "deserving" families and not children who could receive support from fathers who lived elsewhere.[15] During the 1980s, legislators started to speak of "deadbeat dads" to describe neglectful noncustodial fathers.

"Deadbeat dad" is an example of what sociologist Patricia Hill Collins called a *controlling image*, a gendered depiction of people of color that makes poverty appear to be a result of bad personal choices.[16] Controlling images are cultural shorthands for interpreting, constructing, and stigmatizing marginalized social groups, and they inform policies designed to address social problems presumably caused by those groups. Although rhetorically race neutral, characterizations of deadbeat parents were racialized in the popular imagination, reinforcing the belief that negligent Black fathers were promiscuous, predatory, and violent, and therefore to blame for the social ills of communities of color. Increasingly punitive child support policies, including those that criminalized unpaid support, reflected the growing belief that poor non-married families of color were undeserving of public aid and that fathers who did not pay were deliberately avoiding their paternal responsibilities.[17]

These policies presaged the passage of the responsible fatherhood provisions of welfare reform in 1996. Noting that the "promotion of responsible fatherhood and motherhood is integral to successful child rearing and the well-being of children," the law cited that less than half of fathers with a child support order fully comply and that the majority of children receiving welfare benefits "now live in homes in which no father is present."[18] It listed numerous negative effects of being born "out-of-wedlock" and growing up in a "father-absent" home, including lower educational aspirations and higher rates of poverty, abuse, neglect, and school expulsion. The policy also mandated that mothers receiving cash aid establish biological paternity and that states use this information to enforce child support obligations, in part to recoup government costs of cash aid to custodial parents.

The controlling image of the deadbeat dad also played a role in the gendered implications of welfare reform.[19] A major reform goal was to counteract a perceived crisis of masculinity that prevented men from assuming their roles as family breadwinners.[20] One commentator on this purported crisis was sociologist David Popenoe, who argued that by the turn of the twentieth century, masculinity was less about self-control and family obligation—the "family protector-provider" model—and more about competition, assertiveness, and virility. Commitments to women and children, once thought to be "a central, natural, and unproblematic aspect of being a man," must now be encouraged and institutionalized through law, Popenoe claimed.[21] Many within the emergent responsible fatherhood movement advocated for programs that would harness qualities associated with troubled masculinities seen as threats to family stability.[22]

As this movement gained momentum during the 1990s, political and academic discourses about the importance of fathering focused more intensely on masculine role modeling. David Blankenhorn, founder of the Institute of American Values, argued that many major social problems result from living in a society that views fatherhood as superfluous. Without a male parent in the home, he noted, boys look to less positive role models for the meaning of their maleness. When sons must prove their manliness without the help of fathers, they purportedly overcompensate by turning to hyper or protest forms of masculinity. Drawing a direct connection between crime, misogyny, and father absence, Blankenhorn explained: "If we want to learn the identity of the rapist, the hater of women, the occupant of jail cells, we do not look first to boys with traditionally masculine fathers. We look first to boys with no fathers."[23] Involved fathers are presumably necessary to prevent what Maggie Gallagher, president of the Institute for Marriage and Public Policy, termed "father hunger." This refers to "longing for a man, not just a woman, who will care for you, protect you, and show you how to survive in the world . . . [and present] an image of maleness that is not at odds with love."[24] The importance of fathers, and by extension responsible fatherhood policies, these authors reasoned, is grounded in men's abilities to set limits, exercise masculine authority, and teach sons and daughters that they are worthy of male love.[25] Many child development experts have made similar arguments that fathers uniquely contribute to children's well-being through qualities such as masculine play styles and self-confidence.[26] Unstated in this discourse are the highly questionable assumptions that any father in the home is a positive influence, that all fathers demonstrate a similar masculine parenting style, and that children in homes without fathers lack positive role models of masculinity.

Around the time of 1990s welfare reform, sociologist Anna Gavanas found that two major wings had emerged within the responsible fatherhood movement: one focused on promoting marriage as the ideal context for involved fathering and another concerned with marginalized fathers' unemployment as a barrier to marriage and paternal involvement. The "pro-marriage" wing has drawn more on essentialist ideas of gender, while the "fragile family" arm has emphasized the impacts of racism and poverty on men's marriageability and abilities to fulfill paternal responsibilities. Dominant messages in both have strong religious undercurrents, especially calls to promote married two-parent families that include both mothers and fathers.[27] Together the two wings have articulated a shared narrative of fathers' importance to families that highlights the unique and essential contributions of men as parents.[28] As sociologist Philip Cohen has argued, claims that mothers and fathers play distinct and complementary parenting roles and must raise their children to replicate them are at the heart of struggles to preserve the gender binary on which patriarchy fundamentally rests.[29] The ideology of gender complementarity in parenting is a strong common thread that connects many of the most controversial family policy issues over the past few decades, including opposition to marriage equality and parenting rights for same-sex couples, marriage promotion for low-income families, and calls for responsible fatherhood among poor men.

Despite a lack of direct evidence to support it, this political narrative about the importance of fathers *as men* grew to a crescendo by the turn of the twenty-first century when in 2005 Congress created a $150 million annual federal funding stream to support the Healthy Marriage and Responsible Fatherhood Initiative. This funding has since supported hundreds of organizations that offer marriage and relationship education and activities related to fatherhood. Many recipients of government funding for responsible fatherhood programming have been explicitly religious or faith-based organizations with missions focused on reinstating "family values" grounded in the sanctity of married two-parent families.[30] While the George W. Bush administration emphasized marriage promotion, Barack Obama, motivated by a limited relationship with his own father, made fathering, fathers' economic self-sufficiency, and child support enforcement major parts of his presidential platform.[31] Echoing earlier claims about the need for fathers, not the state, to support children, Obama described the "hole a man leaves when he abandons his responsibility to his children [as] one that no government can fill."[32]

Through these various iterations, the political discourse of "father-lessness" has served as a compelling explanation for poverty, crime, and welfare dependency. It also conveniently conceals how inequality and discrimination have fundamentally undermined "responsible" father-ing among marginalized men like Christopher over the past half cen-tury, an issue of growing concern in the field of responsible fatherhood programming.

FATHERING FROM THE MARGINS

The empirical basis for public investment in fatherhood programs is the large and ever-growing number of studies linking fathers' involvement and children's academic, social, emotional, and economic outcomes.[33] Although research finds that children fare better in all these ways when they receive financial and emotional support from their fathers, many issues complicate the link between fathering and children's well-being. This is a case where correlation does not always mean causation, especially given how many factors that predict if fathers are involved—including education, employment, and income—also predict which families do better socially and economically. Most of the research on fatherhood has focused on the parenting experiences of middle-class, white, and married or divorced men. Relatively little has highlighted the parenting perspec-tives of poor never-married fathers of color whose lives do not easily align with dominant cultural scripts of fatherhood embedded in policy. The stereotypical image of the "deadbeat dad" presumes absence, neglect, and deliberate disengagement without accounting for the numerous obstacles marginalized fathers face.

Many social and economic trends have converged in the past several decades to make sustained involvement harder for men like Christopher, including deteriorating work conditions and mass incarceration of men of color. Although middle-class fathers tend to experience parenting as part of a "package deal" of work, marriage, home, and children, fewer low-income fathers follow this script because well-paid work, homeownership, and marriage are markers of economic stability few poor fathers accom-plish.[34] Men with little education especially have experienced declining earnings, rising rates of unemployment, and poor prospects in both labor and marriage markets since the 1960s.[35] Poverty often comes with various kinds of instability—occupational, relational, and residential—that make it prohibitively difficult to be a father who can consistently provide money, time, and care.

Fathers who earn little struggle to support their children financially. They are also less likely to have a middle-class lifestyle, complete with a college degree, a job, and a house, that most people now associate with being marriageable; their romantic relationships also tend to have more tension related to unemployment, infidelity, and addiction. This means that poor men are less likely to marry their children's other parents and more likely to have children with new partners. Many low-income dads are therefore expected to be providers across many families, a situation ripe for ongoing conflict with mothers, who often need all the resources any one disadvantaged father can offer.[36]

Fathers who get along with their children's mothers, regardless of whether they are coupled, are more likely to be involved with children, and contentious coparenting relationships are the main barrier to involvement for many.[37] For this reason, many experts advocate for a stronger focus on marriage and coparenting relationships in fatherhood programs. The problem with this approach is that many relationships between mothers and fathers are already over, troubled, or otherwise irreparably complicated by the time fathers enroll.[38] Fathers often feel that mothers "gatekeep" by blocking access to children in the aftermath of adversarial breakups. Yet research on women who share children with low-income men suggests that many mothers have good reasons to limit access, as they are protecting children from fathers who struggle with addiction and aggression.[39] Family complexity—when fathers share children with more than one partner—also complicates providing couple services. Promoting more involvement with one child can mean less money and time for other children, especially those who do not live with fathers.

Another concern with the focus on coupled coparenting between moms and dads in responsible fatherhood programs is the implication that all fathers parent children in heterosexual relationships. Political and cultural narratives of marriage and parenting, even those focused on marginalized families, are rarely inclusive of gay fathers, who are commonly depicted as white and middle class if they are acknowledged at all.[40] The focus on marriage equality as a flagship issue for same-sex families has obscured how single economically vulnerable gay fathers deal with many challenges that access to marriage rights cannot address. Some government documents outlining responsible fatherhood initiatives mention families headed by same-sex couples and single gay parents, but do not reference the additional obstacles gay fathers often face.[41] Children raised by gay and bisexual fathers of color are particularly vulnerable to poverty, with Black children raised by gay men having the highest poverty rates of any family type.[42] Poor gay fathers of color are likely in even greater need of help with education, jobs, and parenting support given that they tend to face more discrimination at school and work and receive less help from extended families.[43] Gay dads are unlikely to see themselves and their families represented in fatherhood programs when services reflect the assumption that children have mothers and fathers, albeit with varying levels of involvement.

Once narrowly defined by scholars as how much time men spend with their children, "father involvement" has taken on a much broader meaning to include various coparenting dynamics, along with accessibility, affection, and financial support.[44] This reflects how men themselves understand fatherhood as multidimensional, context-specific, and influenced by the larger circumstances of their lives. That is, fathering is not just about direct interaction; it can include anything fathers do to develop a closer relationship with their children. Men parent within constantly shifting cultural norms and political and economic conditions of fathering. The cultural idea of the "new" or "involved" father—one who is nurturing, emotionally connected to his children, present in their lives, and responsible for some, if not an equal portion, of the childcare duties—has become dominant in recent decades as a contrast to the image of the "uninvolved father" who does not provide for or have ongoing contact with his children.[45]

The growing diversity of fatherhood norms and expectations means that men often forge their own understandings of good parenting to account for obstacles they face. This can be particularly challenging for marginalized men who must contend with definitions of responsible fatherhood shaped by middle-class and heteronormative assumptions.

Providing financially, living with children, marriage, and caregiving all have monetary and practical costs that exceed the means of many poor fathers. This is one reason fathers with more education, stable jobs, and higher earnings are more involved with their kids, both financially and relationally.[46]

Nevertheless, many low-income fathers strive to meet their own and others' fathering expectations. They emphasize broader meanings of good parenting that go beyond money, such as defining responsible fathering as "being there" with time and care. [47] Highlighting the emotional and relational components of parenting allows low-income fathers who lack the economic markers associated with being a successful bread-winner to claim a good-father identity in the context of disadvantage. Stressing presence and affection allows marginalized men to bridge the gap between middle-class idealized images of fatherhood and their own experiences limited by economic constraint. That unemployed men are more likely to emphasize time and care over money as key features of good fathering points to how inequality shapes definitions of responsible fatherhood.[48]

Although marginalized fathers embrace these broader definitions, they still struggle to relinquish earning as central to their paternal identities and to develop a sense of themselves as parents with status and value. Part of this is because many policies, especially child support enforcement, still prioritize and mandate through punitive sanctions men's monetary con-tributions to children over other aspects of their parenting. This is where fatherhood programs intervene. By stressing the importance of fathers' presence and emotional involvement and helping men overcome finan-cial barriers, responsible fatherhood policy is a distinct departure from how welfare policies have historically marginalized men as mere wage earners and support payers.[49] It officially recognizes men's commitments to provide care, not just money. This is crucial for men at the center of social scorn and panic over fathering, those like Christopher whom society dehumanizes by casting them as failed providers.

It is difficult to address the underlying issues that make it hard for fathers to be and stay involved, including little education, few job skills, criminal histories, and relationship conflict. It is therefore easy to dismiss these programs as a futile policy experiment. Yet they seek to capitalize on how fathers who enroll in these programs genuinely want to comply with child support orders, cooperate with their children's other parent(s), and see their children regularly.[50] These programs may be successful, not in that they fix the structural issues that undermine fathering, but in how they stand to provide what our society often denies marginalized men: a space to develop and claim identities as good fathers outside the bounds of whiteness, marriage, and money.

Fatherhood programs, most of which are funded through government grants, are constrained by federal guidelines that require activities focused to some extent on "healthy marriage," "responsible parenting," and "economic stability."[51] Pursuant to these top-down requirements, most programs emphasize marriage and two-parent families to some degree. Yet many focus on education, jobs, and fathering classes due to how poverty and unemployment can weaken men's dignity and motivation to be engaged parents.[52] The emphasis on employment also directly reflects how the responsible fatherhood provisions of welfare reform policy underscored "economic self-sufficiency" and child support enforcement as ways to reduce public welfare costs.

These distinct policy priorities signal particular and somewhat conflicting political understandings of the underlying causes of "fatherlessness." While some assume that uninvolved fathers lack family values and personal initiative to maintain contact with children and coparents, others recognize that men's fathering abilities and motivations develop within a larger context of opportunities and constraints.[53] The reality is that most low-income fathers already possess the motivation to be involved, but lack the means and support to do so.

Policy priorities also call into question the true purpose of fatherhood programs. Are job training services about overcoming deficits in fathers' work ethics? Or are they about providing more economic opportunity? Do men need fathering classes to teach them that they should care about and support their children? Or is their primary purpose to help fathers develop parenting and relationship skills (and what must those "skills" entail)? This all points to perhaps the most important sociological question related to responsible fatherhood policy: What is the role of government and public programs in facilitating fatherhood? Is it to supervise and modify men's behaviors in line with dominant social expectations of "responsible" fathering? Or is it to reduce the financial and practical costs of fathers' involvement?

These questions reveal how fatherhood as a policy issue exists at the nexus of culture and structure. Responsible fatherhood policy has a dual purpose: to shift cultural ideas of fathering and to provide resources needed to live up to those ideas. Gauging the policy's full salience depends on asking the right questions that get at how these goals intertwine and how they might diverge. Studies of poverty policy benefit from a cultural analysis; without one, culturally unaware policies reinforce stereotypes of those forced to live in poverty.[54] Polices are cultural products that reflect assumptions about deservingness, responsibility, and a society's structure of opportunity. Cultural values also shape political narratives and the range of alternatives that policy makers envision.

Earlier generations of poverty scholars were associated with the "culture of poverty" model that explained being poor as an outcome of not having the right values. However, numerous studies of fathering among men in poverty reveal that they espouse the same cultural values of paternal responsibility as affluent fathers.[55] More recent poverty scholarship focuses instead on how people respond to poverty using different cultural frameworks and narratives. Cultural concepts are useful for understanding the meanings men bring to and develop within responsible fatherhood programs. Studying fathering frames—the lenses men use to perceive and interpret their parenting—helps us understand how individuals envision what is possible for their lives. Similarly, narratives, or the stories fathers tell that causally link life events, reveal how they make sense of their identities, connections to others, and life chances.

Cultural narratives often involve what sociologist Michèle Lamont called "boundary work," drawing conceptual distinctions between different kinds of people and practices.[56] Individuals draw symbolic boundaries to differentiate themselves from others, create a shared sense of belonging, and make claims to moral worth and responsibility. Sociologist Maureen Waller's research on the meanings low-income fathers assign to parenting revealed that men draw sharp symbolic boundaries between "good" and "bad" dads by redefining responsible involvement in ways consistent with their abilities.[57] Responsible fatherhood programs merge culture and structure by providing resources for the enactment of ideas marginalized men use to claim moral worth as good fathers. Designing effective fatherhood policies and programs requires developing narratives of fatherhood that both resonate with marginalized men and account for the inequalities that constrain their parenting. Without both, there is a risk of reinforcing culture-of-poverty stereotypes and rendering invisible the unequal structural dimensions of fathering.

By focusing on fathers' narratives and the symbolic boundaries they draw around "responsible" fatherhood, this book seeks understanding of how policy shapes the definition, evaluation, and expression of fathering among men central to political debates and directives about paternal involvement. Responsible fatherhood policies were created to target men who do not live with their children, are not married to children's mothers, and do not make consistent support payments. The sixty-four fathers described in the chapters that follow are not representative of all non-resident or non-married fathers or those with outstanding child support obligations. Many did live with their children, several were married, and some made regular monetary or in-kind contributions to their children's households. Still, Christopher and his classmates represent our country's most marginalized fathers. Analyzing their experiences in DADS allows us to understand how policies intended to facilitate fatherhood might help men who encounter the most social and economic obstacles to realizing their parenting aspirations.

Any full and fair consideration of these men's fathering narratives and experiences requires an intersectional perspective that sees race, class, and gender as interlocking forms of inequality.[58] Their accounts of parenting revealed a lot about how the interplay of economic circumstances, racial discrimination, and gender identity led them to DADS. Only by understanding how the program responded to these overlapping systems of oppression can we make sense of the messages of responsible fatherhood programming. Fathers' stories also illuminated the mismatch between political narratives and legislative provisions regarding paternal responsibility and the realities of marginalized men's actual lives as shaped by these inequities. Adopting this intersectional lens requires questioning the gender implications of a policy focused specifically on men's parenting.

FATHERHOOD, MANHOOD, AND GENDERED FAMILY POLICY

A policy focused on promoting men's emotional engagement with children reflects an important shift in the gender dynamics of the U.S. welfare state. Whereas family policies have historically targeted men as fathers tasked with being husbands and breadwinners, responsible fatherhood policy targets fathers as men with caregiving responsibilities. Unlike earlier policies focused on paternity establishment and child support enforcement that prioritized men's biological and financial connections to children, responsible fatherhood policy also focuses on promoting emotionally close father-child relationships, regardless of genetic paternity. For men like Christopher who have few other characteristics that allow them to claim a high social status, the idea that being a caring father makes a man valuable is particularly compelling. It also defies many still-dominant stereotypes about masculinity, gender, and family roles.

Yet just because a policy promotes nurturing father-child relationships does not mean that it necessarily challenges the gendered division of family labor. Promoting a nurturing parenting style for men presents its own challenges. The breadwinning-only father, the dominant fathering model of previous generations, is characterized as emotionally distant and insufficiently caring. However, men who are primary caregivers are also often stigmatized as insufficiently masculine and as not living up to their financial responsibilities. If fatherhood—and by extension manhood—are no longer about providing just money, how do men meet greater demands for caring and emotionality without feeling emasculated? This is a bind for many men and therefore for any policy aimed at men's parenting. How to masculinize domesticity has been one of the key tensions in the responsible fatherhood movement.[59] That is, how can policy and programs make childcare, long associated with mothering and femininity, seem "manly"? If fatherlessness is part of a larger crisis of masculinity, as many have claimed, what specific ideas of manhood do responsible fatherhood programs promote to encourage fathers' emotional involvement?

A broader issue is whether promoting care-focused ideas of responsible fathering actually makes families more egalitarian. Ironically, policies that underscore men's caregiving abilities can reinforce gender inequality if they maintain that parental roles are gendered and distinct. Emphasizing fathers' nurturance, affection, and emotional expressiveness is not the same as encouraging equal responsibility for all aspects of parenting. In fact, as sociologist Michael Messner argued, it is more about changing fathering styles than fatherhood's substance. This stylistic change is reflected in the dominant view that there are two types of masculinity that in turn shape two primary ways of being a father: the emotionally expressive "New Man" who is a highly involved and nurturing father and the stoic, hyper-masculine "Traditional Man" who is emotionally and/or physically absent from his children's lives.[60]

Alas, caregiving ideas of fatherhood labeled "new" have been associated with white, married, straight, middle-class men for decades, while the view of fathers as one of children's primary custodians, caregivers, and teachers goes back to at least the seventeenth century.[61] Sociologist Michael Kimmel explained how it was only after industrialization that "marketplace masculinity" came to define successful fathering as emotionally distant breadwinning.[62] This had the effect of marking poor men and men of color who struggled to be successful financial providers as failed fathers—and failed men. Even for many privileged men, calls for fathers to participate in the direct care of children have resulted in little more than men's symbolic attachment to a caregiver identity, specifically the "new" fatherhood ideal.

This ideal sustains parenting inequalities. Sociologists Pierrette Hondagneu-Sotelo and Michael Messner showed how the cultural image of the "new man"—a white, college-educated, professional who is also a highly involved and nurturant father—assumes race, class, and gender privileges.[63] Qualities associated with the softening of masculinity connected to the "new father" only exist in contrast to characteristics of traditional masculinity projected onto less privileged men, including aggression, emotional stoicism, and "uninvolved" fathering. As a marker of class privilege, "new fatherhood" is not really new at all, nor has it ever questioned the gendered division of parenting labor. Instead, it has redefined patriarchy—a system of power that privileges men and masculinity—at critical junctures to be softer, more emotional, and more focused on care when men's breadwinning abilities falter.[64]

This explains why fathers have anchored their gender identities in nurturing forms of masculinity mostly during downturns in men's economic standing.[65] The actual conduct of fatherhood has lagged far behind these cultural changes. Dominant understandings of fathering now focus on what sociologist Ralph LaRossa called the "culture of daddyhood," the growing tendency for fathers to spend time and play with children.[66] Although fathers' overall contributions to childcare and housework have increased in recent decades, women—mothers and hired caregivers, mostly women of color—still perform the bulk of family labor, with men being viewed as discretionary, part-time secondary "helpers."[67] Ideas of "new fathers" and "new men" therefore tend to serve as cover for gender asymmetry in parenting that perpetuates patriarchy.

Patriarchy has always shaped policy through the prioritization of men's perspectives and needs, but this takes different forms when intersecting with race and class. Although child support laws hold fathers accountable for financial providing, they do not require them to provide unpaid care. Responsible fatherhood provisions reflect yet another way patriarchy has infused family policy. Breadwinning and marriage are the foundation of patriarchal fatherhood. By pathologizing single motherhood, social problems such as poverty, joblessness, and incarceration are seen, not as effects of economic inequality and racism, but as the outcomes of insufficient fathering—specifically insufficiently masculine fathering. Black and Latinx families are more likely to be headed by single mothers and live in poverty, but employment and educational disparities, more than family structure, account for these trends.[68]

The research is clear that, on average, children who live apart from their biological fathers have worse outcomes, including higher poverty rates and poorer school and job prospects. It is easy to assume, as many do, that missing fathers are to blame. Yet doing so oversimplifies the complex reasons families are poor, and political narratives of father absence are quick to conflate missing fathers with insufficient resources and opportunities. The claim that children raised in homes without fathers are lacking because they do not have a man parent—what I call the *"essential father"* *discourse*—rests on a questionable and ideologically motivated empirical basis. Experts tend to agree that women and men exhibit some overall differences in parenting behaviors, but there is not consensus about how much these distinctions matter for children's success. Few studies claiming that fathers are uniquely valuable have examined if the missing parents' sex or gender is responsible for the different outcomes between one- and two-parent families.[69]

This means that we do not know how much parents' gender matters independently of related issues, such as number of parents, lack of a second income, and experiences of family disconnection. Missing fathers tend to mean missing resources—both money and time—and it is difficult to parse out how much hinges on having less of both when a father does not live with his child. The average worse outcomes of kids raised in single-parent homes tend to have much more to do with the effects of growing up poor than growing up without a male parent who identifies as a man.

This suggests that fathers are indeed very important, but not because they are male or men. All who identify as fathers are not male, men, and/or masculine, and many parents who are male, men, and/or masculine do not identify as fathers. The slippage between terms used to describe paternal identity, gender identity, biological sex, and gender expression is part of the problem obscured by narratives about fathering and its gendered influence on children.

Psychologists Louise Silverstein and Carl Auerbach famously challenged the assumption that children need both mothers and fathers to thrive.[70] Those who insist on the importance of fathers tend to believe that men and women parent differently as a result of natural (essential) differences, and that men are necessary (essential) for proper child development due to their ability to model masculine behavior. Essentialist ideas of masculinity as a core feature of responsible fatherhood have their roots in religious ideologies of patriarchal family headship and other biblical metaphors. Evidence for this lies in religiously motivated calls for gender-differentiated parenting roles among many leading advocates of the responsible fatherhood movement.[71] Silverstein and Auerbach's challenge to essentialism grew out of their research on coupled gay fathers, which found that the stability and predictability of parenting relationships matter far more than parents' gender, sexual orientation, or biological relationships to children. The ideology of essentialism, specifically the belief that a child is best off having a mother and father, has contributed to *less* stability and predictability among many families. Non-married mothers, single gay fathers, and same-sex couples raising children have higher poverty rates than families with married heterosexual couples,[72] in part because discriminatory laws and policies have given the latter more benefits and official recognition of their coparenting and parent-child ties.

The political appeal of the essentialist position, Silverstein and Auerbach concluded, reflects social anxiety about changes in family life and gender norms; it is also a backlash against gay rights and feminist social movements that have challenged the power and privilege of heterosexual men within the nuclear family. Research bears out this explanation, as there is little support for the belief that fathers are valuable because of maleness, masculinity, or heterosexuality. As mothers, fathers, and non-binary parents become more similar in how and how much they interact with children, gender is even less salient for how parents influence child development.[73]

Still, there is no denying that parenting is a gendered experience. Despite the lack of significant behavioral differences between mothers and fathers, adults and children are taught to recognize, anticipate, and respond to gender distinctions, especially among their closest caregivers. That is, we learn to think of mothering and fathering as distinct. This conceptual difference, rather than any innate biological distinctions, shapes children's understanding of gendered behavioral expectations. Women's and men's overall different social, political, and economic positions also contribute to gender differences in parenting meanings, processes, and resources. Structural gender inequalities and ideologies, such as the gender pay gap and expectations that women should be primarily responsible for caregiving, shape parenting capacities and patterned differences between "fathering" and "mothering."[74] The ubiquity and taken-for-granted quality of these patterns make them seem like natural expressions of essential differences between men and women. That fathers overall tend to benefit children more economically and educationally does not reflect biologically based parenting abilities. It reflects gender inequality, specifically that men have more authority, earn more money for equal work, and face less discrimination in the workplace. This is likely why there is less evidence for the link between father-child interaction and better childhood outcomes among low-income families in which fathers have fewer economic and social resources.[75]

The view that fathers' masculinity is an important factor in families reflects these socially constructed differences between the meanings and experiences of mothering and fathering. Consequently, many children and parents believe that having male, masculine, or men's parental guidance is crucial. Lesbian and single mothers deliberately recruit men as role models for their children through extended family and support networks.[76] Boys themselves turn to other influential men in their lives, including grandfathers and coaches, as positive masculine role models of good parenting.[77] Participants in fathering programs who grew up without positive paternal role models often enroll to develop the parenting skills they believe they lack.[78]

This all raises key questions regarding political claims about the importance of fathers. Are fathers important because they alone teach boys how to be good men and dads? Research would say no. Adolescents with and without men as parenting role models have similar gender traits, suggesting that gendered behaviors are not imparted only from mothers to daughters and fathers to sons.[79] Moreover, there are no differences in child development and well-being outcomes, such as self-esteem and academic achievement, between children raised in two-parent lesbian families and those in two-parent families with a resident father.[80]

We must therefore consider another angle. How much are men important as parents because our society teaches us that children and families without fathers are inadequate? Beyond grief over a missing parent, how much does the social narrative that "fatherless" children are fundamentally lacking worsen men's sense of "father hunger"? In a society that tasks individual parents with providing for all of children's needs with little social support, is it any wonder that children grow to experience a deep sense of deprivation when a large piece of their small private safety net frays? Finally, how much do claims about men's importance as parents resonate for marginalized fathers because they live in a racist, classist, and sexist society that teaches them they have little else than masculinity to offer their children?

I will show throughout this book why it is crucial to think about these questions in terms of Collins's concept of controlling images. By teaching them to develop self-images as fathers essential for their children's well-being, DADS allowed the men I studied to draw symbolic boundaries between themselves and the controlling image of the "deadbeat dad." This message about the "essential father" is what I call a *valorizing image*. As a cultural idea that assigns unique value to poor fathers, the "essential father" is paradoxical. Unlike controlling images that stigmatize marginalized groups, valorizing images characterize them as centrally important. However, as with controlling images, the intent of a valorizing image is to shape the behaviors of those who experience marginalization, in this case by providing a compelling rationale for poor fathers' non-financial involvement as parents.

Both the "deadbeat dad" and the "essential father" are deeply tied to power relations of race, class, and gender. They blame marginalized men for their disadvantage and provide a compelling cultural narrative that explains inequalities as results of individual pathologies, rather than structural inequities. Understanding this paradox built into the image of the essential father is imperative for grasping the social and political implications of fatherhood policy. This requires an in-depth look at how messages about men's parenting unfold on the ground in responsible fatherhood programming.

STUDYING "DADS": ON THE GROUND OF RESPONSIBLE FATHERHOOD POLITICS

In 2012, the U.S. Administration for Children and Families funded fifty-nine programs through the Pathways to Responsible Fatherhood Grants. Over two years, I studied men's experiences in one of these programs as a unique way of intervening in controversies about the importance of fathers. Men's relationships with their children are influenced by what scholars call "paternal identity," or how invested they are in seeing themselves as parents and how satisfied they are with their parenting abilities.[81] Yet most of the previous research on fatherhood policies and programs has focused more on what men *do* as fathers and less on how men *think* about themselves as fathers.[82] Drawing primarily on the voices of sixty-four men who participated in DADS, I reveal what being a responsible parent meant to marginalized fathers often typecast as "deadbeats" and how they managed identities as good parents amid significant economic and social constraints.

DADS served low-income fathers and expectant fathers between the ages of sixteen and forty-five. Located in a midsize city in the Western United States, DADS was part of a community agency I call the Workforce and Education Program (WEP), which provided education, employment, and job training for the county's low-income residents. Participants had access to an on-site charter high school, paid vocational training, resumé workshops, job search assistance, financial literacy workshops, and relationship and parenting classes. The fathering skills classes offered by the program used the 24/7 Dad curriculum, the most commonly used fathering skills program among federal responsible fatherhood grantees. Services were also available at three additional program sites: a former gang member assistance program, a homeless shelter, and a residential addiction treatment facility. WEP partnered with the local housing authority, the county's Department of Child Support Services, and a domestic violence support center to recruit participants and offer program services.

From December 2013 through November 2015, I conducted in-depth, in-person individual interviews with fifty participating fathers and four focus groups with twenty-one total fathers, including seven who were prior interviewees. All identified as heterosexual cisgender men of color (thirty-two as Black/African American; twenty-three as Latino/Hispanic; eight as multiracial; and one as Native American). They were eighteen to forty-four years old (average twenty-six). The thirty-eight fathers who worked through the DADS paid vocational training program earned between $200 and $600 a month, and another twenty were unemployed. Thus, almost all the fathers I studied qualified as poor—most as living in deep poverty—according to government poverty line measures. Most (forty-seven) did not have high school diplomas. One had an associate degree, and another sixteen were high school graduates. All but three of the forty-seven men who stopped school before graduating were pursuing their high school diplomas through the WEP charter school.[83] Most men had one (twenty-six), two (nineteen), or three (ten) children, and seven had four or more. Two were expecting their first child. Twenty-one fathers lived at least part-time with all their children, and twelve lived with some of their children. Almost half (thirty-one) did not reside with any of their children. All fathers shared children with coparents they identified as women. About a third (twenty-two) of the fathers were single. Thirty-two were romantically involved with women, almost all (twenty-eight) with mothers of at least one of their children. Eight were currently married— seven to children's mothers—and two of these were legally separated.

Fathers who found their way to DADS therefore had unusually dire financial and family situations that drove them to the program. All were experiencing one or more of the following challenges with which they sought support: unemployment; homelessness; food insecurity; stigma associated with criminal records; custody battles; inability to keep current on child support payments; family complexity; and coparenting tension. Simply put, fathers in DADS were mostly young and significantly disadvantaged, and in many cases they had nonexistent or conflicted coparenting relationships with the mothers of their children. Although their experiences are not representative of fathers generally, their stories do reflect the all-too-common extreme challenges of the over five million economically vulnerable fathers in the United States who struggle to live up to political and social definitions of "responsible" fatherhood.[84]

To understand how these definitions reflected in policy were translated into practice, I also interviewed ten program staff and spent fifty hours observing program activities, including community partner/staff meetings and fathering classes. I spoke with: the WEP executive director and DADS program founder; two DADS program managers; the WEP director of employment services; the DADS program assistant; the program manager of the gang recovery program; two DADS case managers/ fathering class instructors; one relationship class instructor; and the program liaison for the domestic violence support center.[85] Talking with staff allowed me to understand how they focused on some aspects of responsible fatherhood discourses while downplaying others. In a highly competitive funding environment, those who administer programs like DADS are constrained by funding guidelines as they work to meet the real needs of struggling parents. Putting fathers' stories in conversation with staff accounts revealed crucial tensions and compromises as top-down policy narratives met fathers' lived experiences.

As a white, highly educated, middle-class woman, I did not share many social characteristics with the men I studied. I was, however, on the verge of sharing one that was crucial for navigating this social distance: parenthood. Fortuitously, I was visibly pregnant with my first child during each of the interviews. My pregnancy was an increasingly obvious quality that men wanted to discuss during interviews, which allowed me to position myself as a less experienced parent in need of advice fathers were qualified to give. As a pregnant interviewer, I embodied a social status that evoked memories of their transition to parenthood and underscored the meanings they attached to parental responsibility. My body visibly prompted them to share with me how they thought about gender differences in parenting. This provided a unique empirical window into fathers' understandings of the differences between fathering and mothering. I discuss this dynamic and the insight I gleaned from it in detail in the appendix.

The sociological story of fathers' experiences in DADS unfolds in two interrelated parts. The first part of this book shows how marginalized men utilized the program to claim identities as responsible fathers. In chapter 2, I focus on how men explained what drove them to DADS and the definitions of "responsibility" they brought to and learned from the program. DADS promoted a broad idea of paternal provision that included financial resources and relational support. This allowed fathers to tailor their understandings of involvement to account for the social and economic constraints they faced, including racism and poverty. Program staff, teaching materials, and especially the fathers themselves used the language of provision to describe men's abilities to meet their children's full needs for care, attention, and opportunity. Focusing on narratives about paternal responsibility that most resonated for men underscores the importance of cultural images that do not discount or stigmatize poor men of color. It also reveals how marginalized fathers uphold perceptions of their value as responsible parents by drawing symbolic boundaries around what it means to "be there" for their children.

Chapter 3 builds on this by delving into fathers' accounts about how social, economic, and relational challenges prevented them from acting on their definitions of responsibility. Much of the previous research on low-income fathers' involvement has emphasized the economic factors that shape men's family relationships, with less attention paid to the stories men use to explain their choices related to those relationships. Gathering their stories while they were in DADS revealed how poor fathers believed they lacked many of the resources and opportunities necessary to forge and sustain bonds with their children. Men's descriptions of the program as a unique situated space for fathering provides important clues for how fatherhood policies can be designed around the cultural and structural dimensions of parenting that make the most sense within the context of marginalized men's lives.

One of the most crucial dimensions is fathers' experiences with and understandings of family complexity and their ties to coparents. Chapter 4 therefore highlights how fathers' goals for better, more cooperative coparenting relationships motivated many to be in the program. A major reason most participated in DADS was to demonstrate their parenting commitments to mothers who they believed mediated access to their children. By showing how the program helped fathers negotiate coparenting obstacles to involvement, the fourth chapter examines how DADS supported men's efforts to forge stronger father-child relationships undermined by weak or conflicted couple bonds. It sheds necessary light on questions of how much fatherhood policy and programs should emphasize two-parent families and marriage.

An intersectional understanding of responsible fatherhood policy and its implementation requires that we go beyond an analysis of how DADS helped men claim statuses as good parents and ask whether such programs promote truly egalitarian parenting. Fatherhood programs are not ideologically neutral contexts for fathers' identity work. They are political spaces with profound implications for cultural understandings of fathering and its connection to race, class, and gender inequalities. The second part of the book therefore takes a more critical stance by analyzing the underside of dominant messages about fathering promoted by DADS. Chapter 5 examines how DADS distinguished paternal care from mothering and emphasized masculine forms of nurturance. It details the narrative strategies fathers used to claim caring paternal identities that merged stereotypically masculine and feminine aspects of parenting—what I call *hybrid fatherhood*—without feeling emasculated. Despite the pretense of more egalitarian parenting, this hybrid construction of fatherhood devalues care deemed feminine and contributes to the durability of unequal gendered parenting arrangements.

In line with political narratives of responsible fatherhood, DADS also taught that fathers, as masculine role models, uniquely contribute to child development. Chapter 6 analyzes how this discourse of paternal essentialism resonated for fathers who found value in messages characterizing them as essential for children's well-being as men, not economic providers. I show how the "essential father" discourse is a response to gender ideologies and race and class inequalities that intersect to shape cultural norms of good fathering that further marginalize poor men of color. Alas, there is little social scientific evidence supporting the "essential father" discourse as a rationale for fathers' involvement. I show how the valorizing image of the essential father individualizes social problems attributed to father absence and culturally scapegoats "fatherlessness" for much more complicated structural inequities.

The concluding chapter discusses the social and policy implications of the book's findings in light of decades-old debates about fathering and its connection to inequality. These implications go far beyond responsible fatherhood programs to the very heart of our national ideas about families, racism, sexism, poverty, and why parenting matters. Policies are counterproductive when they reinforce patriarchal ideologies that children are necessarily worse off without men as parents. There are dangers in the "essential father" discourse, a cultural narrative that ultimately blames marginalized men for the structural constraints they and their children face. But it is hard to challenge an ideology by now so deeply engrained in our political zeitgeist, despite empirical evidence to the contrary.

How might we teach fathers, and all caregivers for that matter, that they are essential without resorting to insidious messages about masculinity that derive their power from the implicit devaluation of mothers, women, and femininity? I provide an answer by outlining a blueprint for a fundamental shift in the political discourse about the importance of fathers, one that emphasizes the value of nurturance and how a father's importance derives from the ability to be a loving parent who can meet children's emotional, relational, and material needs. *Essential Dads* underscores how cultural, social, economic, and political factors shape that ability. Rather than teaching fathers that they are essential to families because they are men, it is essential that we address the unequal social conditions in which fathers like Christopher parent. This book tells the story of how DADS tried to do both.

Admittedly, I started this research expecting to be more critical of responsible fatherhood programs. But after spending hundreds of hours talking to fathers about why they came to DADS, the reasons they stayed, and what it meant for their lives and families, the only book I could honestly write is one that reveals the radically progressive potential of programs like DADS. Ultimately, I endorse these programs. I also make a case for why we must heed fathers' stories so that parenting policies can be even better.

To that end, it is important to acknowledge that DADS was only one program within a much broader national landscape of fatherhood programs scattered throughout the country that have divergent messages, strategies, and goals. Even so, there was much to be learned from studying in-depth one program that reflected and grappled with the major matters at stake in responsible fatherhood policy, including: meanings of good fatherhood, money's role in fathering, marriage, masculinity, and men's value as parents.

Accordingly, each chapter that follows returns to the issues at the heart of Christopher's story with which we began. What did it mean to him to be a "responsible" father? Is it enough that DADS allowed Christopher to prove himself as a parent, even if it did not fundamentally change his economic circumstances? Did DADS help him navigate the constant conflict he had with Chris Jr.'s mother, Monique? What did the program teach him about the unique value of fathers beyond what women caregivers like his grandmother could provide? How did this shape his commitment to compensate for his own father's shortcomings through his relationship with his son?

The answers illuminate how U.S. responsible fatherhood policy unfolded in the lives of real men who stand to gain—and lose—the most from how we ultimately decide to regulate or facilitate fathering through policy. Ultimately, those answers also teach us how politically valuing, not just fatherhood, but all caregiving is vital for addressing race and class injustices, especially those that hinder the essential contributions Christopher and the millions of fathers like him strive to make.

2 Being There Beyond Breadwinning

Responsible fathering means taking responsibility for a
child's intellectual, emotional, and financial well-being.
This requires being present in a child's life, actively contributing to a child's healthy development, sharing economic
responsibilities, and cooperating with a child's mother in
addressing the full range of a child's and family's needs.

Obama White House Archives (2012: 2)

I used to feel like money made me a responsible father, . . .
that being a good father is like cashing your kid out, making
sure they got the best clothes or the best shoes. I've learned
that being responsible is in the love you provide and the
time you spend with your kids, the talking to, the reading.
. . . Just be there for them mentally and physically. If you
can't afford something, you should still be there, listen to
them. If they're scared of the dark, you should be there for
them, laying in their bed with them.

Cayden, age twenty-four, Black father of two, and DADS
participant

The above two definitions of responsible fatherhood both emphasize the
importance of fathers' presence, contributions to children's learning, and
support for children's emotional needs. How they differ is perhaps more
significant. Whereas government definitions also emphasize economic
providing, Cayden learned from DADS to think of paternal responsibility
primarily as loving and caring for his children, even when he could not
afford to provide a lot of money for them.

Cayden wanted to give his children more, both more money and more time, which had led him to DADS. He enrolled with the hopes of finishing his high school diploma and finding steady work. Having grown up in deep poverty, Cayden stopped school before his senior year to care for his newborn daughter, Alisha. Subsequently, he struggled to find and keep jobs, went to jail for selling drugs, and had another child, a son named Cayden Jr., with a new girlfriend. He had not seen Alisha in over two years and owed thousands of dollars in child support. But with no high school diploma and a criminal record that left an indelible mark on his employment prospects, he could barely support himself. This, however, was not the full extent of his parenting concerns. Although he no longer believed that money made him a good dad, he admitted a lingering doubt that he was providing sufficient time and love—the two components he now understood to be central to responsible fathering.

Cayden initially told me that he was a good father because he did everything he could for his son and kept up to date on his child support payments for his daughter. Yet, as our interview continued, he confided to me about his fears that he was not a very good father after all, because two years had passed since he had last seen Alisha:

> It makes me feel sad sometimes wondering what she's doing. . . . I just try to focus on the son I have and keep this going. I go to the courthouse and file paperwork, but I try not to let it bring me down because I can't find her. The police basically say since I don't have no custody that [her mom] can take her. I have dreams of my daughter being a sister to my son. I even moved to [another state] where her mother was, but I couldn't make it financially. I couldn't find work, so I couldn't pay support. I couldn't get food stamps, so I couldn't eat. . . . If I could, if there was a way to be there with her, I would be. I want to be there for her as a father, the same way I'm there for [Cayden Jr.]. I'm not a deadbeat. It's not like I had the baby with her and just left. She left me.

Cayden paused, shed a tear, and reached for his wallet. He showed me a picture of two-year-old Alisha, beautiful with deep, wise brown eyes, in a bright blue dress, smiling up at the camera with arms outstretched inviting a loving embrace. "This is how I imagine she'd look at me if I ever got to see her again." The picture was one of only two he kept with him at all times. The other was of Cayden Jr., taken around the same age.

These side-by-side images mirrored how the two children were equally important in Cayden's estimation of himself as a father. One represented his successes, the other a constant reminder of what he feared were his failures. Noting as he put away his wallet:

> They only take eighty dollars a month for support, and I used to spend over three hundred when I was with her. You can't even buy shoes with that. Your baby mama wants you to be home, she's crying, your baby needs diapers, and you're spending your money on beer and cigarettes. That's a deadbeat. ... In a sense, I feel like a deadbeat sometimes when it comes down to it, but I've got to keep my head up and realize that I'm not. It's not my fault. I'm doing what I can. I'm here.

For Cayden, "here" had a profound and multilayered significance. It meant he was alive after turning away from street life and selling drugs, that he was again living near both his children, and especially that he was in DADS. Motivated by worries over being a failed father, he found his way to the program and met fellow participants who shared these insecurities. There they learned more about the meanings of good fathering that went beyond breadwinning. They were also acutely aware of how, despite loving and wanting to be there for their children in many ways, they lacked the resources to realize the varied components of this broader understanding of responsibility.

Like Cayden, many of the men feared that they fell short of providing the money and resources their children needed. Even more, they worried about how their life circumstances could hinder their ability to provide the things they were learning their children needed most from a father: his love, his time, and the promise that he would remain a constant presence in their lives. Cayden struggled to pay his child support every month. Yet he worried even more about how he was not there to comfort Alisha when she was scared of the dark, as he could do with Cayden Jr.

MEANINGS OF "BEING THERE"

To understand how much responsible fatherhood policy and programming mattered in the lives of Cayden and his fellow participants, I first needed to understand what being a responsible father meant to them. Cayden's explanation was a preview of what I would learn while studying fathers' experiences. In interview after interview, fathers offered the same answer to my question about the meaning of responsibility. It meant *being there* for their children. Without my prompting, thirty-eight of the fifty men I interviewed individually told me that being there was the defining quality of a responsible father. All the others used similar phrases such as "being around" and "showing up." I learned that "being there" was a way of defining responsible paternal involvement even, and sometimes especially, for fathers who had little or no contact with their children. Most importantly, being there was a way of redefining what it meant to be a good provider that did not discount marginalized men like Cayden who made little money.

In this chapter, I show how poor fathers of color justified distinct meanings of paternal responsibility. These men provided crucial insight into how efforts to promote fathers' involvement first require a deep and empathic understanding of how social and economic conditions influence the ability to craft and claim identities as responsible parents. Poor men's life circumstances are least likely to align with stereotypical ideas of proper fathering: being married to one's coparent; living with children in a safe, stable home; and working hard as a well-paid breadwinner. Falling short of these ideas, and consequently identifying as failed providers, can undercut individual initiative, even among the most motivated men. Although policy holds marginalized fathers responsible for the same relational and financial responsibilities as more affluent ones, society does not allow them the same means for living up to these expectations.[1]

Focusing on how men construct identities as good fathers in the context of severe disadvantage is not merely an academic or intellectual exercise. Fathers' parenting identities have profound implications for how involved they are with children, and whether they believe they deserve to be involved. Not surprisingly, fathers who view parenting as central to their sense of self are more involved with their children.[2] Equally important is paternal self-efficacy—how effective men think they are as parents—and if they think others judge them as good fathers.[3] Those judgments depend on the criteria fathers and others use to assess good parenting, criteria that have remained remarkably consistent over time.

Fathering scholar Joseph Pleck outlined four historical phases of father-hood, each associated with a particular idea of what a good father primarily does. These ranged from the moral teacher of the preindustrial era and the distant breadwinner of the nineteenth and early twentieth centuries, to the sex role model of the mid-twentieth century and the nurturing "new" father of the contemporary period.[4] Financial provisioning has been cen-tral to understandings of proper fatherhood throughout all these phases. This "breadwinner ideology" is a deeply gendered understanding of family responsibility that tasks men with financially supporting an entire house-hold through a "family wage."[5] The man-as-family-breadwinner ideal pre-sumes significant economic privilege and obscures how women are primary economic providers in many families, often in addition to being primary or sole unpaid caregivers.[6] Breadwinning is an example of what sociologists Douglas Schrock and Michael Schwalbe called "manhood acts," or prac-tices through which people assert their identities as men.[7]

Given the connection between fathering and masculinity, breadwinning is also a fatherhood act that establishes and upholds men's identities as responsible parents. Job insecurity and the inability to earn any wage, much less a wage large enough to support an entire family, can therefore present a masculinity crisis whereby men's gender and family identities are threatened. Scholars have explored how economically vulnerable men who cannot fulfill the financial expectations of the breadwinner role rede-fine their gender and parental identities in ways that account for what might be called "bread-losing," or the inability to live up to the bread-winner ideology due to unemployment or low wages.[8] Men frequently craft flexible fathering identities in response to their socioeconomic cir-cumstances, especially when they lack the economic markers associated with being a successful financial provider.[9]

Although stably employed fathers tend to maintain high provider expectations, fathers who are under- or unemployed focus more on the relational aspects of involvement that they feel they can more read-ily attain.[10] Part of this is using language that signals a commitment to good parenting and the varied meanings of involvement without defin-ing responsibility solely in terms of money. "Being there" captures this broader understanding of fathering. Sociologist Maureen Waller found that, for nonresidential fathers, being there meant communicating with and seeing their child regularly, providing emotional support and guidance, and being accessible.[11] They accentuated the emotional aspects of their relationships and acknowledged "new" father expectations of quality time and loving interaction. As sociologists Kathryn Edin and Timothy Nelson discovered, being there—which can mean anything from daily contact to occasionally buying diapers, food, or clothes—is an understanding of responsible fathering that allows men to claim the status of good-enough dads who are doing the best they can.[12] Underscoring accessibility and emotional involvement through the language of "being there" helps marginalized men manage and meet parenting expectations in the context of disadvantage.

This calls into question how most political discussions of fathering frame paternal involvement in discrete and dichotomous terms of "presence" versus "absence." Discourses of "absentee" fathers generally assume economic, legalistic, or residential definitions of paternal responsibility, which tend to reduce fatherhood to a relational status dependent on men's connections to women and children. In reality, many fewer men than these discourses would have us believe are completely absent from their children's lives. Fatherhood scholars William Marsiglio and Kevin Roy argued that the "provide-and-reside" model of fathering on which policy is based is out of sync with how many parents, including mothers, express diverse and nuanced definitions of responsibility.[13]

Men doubly marginalized by poverty and racism tend to struggle the most with living up to breadwinning expectations of paternal responsibility. Ideas of responsible fatherhood embedded in directives to support "a child's intellectual, emotional, and financial well-being" incorporate traditional aspects of economic providing with contemporary ideas of emotional and social engagement. I learned that, for poor men of color, these "newer" ideas of nurturing fatherhood meant that they now risk failing in numerous ways as parents. The main problem for the men in DADS was that their social and economic constraints prevented them from achieving either traditional or contemporary fathering goals.

Breadwinning is often talked about as the component of responsible fatherhood economically vulnerable men can least afford. Yet both the financial and emotional components of fathering have costs that often surpass their means. Fathers who do not live with their children, as was the case with many DADS participants, are more likely to spend time with kids when they have more economic resources; those who do live with children are more likely to contribute financially as a replacement for time and care.[14] That money is often a prerequisite or substitute for other forms of involvement suggests that more flexible definitions of fathering rarely translate into more emotional engagement when fathers' breadwinning capabilities falter. As was the case for DADS participants, this signals how broader ideas of paternal engagement can validate men as more than mere breadwinners, while simultaneously setting them up to feel inadequate as both providers and caregivers.

Fathers' stories reflected this harsh reality. They also revealed how men actively used the program to claim identities as responsible fathers and deflect stigma that they were failed providers and parents. A primary way they did so was by co-opting the language of provision, which traditionally denoted fathers' financial responsibilities, and using it to describe the value of fathers' time, love, and existence. By defining a "good provider" as one who gives of himself, especially in the context of deep poverty, fathers were able push back against the controlling image of the "deadbeat dad."[15] Men viewed DADS as an opportunity to improve their job prospects and their children's lives. Even more so, they experienced it as a rare space for the performance of important boundary work. For them DADS was not just a social program. It was a unique place where they could draw symbolic, relational, and sometimes even physical boundaries between the men they used to be and the fathers they wanted to become.

This chapter explores how marginalized men used particular frameworks of fathering and providing to make claims about their moral worth as responsible parents. Sociologist Ann Swidler theorized how people in distinct structural locations develop different cultural "toolkits" they can use to create strategies of action that solve their problems in emotionally resonant ways.[16] DADS gave men additional conceptual tools to understand and justify involvement in nonfinancial terms. They relied on program messages to explain their parenting choices, shape high-status paternal identities, and resist characterizations as deadbeat dads. Ultimately, they selected and interpreted meanings of responsibility that most aligned with their abilities. This signified how marginalized men still feel accountable to breadwinning-plus definitions of good fathering directly at odds with their life circumstances, but also how they make sense of the structural inequalities that shape their parenting.

The "new" father ideal codified in policy may be a more flexible definition for privileged men who can mobilize their social and economic resources to meet (or outsource) the simultaneous demands of providing money, time, and care. However, marginalized men can experience expanded notions of the father's role as more restrictive when deep poverty and racism limit living up to multiple components of responsible parenthood. That Cayden paid little in child support and had no contact with Alisha meant that he feared falling short in multiple ways as a father. DADS helped him manage these insecurities by giving him a space to claim and enact an identity as a good father—"not a deadbeat"—who was "here" and "trying." One of the most significant components of DADS was how it framed the nonfinancial aspects of fathering as valuable forms of provision, allowing men without class and race privilege to assert identities as successful providers.

REDEFINING THE GOOD PROVIDER ROLE

Fathers described how their prior understandings of being there focused on "providing" or being a "good provider," but not just financial resources. DADS validated this breadwinning-plus model of fatherhood that the fathers already valued. They defined providing as giving children money and material goods, such as diapers, but just as importantly time, opportunity, and a father committed to their well-being. Fathering classes offered through DADS reinforced this multidimensional idea of provision, including physical presence, emotional engagement, and monetary support. The 24/7 Dads classes many took explicitly taught men to think of providing in this broader way by noting that "the problem that many dads have is that they allow work to control their lives so much that they lose sight of how much they value family and the relationship between work and family. They think of themselves as providers of money or that providing money is so important that it's okay to not provide in other ways."[17] Although working too much was rarely a problem fathers in DADS had, given their limited job prospects, many explained how the classes helped them better see themselves as providers of all things children needed to thrive. Fathers repeatedly described to me the importance of supporting their children financially, but also insisted that money alone was insufficient for being a responsible father. Men's participation in the program helped them rearrange the hierarchy of responsibilities in their estimations of the father role.

Challenging the idea that breadwinning should be a father's main parenting priority, respondents stressed how time, care, and their participation in DADS were ways of being there that most benefited children. Taylor, a twenty-four-year-old Black father of two, told me that the most valuable lesson DADS taught him is the importance of providing a father's time:

> I'm there. I teach him right from wrong. I buy him clothes. . . . I take him to school. I pick him up, send him to doctor's appointments, help him with his homework, and teach him how to play sports. . . . The classes taught us to be there, not just financially, but physically. . . . Spending time with your kids is the most important. Money goes and comes, but time goes and don't come back. I'm there from the time he wakes up to the time he goes to sleep. I was there to see his first crawl.

Like Cayden and Taylor, most fathers described good providers as those who go beyond breadwinning to be there physically and emotionally. This was something they believed before joining the program.

Still, messages from DADS were crucial for reinforcing their breadwinning-plus script of responsible fatherhood. The program's emphasis on the importance of care and time was symbolically powerful to men who relied on these messages to develop a sense of themselves as good providers, despite the various life circumstances that prevented them from offering children much money. DADS helped men rationalize that their presence was even more important than finances. Fathers learned that time was a finite resource in a way money was not and something only a father could offer. Although money was certainly finite for men in DADS, they came to understand paternal presence as even more valuable and scarce. These messages gave fathers something they never had before: a framework for understanding their worth to children as providers in a way not dependent on education, employment, or earnings.

How men used the language of provision to describe responsible father-hood reflected this new understanding. When talked about in relation to fathering, the terms *provide* and *provider* generally indicate supplying the money or material goods necessary to meet children's needs for food, clothing, housing, and the like. Notably, however, the fathers I spoke with talked about provision in terms of meeting their children's needs for atten-tion, protection, instruction, and nurturance. That DADS staff and the curriculum discussed providing in this way helped fathers conceptualize paternal provision in broader, more inclusive terms. Michael, a twenty-four-year-old Latino father of two, told me: "Some people think that being a good dad is . . . providing stuff for them. I think being a good father is actually being there emotionally and physically and providing care for them, such as when they're sick." For fathers, this redefinition of the good provider role helped them reframe successful fathering around compo-nents of parenthood they could attain.

As part of fathers' identity work, it allowed them to claim identities as good providers in ways that were possible in spite of their economic obstacles. Dustin, a twenty-two-year-old Black father of one, talked about providing as supplying all the tangible and intangible things his daughter needed to thrive: "Being there is the ability to provide for all their needs, being able to pay rent and do things like that, but not only that. It's about preparing for her future, reading to your daughter, teaching your daugh-ter, talking to her, taking her out to the park, having family moments, keeping her away from all the music, all the negative stuff. . . . Providing is not just money. My own dad gave me lots of money, but he didn't really provide because he wasn't really there." According to these men, *providing* was an all-encompassing term that captured the many varied components of responsible fatherhood. They believed it was equally as important to provide things as it was to provide a dependable father-child relation-ship through which children felt safe and loved, created fond memories, and learned to trust others. Facundo, a nineteen-year-old Latino father of one, described providing as being there "at soccer games, taking him out for ice cream, sitting on the couch with him watching Saturday morning cartoons and eating cereal." For Caleb, a forty-year-old Native American father of three, being a good provider meant that "ain't nobody sitting at the award ceremony at school looking for Dad."

Defining providing and being there outside the bounds of breadwinning also helped fathers emotionally manage how work and care responsibilities conflict when time was a limited resource. Curtis, an eighteen-year-old Latino father of one, told me that DADS "teaches you that you're not a bad dad if you can't give your kid what they want, all the extra things. You're not a bad dad for that. You can't get mad at yourself. All you can do is try harder. If you work a lot and go home tired, and you can't really socialize with your family because you've got to get up in a couple hours, you can't hate yourself for that. Sometimes you can only do one thing, either your family or your job. Sometimes in providing for your family you're struggling with your family." Curtis learned that being a good father meant having to make hard choices between the different components of involvement. Like others, he described time spent at work as a way of spending time on behalf of, if not with, his children.

Other fathers talked about providing as what a responsible father should *not* do to be there for his children. As the 24/7 Dads curriculum noted, this included not putting breadwinning and money above children's other needs. David, a twenty-two-year-old Black father of one, explained that being there is about "making sure they have everything they need, . . . being at all their school events, so she can look up and see me there. But it also means not putting work before my daughter." Tanner, a thirty-seven-year-old multiracial father of two, participated in DADS through a residential drug addiction treatment program, an alternative to a second lengthy prison sentence. He described how being there as a good provider was about making a deliberate decision to avoid drugs: "Being a provider means giving emotional support, guidance, and living up to the whole statement of the difference between right and wrong. It means never being on that side of the glass ever again, to not put my kids and my loved ones through that."

Like Tanner, almost half of the fathers had spent some time incarcerated since their children were born. Many also had histories of life-threatening gang involvement. For these fathers, being a provider meant doing anything necessary to stay alive and maintain contact with their children outside penal institutions. Maintaining sobriety, avoiding the streets, and staying alive and out of jail were all parts of "being there" as a good provider who was always present in the most literal sense. "My kid kept me off the streets," explained Marshall, a twenty-year-old Black father of one, "and now I'm in the house daily, trying to create a better future. I play around with him, talk to him, let him know that I love him." None of that would be possible, he concluded, if he went back to "street life" and got killed. Focusing on presence and attention as unique forms of paternal provision was a key way fathers overcame insecurities that they were not worthy of being in their children's lives. Fathers also coped with this fear by claiming identities specifically as providers of upward mobility for their children.

PROVIDING OPPORTUNITY

Men explained how being a good provider meant offering their children very different lives than the ones they had lived. Protection was a recurring theme in fathers' descriptions of provisioning. This meant keeping their children physically safe, but also protecting them from the hardships of poverty. Given their limited means, "responsibility" often entailed significant personal sacrifice from fathers. Caleb told me: "I wear rags, but my son has everything he needs. I save up for his presents, even if that means I only drink one cup of coffee a day and don't eat much." Arturo, a twenty-two-year-old Latino father of one, had struggled since he could remember, especially after his grandmother who raised him passed away when he thirteen. He had to quit school and start working in the fields to support his younger siblings. He was homeless for two years and struggled to find consistent off-season work. After he returned to school, he was expelled for gang-related fighting. Arturo found out he was a father when his daughter was three months old. This discovery, he told me, kicked his "protector-provider reflex" into high gear, a feeling he knew well since he was a teen:

> I had to step up and lose that part of my life of going to high school just to work and pay bills. I was the only kid in the fields. Having [my daughter] brought back the responsibility of when I was thirteen years old, having to pay all these bills and making sure I got money to my mom. Now I have to make sure I make this money so I can provide for my daughter. I don't want her to go through the stuff I went through. . . . I became a dad

in a week. Being there for her means that I'm actually willing to protect my family at any cost no matter what danger they're going to be in. That means that you got to be willing to sacrifice yourself to make sure they're safe and in a good place, which means making sure she has a better life than I grew up having.

Fathers' emphasis on giving children a better life was in part about giving them money and things. More than this, though, for fathers like Arturo, providing meant protecting their children from similar lives characterized by danger and deprivation.

Being a provider in this sense involved becoming a barrier between their children and the hunger, homelessness, gangs, drugs, jail, and early work they themselves knew all too well. To be this kind of bulwark, fathers believed they needed to forge different life paths, which entailed cutting off ties to family members and friends they believed kept them anchored to disadvantage. Ricardo, a twenty-two-year-old Latino father of two, enrolled in the program for this very reason. He was there to get "on the right track for my kids, to start going forward. Being there and being a good dad is not giving up on them for things like drugs and addiction. . . . In trying to move forward, I have to get away from family members that are involved in gangs. Staying on the right path means I got to cut off some of these connections. I can choose to be in their lives or my kids' lives." This was not an easy choice. To cope with homelessness, hunger, and the constant threat of violence that cast a pall over their young lives, many fathers turned to the gangs that made up a large part of their communities—and their families. Many of their own fathers, brothers, and cousins, the men they trusted and often the only men they really knew, initiated them when they were barely teenagers. "Going forward" for fathers like Arturo and Ricardo meant turning away from these support networks that at earlier points in their lives had protected them from worse fates.

Being there and protecting children in these ways would involve, as Ricardo concluded, "making two lives right" out of the only "wrong" one he had ever known. More than providing opportunities for upward mobility, it was about protecting children from disadvantage by providing a barrier between them and the poverty, gangs, and incarceration that hindered fathers' own life chances. As with Ricardo, this goal often compelled fathers

to make difficult choices about long-standing social connections and lucrative, yet illegal, activities. To Keegan, a twenty-one-year-old Black father of
three, being there meant his "kids knowing that I'm coming back at night,"
a sense of security he did not experience due to his own father's perilous
gang involvement and frequent incarceration. He risked this security for
his children by writing bad checks that led to a three-month stint in jail.
Keegan blamed this, in part, on his own pride: "A couple of checks were
just to have money, but I got caught the last time because we didn't have no
diapers. We couldn't afford both diapers and formula, and we needed both.
I told myself, 'I'm going to do this one last time.' I didn't want to borrow
money, so I wouldn't have to owe nobody." Reliving what he saw as a child,
Keegan was arrested in front of his son, the one who needed those diapers.
From that point on, being there was about never going through that again,
even if that meant having to ask for help when money ran out.

When fathers talked about being providers of protection, they meant
keeping children away from physical harm, but even more so, from material hardship and fears of losing their parents. Enrique, an eighteen-year-
old Latino father of one, told me: "To be a good dad is to make sure she
doesn't go where I've been, to provide her a different life. I wouldn't want
my daughter to go through what I did. I want her to graduate, to be successful, to not struggle, not worry about bills. I want her to be happy, to
not live in homeless shelters like I have."

Elias, a twenty-one-year-old Latino father of one with another on the
way, also described how paternal responsibility was primarily about radically changing his life and safeguarding his children from the anxiety and
deprivation of his own childhood. A gang member since the age of ten
after being "jumped in" by brothers and cousins, Elias had been shot three
times and dropped out of school with the hopes of becoming a Marine and
leaving gang life and poverty behind. Although that did not work out as he
had planned, he acknowledged his "luck" that he was still alive. He wanted
most of all to provide his children with more options, ones not limited to
"choices" between gangs, prison, poverty, or death. He explained:

> I don't want my kids raised around this neighborhood, the place where I was
> from, to sit here and see that it would be OK to be a gang member. I didn't
> want to fail as a father. I was scared of getting locked up or getting shot
> again, and my son's father getting ripped from him without him even finding

out who I am. . . . I want them to be in a good, stable environment where his parents ain't fighting or beating each other up. . . . On top of supporting them financially, I want to make sure they can get into a good school, start a little savings fund, something just so that they don't have to struggle in life like I did.

As Elias proudly showed me a sonogram image of his unborn child on his cell phone, he pointed to his heart and said: "I want this child to just fly through life, go to college, do something, pursue a dream. This child will be and have more than me."

Likewise, for his classmate Rodrigo, a nineteen-year-old multiracial expectant father, being there and providing more for his unborn daughter meant being in a position to provide the security he was not able to offer during his girlfriend's first pregnancy, which they chose to terminate:

I was with the wrong people, selling drugs, and got in trouble. Some guys tried to rob me, I got kicked out of school for fighting, and we aborted our first baby. This baby is due in two months. I really wanted that first child, but I didn't feel like I had a say in keeping it because I couldn't provide for it. But now I'm working and back on track to take care of the baby. The abortion fucked us both up. I still dream about that baby. Now I'm working, and I don't want someone else raising this kid. A good dad's first priority is safety. I want my daughter to dream, to have a life, and I'm trying to make that life right.

Rodrigo, still deeply disturbed over the abortion, articulated a particular pro-life stance—that is, that having a life meant having the means to dream. Doing right by his daughter, and really giving her life, would mean providing her with opportunities for upward mobility.

Some fathers were not as critical of illegal activities if those activities enabled them to provide children with these kinds of opportunities. For them, provision was less about things and more about intent. Owen, a twenty-year-old multiracial father of three, noted that "being a good dad has nothing to with money, but with the intention behind the actions you do. If you're selling drugs to help put food inside your family's mouths, not to sit there and buy big chains and a car with big old rims and stuff like that, if it's to help pay for gas or electric bills, then that's the definition of a good dad. You're going about it the wrong way, but it's still the definition of a good dad, someone doing what he needs to do for his family." For these fathers, being there as providers had many components. Parsing them in these ways was a powerful form of symbolic boundary work that entailed drawing distinct lines between responsible fathers who did whatever was necessary to promote upward mobility for children and those who only cared about themselves. It was about giving their children missing social and economic advantages, which included money, but also knowledge, good values, and a father to keep them on the right paths in school and work. Being a responsible dad also meant providing prosperity by protecting children from the circumstances and choices fathers believed had derailed their own lives and plans for advancement. Enrolling in DADS was their attempt to change their children's life chances and to break their link in the intergenerational cycle of poverty. For many, doing so meant providing, first and foremost, a father himself—one who need not be successful by conventional breadwinning standards to have value and worth as a parent.

PROVIDING A FATHER

Most men described fully "being there" as a provision of the self. This was particularly important for those who did not have consistent contact with their own fathers or saw them as mere financial providers. A father who provided of himself was one who gave his children time and attention, but also the cognitive and spiritual components of involvement. Fathers spoke often of providing their children prayers and positive thoughts and feelings. Ricky, a twenty-two-year-old Black father of one, put this most pointedly when he told me that being a good father and provider meant: "just being around. That's it. You can be the brokest, the dumbest, the ugliest, the cutest, the baddest, the goodest. I don't care, just be around your child. I'm around my child every second I can. I ain't never had the big stuff, and all I wanted from my father was for him to say, 'Hey, son.' I think about my kid every second, every hour, every day, every week, every month, every year. He's on my mind. How I think and feel is what makes me a good dad." Ricky regretted that he saw his son, William, only on the occasional weekend and that his low earnings prevented him from buying more. That he thought about William the rest of the time and bought what his meager means would allow, however, made him feel like a good father and provider. The program's emphasis on the importance of paternal presence, despite low earnings, reinforced men's beliefs that responsible fatherhood is not necessarily about providing money, which is often out of fathers' control. Rather, they told me, it is about doing the best one can, especially by making personal sacrifices on behalf of their children.

Randy, a twenty-nine-year-old Black father of three, talked about being there in this way and explained that taking care of his kids entailed "spending time with them, buying what I can, trying to hang out when I can, and just talking to them about life. I ain't really got no money, but I do what I can." Homeless and often hungry, Randy proudly confided to me that he used some of his food stamps to buy milk for his children and sold the rest to get his daughter diapers and wipes. He skipped many meals to do so. He provided for his children, he reasoned, using the currency of his own comfort and well-being. To Ricky, Randy, and others, responsible fathering emerged from these kinds of "doing what I can" sacrifices. In acknowledging that they gave their children relatively little compared to better-off fathers, they also highlighted that what they gave was a greater portion of the very little they had, usually at the expense of meeting their own basic needs. This emphasis on selflessness and the idea that children need fathers' presence as much as they need money was one way men claimed identities as worthy fathers who provided value to their children's lives. To echo Ricky, even the "brokest" and "baddest" fathers had a lot to offer by just being proximate to their kids.

From fathers' perspectives, time and presence were the most valued assets they, and only they, could offer their children. Jonathan, a twenty-three-year-old Latino father of two, communicated this when he told me: "If you can imagine a kid, and you just send them money and keep a roof over their head, and they're just there growing up on their own, they have some of what they need, but they're missing out on you. How would they know right from wrong?" Other kids may have more money and things, Jonathan noted, but his children were "more privileged" than those with breadwinning-only rich fathers. He believed that such kids were impoverished in terms of what really matters—a father who loves and values them enough to be around and spend his precious time with them.

In drawing symbolic boundaries between themselves and other fathers who provided only money, albeit a lot more than they could, fathers in DADS stressed how money could not replace the value of fathers' time, attention, and wisdom. Anyone, they rationalized, could provide money and things, but only fathers could provide a guiding paternal presence, rendering them uniquely important. Tomas, a thirty-three-year-old Latino father of three, learned this through DADS and life experience: "Don't just tell them go outside and play, but actually try to get involved. A lot of dads aren't active anymore. Go to a park, just play with the child, and just be there for them. The most important thing is time. You may not have a lot of money to take them to fancy places or to the mall, but if you can spend time, that would be an invaluable kind of thing you can't replace. I'm learning from [DADS] not to just say, 'Here's ten dollars, where do you want to go spend it?'" Estranged from his two older children whom he saw only occasionally when they were young, he was trying to be a better parent with his youngest by spending time, not just money. Tomas hoped spending this time would prevent his younger child from resenting him like his older siblings did.

His classmate Maxwell, a twenty-one-year-old Black father of one, also emphasized time when describing what fathers were specifically equipped to give their children: "Being a good dad is stopping what you're doing to spend time with your son, to teach him things, like talking, to read him books, to teach him the ABCs, and to teach him to cope. I do my money part as a father, the clothes, the diapers, the wipes, and everything, but buying diapers, clothes, and food is something that anybody can do for him. I'm the one who has to spend time and teach my son. Anybody can buy something. That's just money. That's not a father." Men reasoned that they, and they alone, could give children confidence by proving that their fathers loved them enough to be and stay around.

By stressing this message, DADS helped men overcome the insecurities of being failed financial providers. Many told me that they came to the program believing they were lacking as fathers because of their inability to earn a lot of money. Harris, an eighteen-year-old Black father of one, described this feeling of inadequacy:

> I came in believing I don't have a lot to offer, but I was going to make sure I'm in my kid's life. I don't have a big house and a lot of toys to give my son. All I can give him is love and quality time and show him I really care about him. . . . I don't have a spot. I don't have a house. I don't really have anything. But I now know I was worrying about the wrong things, about how I was

going to provide for him, instead of being a father. That's how my dad was, a financial father spoiling me with money, not with time.

Through DADS Harris was learning to challenge benchmarks of good fathering that depended on privilege. With dreams of taking his son fishing and being more than the "financial father" who raised him, Harris now felt he had a lot to offer by committing his life to his son's well-being and "spoiling [his] son with attention and quality time."

Providing this time and attention meant facing the omnipresent threat of violence, death, and incarceration these men faced. The realization that staying alive and being around for one's children were accomplishments and forms of provision was a catalyst for changing their lives. Ambitions of being responsible fathers who continued to defy these odds motivated them to change into the kind of people they aspired to be. This came up in the third focus group I conducted when men discussed the meanings of responsibility they were learning in DADS:

RODRIGO (nineteen, multiracial, expectant father): A daddy is a sperm donor who just hits it and leaves, but a father is responsible.

JAMES (nineteen, multiracial, father of two): We sit here and talk about ways to become better dads and how some dads do nothing. Dudes make babies and just leave their babies with the moms, and somebody else comes and takes responsibility.

XEO (twenty-one, Black, father of one): Responsible fathers play a direct role in taking care of a child.

JAMES: Right, a good dad is a person who's there to provide and protect and love their family when they need it.

RODRIGO: Yeah, we're always talking here about how a father balances that with the ability to show them affection, to show them love from their father. It's not the same as love from the mother.

JAMES: Right, man, you got to be there to provide anything you can when you can and not just money but love, basically everything that a child needs. A dad should be there to provide for them, and they should want to be there.

XEO: Right on! It's just actually being there, being present, taking care of duties.

JAMES (interrupting in agreement): Through play time, bath time, all that time with your kids.

RODRIGO (interjecting excitedly): Yes, actively do *everything*!

MANUEL (nineteen, Latino, father of one): That's why I consider myself a good dad because any chance to be with my daughter I spend with her.

RODRIGO: You got it, man! [DADS] is teaching us that being a father is that whole other mindset, another mentality entirely. It changes who you are. It has to change you. [Everyone nods in agreement].

JAMES: Everything about you—moneywise, who you hang around, the stuff you do, dropping a lot of the stuff you used to do—you got to change it all.

MANUEL: I would be at home doing nothing without my baby.

JAMES: And I'd be in the streets kicking it if I didn't have my kids. When she was born in the hospital, they put that ink on her feet. They put her footprints on my shirt. Right then, right there, I'm thinking, "Damn, I got to start doing something right now. Everything has to change. Everybody I hang out with got to go."

MANUEL (shaking his head and sighing in deep agreement): The only thing that stops me from being a better dad is not being able to live with my daughter. I got to change that.

XEO: I have chills right now. [JR: Why?] They're in my head. They're talking about what I'm going through, what I'm living through with my kids.

A consensus emerged around the belief that responsible fatherhood necessitated a fundamental shift in how men spent their time, who they spent it with, and essentially how and why they were living. DADS helped men redefine fatherhood and fathers' value to children in emotionally resonant ways that made sense given their social and economic constraints. By validating this multifaceted understanding of responsibility, namely the idea that "good providers" offer their unique love, care, and time, DADS gave men conceptual tools to make claims about their moral worth as responsible parents. This allowed men to understand and justify their paternal involvement in nonfinancial ways. Beyond this, it helped them develop and claim a high-status paternal identity not grounded in the exclusionary white middle-class breadwinner ideology. Program messages co-opted the language of provision to challenge the notion that responsible fatherhood requires race and class privileges. In doing so, they helped men resolve identity challenges rooted in fears of being failed fathers.

Hence "being there" was not just about presence. It was about becoming and being a different kind of person who put their children first in terms of money, time, and identity. A responsible father is someone who identifies foremost as a provider, protector, and teacher of his children. Living up to this identity entails changing into a person worthy of these responsibilities, a goal that drove many men to DADS. Alex, a twenty-four-year-old Latino father of one, described in another focus group to passionate nods of agreement how society expects so little of poor fathers of color: "It would be easy to walk away from being a dad and confirm all those stereotypes. But we're here, we're students, we're making money, which can take us away from our families. We're trying to actually take that step forward and raise a kid in spite of all of it." To Alex and his fellow participants, being there as responsible fathers involved more than just being around. It required defying racist, classist, and gendered labels about who they fundamentally were and what they were capable of for the sake of their children. "Being there" meant not confirming stereotypes about men of color being mere "sperm donors" who "just hit it and leave," even when others believed that was all they were fit to do.

Like James, who felt changed the moment his daughter's footprints were stamped on his shirt, most men described becoming fathers as the most profound experience of their lives. This was true even for those whose children were unplanned. Children's existence—and their fathers' reckoning with such an awe-inspiring responsibility—altered the fathers and their sense of self, despite how much they were able to see their kids. Peter, a twenty-three-year-old Black father of two, did not find out he was a father until his oldest son turned a year old. This discovery filled a void in his life and in his identity: "I prayed for this child. I just wanted someone that I can love, support, and everything. My son filled a hole. . . . A good dad is a provider. He also knows how to relate to his child. He always knows what the child is doing, what they can do, what they can't, their personality." This deep knowledge of his son gave Peter's life meaning it was missing before. Unfortunately, that was tempered by the reality that he barely saw his children after their mother got a new boyfriend. "It's been three weeks since I last saw them, and when I leave, I don't know when I'm seeing them again." This uncertainty devastated Peter, but it did not undermine his motivation or identity as a parent. He concluded after describing to me the pain of separation from his children: "You still got to wake up. Either way it goes, you're a father." For Peter, being there as a responsible dad meant persevering in the face of extreme hardship and having someone to love unconditionally, someone whose mere existence rendered you valuable despite any personal, social, or economic short-comings. This life purpose was a gift, one that fathers believed they were beholden to give back by being there in mind, body, and spirit. As men talked about what they believed fathers should provide for their children, they also revealed what children provided for them: a sense of purpose and a vicarious upward mobility.[18]

BRIDGING THE GAP BETWEEN IDENTITY AND INVOLVEMENT

Although almost all the men told me they identified as good fathers com-mitted to being there for their children, many were involved much less than they wanted. Several indicated that participating in DADS was a way of "being there" because it meant they were working to improve their par-enting skills, employability, and coparenting relationships. This aspira-tional way of thinking about involvement came up most when talking with nonresident fathers who believed that time spent away from children now because of work or school would ultimately allow them to be better, more involved dads in the future.

One particularly poignant conversation about this was with Emmett, a twenty-four-year-old Black father of one deceased child, who described through tears how participation in the program allowed him to maintain his identity as an involved father. He was grieving the death of his daugh-ter, Shannon, who died of Sudden Infant Death Syndrome when she was twenty-eight days old. During our interview eight months after her pass-ing, he expressed deep regret that he did not spend more time with her during her brief life: "I came for [Shannon]. I didn't come back for myself at all. . . . I continue on the right path to better myself and live, or I go back to what didn't get me nowhere . . . , making me more depressed. Now I'm here for myself to better myself and possibly for my children in the future. . . . I don't have her, but I am a spiritual dad. I'm not a dad on this earth, but I'm a father to a child in heaven." Being in the program allowed fathers like Emmett to claim identities as good dads and providers who showed up to work or school each day and strove for upward mobility for their children. DADS offered men a way of being there when they were unable to see or spend more money on behalf of their children.

Thus, to fathers, being there was not always about direct interaction with children. It could even mean the opposite, in the sense that long stretches of time away from children, especially due to work, indicated commitment to families. The reasons for separation determined if they were "there" or not. Fathers believed they were involved dads even when they were incarcerated or otherwise rarely saw kids. They rationalized that intent mattered more than the level of interaction, especially when they were trying to improve their own lives on behalf of their children. Orlando, a thirty-five-year-old Latino father of five, told me: "Kids need to *know* their father's time." By this, he meant that children knew where their fathers were and when they would see them next. Childhood memories of not knowing when and how much they would see their dads motivated men to prevent this doubt and disappointment for their own children. This is also why men understood participation in program activities as time spent physically away from children, but emotionally and psychologically with them. Knowing a father's time meant children knew that their dads were safe and doing something for their benefit.

Still, money was central to men's understandings of responsibility, and many felt demoralized as failed providers when they lacked the means to give their children more. Despite fathers' efforts to rationalize their relational, rather than just financial, value to children, many still grappled with the breadwinner ideology. Aaron, a twenty-one-year-old multiracial father of three, tried "not to shut myself out of their lives because I'm not providing enough." His children's mother would give him a list each month of the items his children needed. He was proud of the times he could afford to buy every item. Yet some months he came up short, prompting him to look for a second job. He too emphasized the importance of being there by "listening, physically and mentally, and understanding my kids' habits." But he dreamed of being able to buy anything his children needed or wanted. When their mother gave him that list, he wanted to be able to "tell her, 'OK, sure, give me a second. I'll go get the money and bring it right over,' without even really thinking or worrying how I'm going to make it and help them pay the bills." A truly responsible father, he concluded, was the kind who could take his child to a store "and say, 'Pick out anything you want,' without giving it a second thought. He's not someone who encourages their child to want less than the best because that is all he can afford." Like Aaron, many fathers described being there in aspirational terms, as in what they would do if unconstrained by lack of money. These descriptions conjured up images of possible selves who were successful earners and financially comfortable family men. They saw DADS as their only route to making these aspirations a reality.

This is likely why forty-five of the fifty fathers I interviewed told me they believed they were good fathers doing their best to fulfill their parenting responsibilities. Four others told me they were at least moderately good fathers. Only one said unequivocally that he was a bad father. Alas, almost everyone admitted they had doubts about their claims of being good dads, sensing that their actions did not always fully align with their understandings of being there in terms of how much they gave to and saw their children. Fathers blamed themselves for these shortcomings, while simultaneously acknowledging the barriers that prevented them from living up fully to their own definitions of responsible fatherhood. Low wages, geographic distance, homelessness, lack of transportation, custody arrangements, restraining orders, tense relationships with coparents, and addiction, among many other reasons, prevented men from realizing their parenting ambitions. The DADS program was essential in these cases for bridging the gap between men's paternal identities as involved fathers and their actual behaviors influenced by multiple and often insurmountable barriers. It was a unique situated space where they could redefine being a good provider as not just a parent committed to giving children financial support, but a father who loved them enough to change his life and life chances for their future well-being.

BEING THERE AS BEST THEY CAN

The men's stories aligned with Edin and Nelson's finding that marginalized fathers espouse a "doing the best I can" ethos that justifies providing materially only on an as-able basis, often through highly visible or essential items such as expensive sneakers or formula and diapers.[19] Given that this rarely covers half the actual costs of raising a child, mothers and others still believe that fathers' attempts to do what they can often fall far short of enacting the responsible parent role. Fathers' narratives indicated that they too were acutely aware of these perceived inadequacies and worked hard to develop identities as responsible fathers who reject narrow expectations of financial provision. On the surface, the result is a flexible and vague conception of responsibility whereby "being there" can mean doing anything on behalf of children.

Yet, considering the inequalities that structure the lives of marginalized fathers, being there—even its most essential component of staying alive—was no small feat for the men who found their way to DADS. It entailed resisting the pressure, both economic and social, to participate in illegal underground economies and gang activity, which risks cutting off paternal involvement if a father is incarcerated or, even worse, if he is killed. This resistance often requires fathers to cut off ties with close friends and family members. It also resigns them to the very low-wage sector of the formal labor market where even full-time work rarely earns enough to support a lone individual, much less a family. That these were core concerns of most of the men with whom I spoke revealed the inherent limitations of using definitions of paternal involvement based on white middle-class men as a starting point for political discussions of fathering. These accounts compel the question: What does "responsible fathering" look like when a man must worry that he may not make it to his child's next birthday?

These findings also showed how government programs enhance marginalized fathers' abilities to devise parenting scripts that allow them to resolve fundamental identity conflicts resulting from inequality. More broadly, they suggest how definitions of responsible fatherhood focused on time and care can be as problematic as those that emphasize breadwinning. Racism and economic vulnerability do not just undercut the ability of poor fathers of color to provide financially for their children. They prevent many from "being there" according to any definition.

Programs that focus on fathers' identity regarding issues of breadwinning and caregiving represent a radical shift in how policy intervenes in fathering. Political definitions of good fatherhood in the United States have hinged on economic self-sufficiency and family financial support. In a significant departure from these criteria, responsible fatherhood programs may be one of the most important political and social contexts for developing men's abilities to assert identities as successful men and fathers who circumvent singular expectations of economic providership.[20]

Offering fathers a space to connect with similarly situated men allows them to share and confide with others who empathize with what it is like to be on the margins of families and society.[21] By increasing men's sense of belonging and promoting a more inclusive understanding of family, fathering, and masculinity, programs can also be catalysts for changed perceptions of the gendered attributes of parenting.[22] They are also politically redefining what fatherhood means outside the narrow bounds of biological paternity, marriage to children's mothers, and financial child support. Shifting the perspective about the intended goals of fatherhood policies—from one solely focused on fathers' finances and children's outcomes to one that also acknowledges the importance of validating how men define, negotiate, and manage fathering expectations—is a powerful strategy for reducing the marginalization of men in family policy.[23]

Fathers' stories also reinforced the importance of designing policies and programs around the cultural dimensions of parenting that most make sense in the context of marginalized men's lives.[24] We must understand how and why particular models of fathering resonate more with low-income men because they account for the inequalities that profoundly shape their lives. Without this insight, definitions of fathering embedded in policy risk reinforcing those inequalities and culture-of-poverty assumptions about marginalized men's parenting. Fathers' narratives specifically point to the need to rethink paternal "responsibility" in the context of deeply entrenched structural constraints. Government definitions that task fathers with addressing children's full needs obscure how living up to one component of responsibility can jeopardize fulfilling others. Like Cayden, who quit high school to care for newborn Alisha, numerous fathers I studied experienced social and economic setbacks as the results of putting their children's needs first. Many had to choose between higher-paying illegal and life-threatening activities and making much less to ensure that they would live long enough to see their children grow up. This suggests that marginalized fathers emphasize care and time not only because they are the components of fatherhood they can actually achieve, but because it is the most emotionally resonant way marginalized men can justify making impossible parenting choices.

"Being there" signals more than a greater focus on time and love over money in men's descriptions of good fathering. That almost all the fathers I studied used this language indicates that it has become a common conceptual shorthand for reconciling the growing expectations of fathering and marginalized men's inabilities to realize them. Both ubiquitous and amorphous, "being there" can refer to any level and type of involvement, even enrolling in a fatherhood program like DADS. Lest one should think this renders the phrase meaningless, I argue that the opposite is actually true. Men across lines of race and class have embraced the "new" fatherhood cultural ideal that dads should be financial providers *and* nurturing caregivers.[25] That marginalized men equally espouse this multifaceted understanding of responsibility, despite the many more obstacles they face in fulfilling it, challenges culture-of-poverty assumptions that poor fathers of color hold different parenting values.[26] I found that "being there" captured how men used a fatherhood program to perform paternal identity work, especially by aligning their challenging lived experiences with culturally ascendant ideas of being worthy men and fathers.

Ultimately, in carefully listening to these men, I discovered how DADS helped them tailor their definitions of good parenting and providing to account for the socioeconomic constraints that eroded connections to their children. The program was an opportunity to abandon lifestyles, relationships, and disadvantages that undermined their fathering capabilities. As importantly, it helped them negotiate definitions of "good" versus "bad" fathers and reconfigure dominant fatherhood scripts—especially that of the good provider—based on the experiences of white middle-class men and the implicit exclusion of men like them. Cayden and his classmates pursued the program to align their identities as responsible fathers based on a breadwinning-plus script with their behaviors. As I show in the next chapter, what they found was a group of people who validated these flexible, more inclusive meanings of "being there" and helped them access the resources they needed to live up to them.

3 Resources for Responsibility

The lot where the DADS building was located contrasted noticeably with the surrounding area. Driving to the main program site took me through one of the poorest neighborhoods in the United States. Known locally as a hub of gang activity, the streets around the fenced property were just off the city's major highway. Dotted with corner stores, untended vacant lots, and houses with boarded windows, the location was not far from a rapidly gentrifying downtown. Lush parks and expensive suburban housing developments in the oft-described "family friendly" affluent part of town were only a few miles away. This area had a reputation for "bad" schools, blighted housing, and crime. As my car approached the DADS building, I saw billboards with images of happy children reminding parents of the importance of daily reading and eating fruits and vegetables. Yet, on this drive, I saw more police cars than libraries where parents could get books to read to their children. Although many of the community's residents were local fieldworkers who picked produce, often for less than minimum wage, there were no farmers markets or grocery stores nearby.

On my way to meet the DADS program director, a uniformed security guard greeted me at the gate and directed me to park near the front entrance of the well-kept main building. I noticed a garden on the east side budding with vegetables and a play yard for kids. The waiting area right past the front door had several computers, a couple of phone stations, and a printer. An orientation for a job training program attended by about fifteen men was taking place in the large central conference area. The leader was going over dress requirements and penalties for showing up late. Otherwise, the building was quiet, except for the occasional person walking through in work uniform—green shirt, khaki pants, and dark work boots.

I met Amber, the program director, in her office. Along with typical furnishings of a desk, chair, and computer, the office had shelves stocked with hundreds of children's books and diapers and an area filled with car seats and a refrigerator-sized box of baby clothes. Amber offered me a tour of the rest of the campus and introduced me to other staff and fathers in the program. Everyone was friendly and conversed with a sense of familiarity. Amber guided me through the community kitchen and invited me to peek into classrooms where fathers in DADS were taking high school English, math, and history classes. Teachers seemed eager to answer questions from the men, who in turn appeared happily willing to pass along this information to their classmates. As the tour continued outside, we walked through a basketball court surrounded by additional classrooms. Other men in green uniform T-shirts walked around the building, chatting with one another. Some were mopping the kitchen and bathrooms and tending to the trashcans around the periphery of the buildings. I overhead a father with two young children inquiring at the front desk about DADS.

When we returned to her office, Amber, twenty-eight and Black, eagerly described for me how she understood the purpose of the program: "We start with the assumption that dads want to be involved but have many obstacles in their way. It may be because they don't know how or don't feel comfortable, or for many they don't feel deserving. The program gives them a sense of belonging, to see the importance of their role and understand they're not alone. Just because they weren't there the whole time doesn't mean they can never go back. It doesn't mean they're deadbeats and all the other derogatory things they've been called." Amber ended by explaining how DADS was about getting fathers to acknowledge their worth and grasp that they deserved to be in their children's lives.

I would soon discover the importance of this space for how men in DADS, many of whom came from the poor neighborhood surrounding the building, experienced and thought about responsible fathering. Most fathers enrolled to complete their high school diplomas while working in paid training programs in landscaping, recycling, and janitorial services. About two-thirds—forty-two fathers—were attending the DADS high school, and many of these went to school and worked on alternating weeks. Depending on whether they were full or part time, those working for DADS earned $200 to $600 a month. Although all program services were voluntary and fathers could leave DADS at any time, some participated to meet court-ordered child support requirements and to bolster their claims in custody disputes. Wages, academic credit, and support services were contingent on fathers being on time, wearing uniforms, following directions from teachers and work crew bosses, and attending twenty to forty hours per week.

As I showed in the previous chapter, almost all of the fathers I studied defined themselves as good dads who were striving to become even better fathers. This was the case despite how much money they earned, how often they saw their children, and whether they were on good terms with their children's mothers. Nevertheless, many fathers also had a sense that their actual behaviors did not always align with or live up to their understandings of "being there." DADS was essential in these cases for bridging the gap between their identities as responsible fathers and their constrained realities.

One of these fathers was Cayden, whom we met at the beginning of chapter 2. By setting him up to work and go to school, DADS allowed Cayden to offer more for his son, Cayden Jr., and to pay his monthly $80 in child support for his daughter, Alisha. It also enabled him to make progress toward a high school diploma that would likely improve his earning potential. As importantly, Cayden noted, DADS offered social support and symbolic resources. Taking classes focused on valuing fathers increased Cayden's confidence in his parenting abilities and, he hoped, signaled that he was a devoted father who challenged the "deadbeat" dad label so often applied to poor men of color. He told me: "You got to wonder how it feels as a father to wake up in this skin every day. You're already stereotyped. I might get shot in the neighborhood I'm walking through to get here, but I'm still taking that risk to get to work, to get my kid some diapers." Through DADS, Cayden came to see himself as a responsible father and worker committed to being there and providing for his children. He hoped a DADS graduation certificate would allow future employers, Alisha's and Cayden Jr.'s mothers, and the judge overseeing his child support case to see him in the same way.

Men in DADS struggled to realize their definitions of responsible fathering that combined expectations of breadwinning, caregiving, and providing opportunities for their children. Because all these components of involvement require resources that marginalized men are unlikely to have, they often feel like failed fathers. As shown in the previous chapter, a primary benefit of the program was how it validated men's multifaceted understandings of paternal provision, including the idea that a man was a "good provider" as long as he offered his children a father committed to their well-being and future prosperity. Yet men often experienced a conflict between this idea of good fathering and their social and economic constraints.

This chapter draws from fathers' narratives to show how DADS helped them overcome those obstacles by giving them financial, social, and symbolic resources. Fathers believed that participating in the program was itself a way of being there for their children because it offered a physical and social context where fathers could claim and enact their identities as responsible dads. Inside the program, others recognized fathers foremost as parents, employees, and students. This was a marked contrast to the stigmatized statuses—gang member, ex-convict, drop out—they carried outside it. It was these negative labels, they believed, that hindered their economic opportunities, paternal involvement, and ability to see themselves—and have others see them—as responsible, hardworking family providers. In describing what DADS offered him, Cayden explained how the program supported his goal of becoming an even better father:

> The program gives you focus. It keeps you away from these people that are your age that are not doing nothing, the ones that are making fun of you when you get off work, calling you a sucker for being a dad. . . . It gives you something to look forward to and to do. It keeps your life on track. It gives you a schedule. You've got to be in bed by this time if you want to go to work by this time. . . . It sets a certain standard in your life. It feels good to come home in your suit and see how your mother-in-law is looking at you. You're getting off work, you got your boots on, and you're walking proud. . . . Even

though this job doesn't pay that much, it's just the fact that you're willing to work. You're willing to learn.

Like Cayden, most of the men I spoke with described how DADS allowed them to become the kind of men who show up to their jobs every day, bring home a paycheck (however small), and strive for a better life by finishing school and earning the credentials they needed for stable, legal, better-paying work. For some, the program allowed them to stay alive and out of jail because it provided just enough money for them to justify ceasing dangerous and illegal activities, namely being in gangs and selling drugs. The program also enabled fathers to demonstrate their parenting commitments to those who controlled access to their children, including judges responsible for deciding custody and child support cases and mothers who were primary custodial parents. DADS did not necessarily reshape how marginalized men defined responsible fatherhood. What it did was allow fathers to live up to their definitions.

Still, many fathers admitted that the program did not always enable them to provide as much or see their children as often as they wanted. The money they earned from work was rarely enough to meet their own basic needs, much less fully support their children. As Christopher described in chapter 1, even with his DADS certificate, he struggled to find work, as did all the other fathers he knew who went through the program. Some men were also worried that, even with their new diplomas, they would be competing in the job market with others who had some college, more work experience, and no incarceration histories. Half of the fathers did not live with any of their children due to homelessness, tense relationships with mothers, or in a few cases, restraining orders after incidents of assault.

This raises important questions about how much programs like DADS meaningfully change marginalized fathers' life circumstances and if programs actually have tangible impacts on their children. Most fathers I studied were in the middle of their two-year terms in DADS and did not yet know how much the program would really enhance their economic opportunities. Although optimistic, many confided that they were uncertain they could increase their earnings beyond poverty-level wages, become stable financial providers, and be consistently present in their children's lives. What they knew for sure was that being in the program gave them a rare chance to prove that they were working toward these goals. Fathers' beliefs that DADS was the only option for changing their lives is key to understanding fatherhood programs' benefits and limitations.

A SOCIAL SPACE FOR FATHERING

Some have criticized responsible fatherhood policy for assuming that poor men lack a mainstream work ethic and therefore need government programs to supervise and modify their behaviors in line with dominant social expectations of responsible fathering.[1] Relatedly, one of the key issues raised by responsible fatherhood programming is whether policy and state-supported programs can encourage marginalized men to develop alternative views of successful parenting and act according to these viewpoints. However, as we saw in the last chapter, just like fathers across the class spectrum, men in DADS defined *providing* more broadly than just financial support. They called into question middle-class assumptions that shape political understandings of good fathering and highlighted how the costs associated with providing—whether it be the provision of money, time, or care—often exceed the means of poor fathers.

Much of the "crisis of fatherhood" has been construed in terms of values or culture, which overestimates how much autonomy individual fathers have to act in line with their definitions of responsibility.[2] This feeds stereotypical portrayals of "deadbeat" dads who are unmotivated to work hard to meet their children's needs.[3] These stereotypes in turn support individualistic explanations for social problems that blame irresponsible fathers for everything from poverty and crime to prostitution and low graduation rates in communities of color. Many fault government policies on responsible fatherhood for perpetuating a deficit perspective that focuses on what men lack personally rather than what society denies them structurally.[4] These criticisms compel us to question how institutional arrangements, including policies and inequalities, either promote or prevent parental involvement. This requires a situated understanding of fatherhood that links context, values, and experiences to reveal how the social and symbolic dimensions of particular physical settings shape how men enact and express their fathering identities.[5]

Responsible fatherhood programs are therefore an important case for understanding the contextual nature of fatherhood.[6] Prior research has highlighted how fatherhood programs provide spaces for marginalized men to develop views of successful parenting that are achievable within the context of their economic constraints.[7] Yet little of this prior work has sufficiently addressed the role of resources and opportunities in shaping the identity work fathers do as they seek to sustain, strengthen, or repair relationships with their children. By exploring how fathers experienced DADS as a situated space where they could overcome obstacles to involvement, this chapter reveals how fathering is a social process shaped by state practices, as well as intersecting inequalities of race, class, and gender.

Laura Curran and Laura Abrams criticized responsible fatherhood policy for assuming a deficit perspective "that understands poverty's consequences as lifestyle choices and does not acknowledge the rigidity of the social and economic barriers that the men face."[8] By attempting to "mold both the behavior and inner psychologies of men," they claimed, fatherhood programs ultimately do little to address larger race and class inequalities that undermine paternal involvement.[9]

Other assessments of fatherhood programs have analyzed how they account for the intentions and circumstances of fathers in poverty. Kevin Roy and Omari Dyson found that fatherhood programs were rare spaces where low-income men could shape positive paternal identities in the context of "unpredictable and risky local communities and long-standing social stigmas due to race and class."[10] By facilitating a network of mentors and peers that help participants avoid isolation and stigmatization as deadbeat dads, some fatherhood programs explicitly challenge an individualized discourse of irresponsibility that construes low or no involvement as a personal lifestyle choice.

I add to this debate by showing how fatherhood programs have powerful potential to illuminate how fathering suffers when men lack resources and opportunities. Responsible fatherhood policy was a response to concerns that many men deliberately refuse to take individual responsibility for their children. In an ironic twist, the programs this policy supports have become one of the most important political and social spaces for revealing how systemic factors enable or constrain what policy prescribes as responsible parenting behaviors. As Amber explained to me that first day in her office, DADS structured services based on the assumption that fathers are already motivated to be involved, but lack the means and support needed to develop, express, and enact statuses as responsible parents.[11] Studies of similar fatherhood programs have also found that men voluntarily enroll because they want to be there for their children and become better fathers.[12] This suggests that an aspiration to be a good father is a strong predictor of enrollment in fatherhood programs rather than an outcome of participation.

Nevertheless, it is difficult for any single intervention to address the individual effects of social and economic trends that have prevented marginalized fathers' involvement in recent decades, including bad job markets, high rates of incarceration among men of color, and growing family instability.[13] Men who enroll in fatherhood programs face significant obstacles, including strained relationships with coparents, low wages, and the stigma of criminality.[14] Prior research has found that fatherhood programs rarely advance fathers' long-term employment opportunities and often fail to help men secure a status as consistent financial providers.[15] This raises important questions about responsible fatherhood programs' efficacy and the metrics by which we deem them successful. Are programs effective only if they produce tangible benefits in terms of fathers' earnings, employment, child support payments, and time spent with children? How much does their impact on fathers' self-images and sense of paternal self-efficacy matter independently of these measures?

As I will show, the answers to these questions are crucial for grasping fully the social, political, and economic value of fatherhood policies. It should also be noted that these different ways of thinking about the success of fatherhood programs are not wholly distinct. Fathers' involvement is strongly associated with how much men are invested in and satisfied with their paternal identity and how much value they ascribe to the fathering role.[16] In other words, identity motivates behavior. Men are also more likely to be involved fathers when they think others believe they are doing a good job. Therefore, having access to a space that affirms criteria of good fathering they believe they can achieve—and especially where others recognize and praise them as responsible fathers—could motivate further involvement. As time-limited opportunities that target select groups of individual men, fatherhood programs are ill equipped to address larger structural inequalities that undermine fathering. Still, they have potential to counteract how these inequalities shape men's fathering identities and some of the individual-level consequences of poverty and racism.

Drawing from fathers' narratives about their experiences in DADS, I propose an alternative way of understanding the value and efficacy of fatherhood programs. DADS was informed less by the logic that poverty is the result of cultural values or lifestyle choices than by the recognition that poor men of color face deeply entrenched social and economic barriers. DADS provided a situated space where marginalized men believed they could cast off the controlling image of the deadbeat dad label by claiming a broadly defined provider status. I show in this chapter how this challenges an individualized and deficit-focused discourse of paternal irresponsibility.

Given that I studied only one program, I do not suggest that DADS was qualitatively different from other programs researched to date. What my in-depth study of DADS did reveal is a new perspective on the value of fatherhood programs, especially their ability to provide men with the basics necessary for what policy and social norms define as "responsible" fathering. More generally, this case indicates how the actual conduct of fathering is shaped less by role expectations than by the resources to which fathers have access.

For participants, DADS was a rare space where they could legitimately identify as providers who offered children money, opportunity, and care. It was also a place where they could prove they were actively trying to alter their lives and life chances for the well-being of their families. Rather than reshaping their paternal identities, men emphasized how the program provided an opportunity structure in which they could more readily achieve their ideas of good parenting. This illuminates how marginalized men work hard to tailor their parental self-images in accordance with their challenging circumstances. It also points to the need for policies to focus more on the social and economic contexts of fathering and less on shaping men's views of themselves as fathers, which already align with dominant expectations of paternal responsibility. Chapter 2 offered insight into the meanings and goals marginalized men attached to fathering. Building on this, here I show how DADS became a social environment in which men could actually act on these aspirations.

DITCHING THE "DEADBEAT" DAD LABEL

Fathers explained how DADS ascribed great worth to men's parenting, something devalued in the other social spaces where they lived. Outside the gates of the program, fathers felt that others automatically judged them as irresponsible parents because they were poor men of color. Inside the program, they received praise from staff and other participants who lauded their commitments to doing and being better for their children. Their time in DADS allowed them to challenge race, class, and gender stereotypes embedded in the deadbeat dad controlling image.[17] This was the main topic of conversation in the first focus group I conducted. Five fathers—Keegan, Douglas, Cayden, Jesse, and Saul—poignantly discussed how they were always falling short of others' expectations about what kind of parents and people they should be. DADS connected them with others who deeply empathized with this perpetual struggle. It was a place where they could prove that they were not deadbeats who neglected their kids.

KEEGAN (twenty-one, Black, father of three): You can't even get a job at McDonald's if you don't have your high school diploma. But now I know I ain't the only one going through these issues. Other guys here, you're going through it too. Yet every time you turn on the TV or hear something on the radio or in the newspaper, you hear about a dad ain't doing this. The dad done this, but it's always something negative. You don't hardly hear anything good about a dad.

DOUGLAS (twenty-three, Black, father of one): Yeah, especially with minorities, you hear a lot of things like, "Oh, you Black or Mexican, you don't raise your kids."

KEEGAN: Yeah, like Black guys are never there, or Mexicans neither.

DOUGLAS: But [DADS] is like a trophy. This is something we did as fathers. We're learning. We're becoming good fathers. Can't nobody put us in the minor league right now. We know what we do every day. Most fathers ain't doing it. A lot of people don't really want to come out and say, "I need help as a father."

CAYDEN: Yeah, because people think Blacks are always going to leave, and Mexicans too. It's like they think all we do is drink, beat our women, and hit our kids.

KEEGAN: Right, like all Black dudes do is they just get girls pregnant just to have kids, and that we don't want to take care of them.

As this part of their conversation revealed, men knew others judged them harshly for being poor men of color without degrees or jobs. Yet, in the program, men felt valued as employees, students, volunteers, community members, and especially devoted dads.

As fathers continued talking, they discussed shaming from peers outside DADS for being committed fathers, which others interpreted as meaning weak men. This left fathers in a bind. If they were highly involved, some questioned their masculinity; if they were not, others deemed them deadbeats. Outside the program gate, fathers received contradictory messages about the connection between manhood and fatherhood, especially from other men who negatively judged them for parenting behaviors regarded as feminine. Immediately after Keegan's comment in the focus group about stereotypes of Black men, Cayden continued: "Yet, when I walk down the street in my uniform, people make fun of me, like, 'Oh, Cayden, you're still up there?'"

> JESSE (twenty, Black, father of two): You're already labeled.
>
> CAYDEN: I'm taking a risk even walking home from here to get to work, just to take care of my kid. A lot of people don't want to go through that. That's why they're stuck in a circle.
>
> JESSE: This has been the only place we can have positive conversations about fatherhood. . . . The conversation we're having now, we're not going to sit up and have this same conversation on the street.
>
> CAYDEN: Yeah, I take all this home with me.
>
> SAUL (twenty-two, Latino, father of one): Pushing your stroller down the street, somebody ride by and call you a sucker. You with your baby mama, and they say, "Oh, you cupcaking."[18] But this is my baby mama, and now you're making it feel awkward.

Men described having unique interactions with fellow participants around fatherhood issues. They lauded and affirmed one another for being devoted dads. In doing so, they co-constructed a communal space where being an engaged father was considered a high-status masculine activity.

Their mutual recognition of one another as legitimate fathers and men moved them to challenge racist, classist, and gendered stereotypes of good parenting. Returning to the focus group conversation:

KEEGAN: It takes a lot to be a father when you're poor and Black. You don't even know.

DOUGLAS: Yeah, the money, the home, the food.

JESSE: And it ain't easy living your life knowing at any moment you're going to have to give it all up. Right now, my son and baby mama, she needs some money. If that's my last money, I got to give that up. If somebody hurts them, I'd give up my whole life. I grew up with nothing, so it wasn't hard for me to give my child more than what I had because I didn't have anything.

CAYDEN: [DADS] let me get out of the game, get me a job, so that part of my life, the gangs, my son won't even know about. I got seven certificates from here for different trainings, and that's all he needs to see.

DOUGLAS: I got to get one of those so I can put it on my resumé.

CAYDEN: It shows you accomplished something.

SAUL: I've worked sixteen hours a day to support my kids and baby mama. I do it, and I'm here because I want to be the kind of dad that can just take my kid into a store without counting my money and shit, thinking about what else I got to pay for. I want him to know that he can get whatever he needs, and that he ain't sitting there looking up at me asking, "Which one, Daddy? Can I get that one?" And you got to sit there and look at him and question it all. You'll be thinking, "Oh, I'm the only person going through this. Ain't nobody else know what this is like." [Gesturing to others in the group] But they do.

KEEGAN: We all either been through the same thing or going through it at the same time.

JESSE: It feels good when you're not alone.

DOUGLAS: They make you want to be here.

CAYDEN: I didn't know I could do this. But now I get up every day, take that risk, have a routine of coming to work. Then when I leave work, I go home and learn how to be a better father, all in one day.

This conversation captured the many reasons men came to and stayed in the program. It provided social support from both committed staff and similarly disadvantaged men coping with the same family and financial challenges. DADS was also the only opportunity men believed they had to disprove that they were fathering failures. To them, DADS was both a community of accountability and a badge of accomplishment.

Men also often spoke of how other fathers and staff rarely judged them for not conforming to normative definitions of successful fatherhood shaped by classist and racist assumptions. It was the one social space where they did not feel stigmatized for not living with their children, having a criminal record or gang affiliation, sharing children with more than one woman, and especially for being men of color. Darius, a twenty-three-year-old Black father of one, explained:

> When I come here, they don't see my tattoos. They really care about me the person. . . . You don't need to go robbing anybody, don't have to go shooting no one. All you have to do here is work. It's easy. You're not judged here for being Black or having a past on the streets. . . . When I leave the gate, it's a whole different program. When I walk past people, they grab their purse. I walk by a hotel, they grab their phone. Second chances are rare out there. . . . This program will hire people regardless of race. I tell other guys, "If you're really trying to work, if you're really trying to get your diploma, trying to get your life right, this is the place you need to be." This program is not a gamble like other jobs.

This remark prompted other men in the focus group to admit that, because they were members of rival gangs, DADS was the only place they could interact and bond over their shared commitments to children.

In response to Darius, Cristobal a thirty-seven-year-old Latino father of five, confided: "People here actually care about if you're OK and your kids. There's a lot of negativity at home, but they don't judge anyone here. [Pointing at Darius] He can't go to my neighborhood. I can't go to his. But here it's neutral. Here there's people from all different gangs and neighborhoods. They can come into this campus and work together, not have any conflict, any fight. They work at everything side by side. But when you leave the gate, you're on the streets, and you can't let your guard down. You don't have to watch your back here." Darius worried that the end of his time in the program would throw him back into the streets, where he would fear for his life and lose contact with his children. As the conversation ended, it became clearer what Cristobal meant by letting his guard down in DADS. It was a place where men could focus on work, school, and fathering and worry less about getting shot, stabbed, or arrested. It was not just a space for the kinds of "second chances" Darius mentioned. For many fathers, it was their first real opportunity to be given the benefit of the doubt as dads doing the best they could for their kids.

Even those who had no prior or current connections to gangs feared for their lives and getting caught up somehow in the prison system. Randy, a twenty-nine-year-old Black father of three, lost a close friend to a "shoot out" two days before our interview. He said, "I ain't no gang-banger or nothing like that, but as a Black man, I might as well be, based on how other people see me." For Randy, being in DADS was about getting others to see him differently. He wanted people to look at him and see a strong Black man, a hard worker, and a loving father on his way up the social ladder. He did not want people to see a "gang-banger" or criminal destined to be shot on the street or spend his days away from his three young children locked in a jail cell. Until he enrolled in DADS, he spent a lot of time worrying that his fate was one or the other. As it did for Randy, the program freed up men's emotional and psychological resources to think about their children and future family goals. For most, it was one of the first times they were thinking about any long-term future at all.

In DADS, no one questioned men's pasts or the routes they had taken to fatherhood. Being an involved father was a highly valued identity in the program. This is why many fathers I spoke with told me that the program felt like a "family" and "home" where you could vocalize your troubles without being blamed for them. Because fathers came from similar backgrounds, they deeply understood how life was not always within an individual's control, especially when that individual grew up in a poor family and community with few resources to protect them. In DADS, the only life decision that mattered was whether someone was trying to become a better father in spite of any setbacks. Alex, twenty-four, Latino, and a father of one, powerfully captured this when he told me: "Children are not something you make and forget about, but people used to assume that's what I did. People look at me differently now that I'm in the program."

Similarly, Facundo, a nineteen-year-old Latino father of one, explained: "I feel like this is home to me. . . . We actually come together and have fun. We sit together at lunch and talk about what we're going through. We sit in our groups. We play basketball." When I asked Facundo why this sense of camaraderie was important to him, he got teary-eyed and explained that other spaces of connection, especially with fellow men, were risky and often life threatening:

> I grew up seeing my family do a lot of gang banging and [drugs]. All I can worry about is now, how to finish out today, get to the end of the day. . . . I've seen friends go and come. For drive-bys, all you have to do is be at the wrong place at the right time. It's not a pretty sight. I've seen blood on my hands, not my blood, at least not yet. . . . I've had to cut off a lot of my homies. I tell them that they can come to my house whenever they want if they need something like food, clothes, a drink of water, but don't come to my house disrespecting. . . . I have too many priorities on the line. This program is keeping me straight and busy. I'm not at home fucking around with my friends on the street. I have a full plate to take care of, and I have to eat one thing at a time. As long as [my son] is taken care of, he has his clothes, his food, his Pampers, anything he needs. This program keeps me from having to sell drugs for that money. Otherwise we're stuck in the ditch. We're all stuck in a box we can't get out.

As part of his promise to turn away from street life and do anything to support his son, he enrolled in a program through DADS to have his gang tattoos removed. He had already chosen the picture of his son he wanted etched on top of the first tattoo he got. To Facundo, this would be a fitting symbolic reminder of how his new life as a responsible father would soon overshadow his dangerous and impoverished past, that metaphorical ditch out of which he was working so hard to crawl.

Facundo's classmate Elias—twenty-one, Latino, and a father of one—had a similar plan. He was covered fully from the neck down in gang tattoos, the first of which he received at age ten. Elias was mere hours away from doing something that would have likely landed him in prison for the rest of his life when his girlfriend sent him a picture via text of a positive pregnancy test. Reflecting on the memory of that moment, Elias described his unborn son as having "saved my life." DADS was an important part of that redemption: "I don't want to do anything now except work or school. Outside everything else means trouble. People in other parts of my life want me to fail. Here they want me to succeed. They want me to end up alive with that baby, not dead on the streets."

For these men, DADS conferred self-respect and gave them a basis from which to challenge racist assumptions that they lacked motivation to be involved fathers and hard workers. Once they enrolled, and especially the longer they stayed, the more they believed others' perceptions of them changed. They readily shared with others in their lives about their progress through the program, and fathers often showed me crumpled certificates earned from DADS that they carried with them in their wallets and backpacks. Justin, a thirty-four-year-old Black father of three, noted: "We have a strike against us already because we're African American. We've got to be out to make people see us differently. With that strike, you've got to do well in school, and you've got to buckle down." Justin further described how the support he gave to and received from other fathers kept him going. Race, he noted, did not often come up in classes, only that "It's a little rougher on Black men."

However, he also indicated that he and his fellow participants had an unspoken understanding that being in the program was one of the few ways that Black men like him could prove their parenting. DADS gave them hope that others could see them differently, which meant viewing them as responsible fathers who were as committed to their children as any white man with a college degree, a steady job, and a big paycheck. When one father was down on his luck, the others rallied to help him out. This is why, more than once, Justin bought diapers for his classmates. Based on his own experiences, he was well aware of how his peers would be deemed "deadbeat" if they showed up to see kids empty-handed. This, Justin told me, was the power of the program and the most significant indicator of their shared commitment to fathering: Men who would otherwise risk getting into life-threatening altercations on the street were buying diapers and food for each other's kids.

These perspectives and experiences poignantly illustrate the importance of context for claiming and enacting responsible father identities. Marginalized men are often missing far more than the material resources for escaping poverty and what they described as "street life." They were also deprived of social status as successful and devoted fathers. Waking up in their skins and in their neighborhoods every day meant that they were immediately judged as men who made babies, left, and confirmed the deadbeat dad stereotype central to social and political discourses about poor fathers of color. They were acutely aware that the deadbeat label was a controlling image of poor Black and Brown fatherhood that shaped others' perceptions of their parenting priorities, intentions, and identities. They used the program to reject this label and related culture-of-poverty assumptions that they did not value hard work and their paternal responsibilities.

Fathers' stories captured how prohibitively difficult it can be to live up to these values when faced with the daily threat of violence, incarceration, deprivation, and death. In describing how the program enabled him to be a better dad, Harris, eighteen, Black, and a father of one, simply said: "I'm eighteen, and I'm not in jail. . . . Just to make it to eighteen was an accomplishment. I wasn't locked up or in the grave. [DADS] is a great opportunity, a safe environment where you can work. It opened a lot of doors for me. I was at that door, but not walking through it. Coming to this helped me walk through that door. I don't have a lot to offer, but I'm going to make sure I'm in my kid's life." By automatically conferring respect and recognizing them foremost as devoted fathers for walking through the door, DADS became a situated space where trusted others supported their efforts to be responsible fathers. In essence, the program gave them what more privileged men tend to develop merely by virtue of their race and economic position: self-images as good parents and men not marked deficient.

BEING THERE AS GOOD PROVIDERS

Although fathers redefined the good provider role to include the provision of time and care, breadwinning was still central to how men understood their paternal responsibilities. Being a productive worker who earned a good, legal wage and set an example for his children was a major goal for most men. This became especially clear when fathers talked about how DADS enabled them to "be there" for their children. Fathers described their participation in the program, whether through work, school, parenting classes, or a combination of the three, as ways of being involved in their children's lives. These activities allowed men to align their behaviors with their definitions of good fathering. Marcus, a twenty-one-year-old Black father of one, explained: "My son knows Dad goes to work. He gets up every morning. That's the thing I want him to see. 'If Dad gets up and goes to work, maybe I should get up and go to work. My dad gets up and goes to school. I should get up and go to school.' That's what I think makes me a good father because I try to be there like that." Marcus did not have a driver's license, could not afford a car, and did not trust the bus to get him to the DADS building by 7:00 a.m., so he biked four miles back and forth each day. He was jealous of other fathers who had a car and could increase the geographic range of their job searches. He was desperately hoping that another position would open up at the Mexican fast-food restaurant a short block's walk from his house. In the meantime, he was proud to work through DADS, which gave him the bicycle he used to commute. He concluded: "It does make me feel like less of man because there are other dudes out there who got the car and the better job because of it. It makes me really low sometimes. Then again, I keep reminding myself that I'm on the stage to get there. When I put on my hardhat and my vest, and I'm out in public walking around, I feel good, like I'm doing something good, that I'm part of something. It makes me feel important, like I'm being a role model for my son." Seemingly simple things like bicycles that enabled them to get to work faster were profound to the fathers in DADS.

Men were equally proud of transmitting a strong work ethic to their children as they were of financially supporting them through wages earned from work. Many men spoke about the power and pride of wearing the DADS work uniform. Some described how they kept their soiled and sweat-soaked green program T-shirts on well after the end of the work day when they knew they would see children later that night. Jonathan, a twenty-three-year-old Latino father of two, expressed what coming home in his uniform meant to him and his six-year-old son: "When I'm in that shirt, he knows that I'm at work making money. In the future, he's going to be like, 'Oh, yeah, I saw my dad go in to work every day. He was a hard worker, and I want to be like him and follow in his footsteps.'"

For some fathers, especially those who had little or no contact with their children, being in the program prevented social isolation and provided hope that they would be together in the near future. Udell, a twenty-three-year-old Latino father of two, had not seen his children in three weeks when we spoke and was using the program to "get my head straight and work out a lot of pain and bad experiences." He desperately wanted to get his life in order before his three-year-old daughter and one-year-old son would start to remember the long stretches of time they were separated. As long as he earned some money, he could see himself as a successful breadwinner who was working to remedy this situation. "When they get older, they're gonna realize Daddy tried his best and is still trying to keep contact with them. They have to see me as a positive person, a hardworking man, not just a guy on the couch all day and a do-nothing or drug dealing and hustling. This keeps me busy, and I'm not home by myself." Udell dreaded what might happen if he was not accountable to the program. The thought of being at home alone and anxious over whether he would soon see his children was too difficult to ponder. Until he could see them again, the program conferred self-respect, allowed him to earn something, and kept him from "doing something stupid" that might jeopardize their reunion.

Fathers knew they were beholden to breadwinner expectations and that their kids had to eat and have a roof over their heads. Men explained how living up to any component of responsible fatherhood—time, care, or money—required resources they simply did not have. Most of the fathers I studied were many credits shy of their high school diplomas. Given their limited formal education and its effects on their legal employment opportunities, they experienced extreme pressure to make money through informal underground economies and gang activity. These were ways to make significantly more money than in the minimum-wage jobs they could get, but they risked cutting off paternal involvement if incarcerated, or worse, killed. Men were acutely aware that such methods of providing their children with more money meant taking life-threatening risks. They also knew that the multiple components of being there required them to make impossible choices between providing their children money and providing the care and time associated with a consistent paternal presence. For this reason, fathers often described the program as a way of "being there" for children because it kept them alive and out of jail.

DADS was not equipped to help directly with expungements or navigating parole requirements, criminal background checks, or job applications requiring the disclosure of prior felony convictions. Yet it was a documentable activity useful for job searches and court proceedings, as it could attest that a father with a criminal record was actively trying to turn his life around. Beyond this, many fathers specifically noted that DADS paid just enough for them to stop illegal and dangerous money-making activities. Lester, a forty-year-old Black father of four, confided that the program enabled him to offer money and care for his children without risking his life. He had been shot, stabbed, and incarcerated for selling drugs, all in an effort to feed his children. He wanted to:

> be there to answer the kids' questions, discipline the kids, basically be in tune with the kids' feelings. . . . With the program, I'll take two hundred dollars every two weeks instead of two thousand. . . . With that two hundred dollars every two weeks, you don't have to worry about the same thing when you're making that two thousand. You don't have to worry about going to jail. You don't have to worry about looking over your back. You don't have to worry about people breaking into your house, thinking you're doing something more than you are. . . . It's going to kill you in the long run, that two thousand dollars, but the two hundred keep you safe. It helps you get closer to your kids.

Like Lester, almost half of the fathers I interviewed told me they had a criminal record and had served at least one prison or jail sentence. Upon release, they faced significant obstacles to reenrolling in school and finding legal, well-paying jobs. DADS did not penalize or stigmatize them for having a criminal record. Instead, it gave them an opportunity to stay off the streets and away from the temptation to earn more money in activities that jeopardized their lives and sustaining relationships with their kids.

Alec, twenty-one, Black, and a father of one, understood this all too well. After his mother went to jail when he was fifteen, he was forced to quit school to work in the fields and care full-time for his five younger siblings and disabled father. As he showed me a picture of his infant daughter, he lamented:

> You go out and try to find a job, but if you don't have that diploma, nobody wants you. . . . We got a long life to live, and you can cut it short, or you can have it long. Out hanging in the streets, doing the wrong thing, selling drugs, gang banging, talking about this side, that side, when everybody should be on the same side. It wasn't the life I wanted to live. [DADS] got my head more focused, and I know what I want for myself and for my kids. You can hustle and do all the stuff you want day by day, but when it comes down to the long run, you get locked up or anything, you don't got no bank account, you have no income, you have nothing to back you up. That six

hundred dollars a month I take from here is tight, but it allows me to get by, to buy diapers, to have a future with my kids.

On the streets, fathers lived in the present because money and the assurance that they would come home to their kids at night were not guaranteed. DADS allowed them to envision and plan for a future where they supported their kids and watched them grow up.

Many men also spoke of how the program provided structure for their lives, gave them a reason to wake up, and channeled their energy toward being involved fathers. They took pride in getting to work on time and knowing that their case managers, supervisors, and fellow work crew members and students would be worried or upset if they did not show. The program gave Peter, a twenty-three-year-old Black father of two, a positive way to spend his time and earn money: "The program keeps me too busy to think about revenge for my baby mama. I wasn't doing nothing, and now I'm doing something."

Similarly, Christopher "lost everything" and hit rock bottom right before he enrolled. Without housing, a car, a job, a girlfriend, or access to his son, he found himself without much to live for after he was arrested for selling drugs. He told me that he could spend a "day in the street lifestyle and make a couple thousand," whereas a long day's work in the program with overtime was only worth about one hundred dollars. Those thousands, however, came with a steeper cost: the threat of more jail time and lost years not watching his son grow up to know him. He was no longer willing to take that chance. When I asked if the lower pay was worth it, he did not hesitate:

Most definitely, not a doubt in my mind. Because I get to come home and see my girl, see my son. I don't have to worry about looking over my shoulder. No, it's not as much money, but I work for it. I'm proud of it. I *am* working for it. It's something that I had to get up and devote my time and myself to get. I'm not depending on anybody else to give it to me. I'm getting up on my own every day and doing what I have to do to take care of my responsibilities. . . . You just have to get in the mentality of getting yourself into a schedule, a routine, being on time, and making it a priority. . . . As a man, it made me feel like I was doing something with myself, not just making a couple of dollars. . . . I make less money now, but that money is guaranteed. I'm more at ease, at peace, because at least I don't have to worry about if someone is going to rob or shoot me.

For fathers like Christopher, donning their DADS uniform and displaying their DADS certificates allowed them to embody a responsible worker and father identity previously denied them.

Being in the program was also a powerful status marker for dads. Ricky, a twenty-two-year-old Black father of one, explained as he pointed to the paint and perspiration stains on his uniform: "I'd much rather be coming home looking like this from working hard than from hustling in the damn streets. I ain't going to be lucky enough to wake up every morning to just sit there." Living with the daily threat of violence and death was not conducive to being attentive fathers who could focus on caring for and supporting their children. In contrast, DADS offered a structured social context in which fathers could access education, safe employment, and social support in the form of case managers, supervisors, teachers, and other fathers who cared about them, held them accountable, and saw them as responsible parents and successful breadwinners.

Although DADS was a government-funded program, which most fathers knew, it was notable that none viewed it as a government handout, but rather as a source of money and opportunity earned through labor. Fathers spoke about wanting to get off other forms of assistance, such as food stamps and cash aid, but they did not describe DADS as having the same stigma of dependency. Instead, they saw the program as a place where they could prove they were dedicated to the values of hard work and individual responsibility. As importantly, they described how others also viewed their participation in this way, as an expression of their commitment to self-sufficiency and familial accountability. For all these reasons, DADS conferred on marginalized men a sense of earned dignity and respect as good providers.

THE MEANS TO PROVE THEIR PARENTING

Men also described how DADS offered many of the basic needs they and their children required, including resources and items necessary for seeing their children. The ability to combine paid work with school was the biggest draw for fathers who participated through the main program site. The job component was officially classified as vocational training by the government. Therefore, none of the money fathers earned counted as part of their income when determining eligibility for public benefits such as food stamps, Section 8 housing, and welfare cash assistance. Many fathers described this as crucial for allowing them to earn a small paycheck without decreasing other benefits necessary for their, and often their children's, survival.

DADS did not always enable men to provide as much money or see their children as often as they wanted, but it did allow them to demonstrate that they were trying, especially to those who controlled access to their children. While men with steady jobs provide more financial support, fathers without stable pay tend to offer their children more experiences and in-kind items, such as outings and diapers.[19] These items are often important for negotiating paternal access through children's mothers, who are more likely to be custodial parents.[20]

However, money earned through DADS was included in calculations of fathers' child support obligations. Although only five fathers reported having a formal child support order, almost all told me that they gave a certain amount to their children's mothers from each DADS paycheck. Most noted that they preferred an informal child support arrangement to a court-ordered one. For those who did have a formal order, the DADS program provided on-site access to enforcement officers from the county child support office who would work with fathers to file paperwork, modify support orders, and work out payment plans to address arrears. DADS case managers also advocated on fathers' behalf during child custody hearings and documented their program involvement as indication of being a proactive parent. Joe, white and fifty, was the DADS community outreach coordinator who worked with fathers to help them understand and comply with support orders. He shared that: "Dads get paperwork from the child support system and don't know what to do with it, which is why they may ignore it. [DADS] helps them with paperwork, with modifying the order, and encourages fathers to talk directly with a child support agent to work things out. Then they can take their certificates from here to child custody case hearings to show that they're trying to be more involved." Fathers knew that their participation in DADS was a highly visible activity to judges responsible for deciding custody and child support plans. Many tried to leverage their time in the program for visitation or shared custody.

Joe and other staff understood that fathers also needed items to offer their children when they showed up for formal or informal visits. Melanie, forty-one and Black, was a program manager and had the most direct interaction with fathers. She explained how giving dads these items as incentives for participation built up their confidence as parents in a society that marks them as deadbeats:

> Dads come in defeated. They've encountered others, teachers or somebody, who said, "You're a failure, you won't make it. I bet you'll be imprisoned as soon as you turn eighteen." Many of them don't have a support system. They come here because they don't want to be locked up anymore. They want to get money the right way so they don't have to be involved in this high-risk lifestyle that leads to either prison or death. They don't want to be out of their kids' lives, but it's a series of factors that play into them being absent. Very few times have I heard a dad just say, "I don't care. I've got other kids. I'm not thinking about those kids." It's rare that he really qualifies as the definition of a deadbeat dad. He's usually thinking about the kid and worried about serving his and their needs. It's unlikely that he's going to have a job that earns enough to truly, realistically support his family. So it's about establishing what he can do until he can do better and letting them know it's not just the money, but that mothers need help.

Melanie plaintively concluded that we need programs like DADS to "build fathers up" in a society that is constantly beating them down. Samuel, the fifty-year-old Black program director, agreed: "Everything we do here is geared towards making these men see themselves as contributors to their family and community, that they belong to something, that they have value."

Building fathers up in this way entailed defraying the direct and indirect costs of involvement. To spend time with children in their homes and make a stronger case for shared custody, fathers needed a safe place to live. If they were homeless, DADS case managers connected fathers to transitional housing services. Working and going to school at the main site meant fathers had daily access to phones and computers with internet. Many fathers used them to stay in contact with children and potential employers, especially when their personal cell phones were disconnected due to lack of payment. Once a month, if fathers helped organize a food distribution program, they could take home a food box. Other weeks, fathers received single food items such as loaves of bread and formula packets. When there was a harvest from the community garden near the building, they could take home fresh vegetables. Many men were also using their time in DADS to accumulate volunteer and service hours to qualify for a $4,000 college scholarship through the federal AmeriCorp program. Otherwise, college tuition far exceeded what fathers could ever hope to afford.

Fathers also met regularly with their case managers for needs assessments, which is how many of them got access to low- or no-cost medical and mental health care. Several men shared with me that they struggled with alcohol and drug addiction. The program not only connected them to counselors who helped them process their trauma and achieve sobriety, it also gave them a way to pay the exorbitant fees for court-mandated drug testing. Nicholas, a nineteen-year-old Latino father of one, could see his three-year-old daughter, Olivia, only on Saturdays and Sundays from 10:00 to 3:00 per the terms of his court-scheduled visitation agreement. This was conditional on biweekly mandatory drug tests that cost him $70. His $600 monthly paycheck from DADS was the only way he could cover the costs. If not in the program, Nicholas would have been in a perilous bind. Without his earnings, he feared that he would have risked going back to the streets to sell just to cover the costs of the drug tests, which he needed to meet the conditions of his visitation and parole agreement. If police caught him, he would be back in jail and lose his rights to see Olivia. Worse still, the temptation from being around drugs would put his sobriety at risk and therefore his ability to pass those tests.

Other program incentives were required for some fathers' contact with children. In exchange for attending DADS parenting classes, fathers received high-demand baby items, including diapers, wipes, clothes, formula, gift certificates, and car seats. Their case managers would usually give them more if there was a desperate need, which there often was. For fathers who rarely saw their children, delivering these items gave them an opportunity to be with their kids. For fathers who relied on in-kind support to successfully negotiate access through children's mothers, these incentives were essential for father-child contact. They also allowed fathers to feel as though they deserved to see their children and to avoid the stigma and shame of showing up for visitation with nothing to contribute to their children's households. Peter poignantly described how the money he earned through the program combined with the goods it gave him allowed him to be the kind of father he aspired to be, despite seeing his kids only occasionally. He paid $153 per month in child support, which was more than half of the money he earned through DADS. According to Peter, his children's mother demanded diapers, wipes, and formula each time he saw them:

> When I leave them, I don't know when I'm seeing them again. When the diapers are low, then "Oh yeah, you can come give me some diapers," and then the next week I have to ask, "Where are my kids?" . . . When I found out she didn't want me to see my kids, I had to get a job. When I gave the diapers, it felt good because I did something responsible. That's my kid. Nobody else can do that. . . . I'd rather do more than just getting the diapers. I want to be the one they call on. I want to be more than the diaper man.

Peter saw his kids a lot more since joining the program because his DADS job allowed him to pay child support and show up more often with diapers and wipes. He was confident that earning his diploma through DADS and eventually finding higher-paying work would allow him to realize his dream of being a father who provided more than just diapers. He hoped that, with a better job, joint custody was a possibility and that he could "quit paying to seeing my kids." This would only be possible if he kept working while going to school. How else could he afford those diapers? They were, in Peter's words, his "admission ticket" to fatherhood.

Like Peter, many fathers had tried to go back to school before but found it prohibitively difficult to find jobs that would accommodate their academic schedules. Transportation between work and school locations was costly in terms of both time and money, and most fathers simply could not afford to cease working long enough to finish their diplomas. As Isaac, a twenty-three-year-old Black father of one, explained: "This is the first place I ever heard of that they actually let you, like people my age, still get my high school diploma. And I was able to work at the same time!" Prior to enrolling in DADS, Isaac had an eighth-grade education and found it difficult to get hired even in very low-wage jobs. He wanted a high school diploma that would permit him to provide more financially for his two-year-old daughter, Leah, whom he had not seen in over a year. Consistently working and attending school through DADS enabled him to demonstrate to Leah's mother that he was committed to being an involved father who could help support their child. She finally agreed to let him see Leah the day after I interviewed him. Isaac could not wait to introduce her to hot dogs, his favorite food. When next I saw him, he eagerly shared that she loved them and drew him a picture to keep. "Without DADS, I would never have this," he said holding up the crumpled picture pulled from his pocket.

Other than showing up empty-handed for visitation, transportation was the most commonly mentioned obstacle to seeing nonresidential children on a regular basis. To address this, DADS gave fathers bus tokens and occasionally helped offset the cost of automobile registration fees and car repairs. Curtis, an eighteen-year-old Latino stepfather of one, explained how his twice-monthly $270 check did not stretch far, which made the transportation incentives he received even more important for supporting his son: "Whenever she runs out of diapers, she has to call me. The only thing is she has to drive over to my house. I can get a ride, but me getting around means I have to pay for gas, and I have to give her money. You can't go to that many places, and they'll give you a diploma, and they'll give you a job. Then it's all in one place. You don't have to go to different places every other day. Then they help with bikes and buses so you can see your kids." Curtis told me that going to multiple locations to get the resources he needed would have been prohibitively difficult in terms of money and time, especially because public transportation was crowded and often late. He was working with the program to get his driver's license and trying to save a little from each paycheck to buy a car once he graduated. He hoped that this would allow him to see his girlfriend and son more frequently and show up with enough diapers, milk, and wipes when he did. For Curtis, DADS was a "one-stop shop" for what he needed to become a better father.

The incentive structure of the program, which enabled men to make more monetary and in-kind contributions to children's households, contributed to their sense of being responsible fathers, despite low earnings. Many of the fathers reported using a significant portion of their paychecks for children's housing, food, and clothing. Most also described setting aside a portion of each check for special outings with their children, such as going to restaurants, visiting amusement parks, and shopping trips for school supplies, shoes, and clothes.

DADS also provided free father-child activities, including visits to a local planetarium, games of the local minor league baseball team, and holiday-themed events, such as indoor trick-or-treating for Halloween. Randall, a twenty-three-year-old Black father of two, explained how the program helped him be there for his kids because it provided free, safe activities he could do with his children, a rarity in their crime-ridden neighborhood. "People that grew up in here can't afford it, and it shows them something better than just the average everyday stuff that they see walking. The area we stay in, you can see people using drugs. I'd rather take them and see stuff they can remember, something better than where we're at."

This signified how fathers understood their contributions to children in relational rather than financial terms. They were more concerned with giving things that could help forge and sustain stronger bonds than providing for an equitable share of the total costs associated with raising a child.[21] Still, DADS enabled fathers to "be there" for children in ways they would not have been able to afford otherwise. Keegan, a twenty-one-year-old Black father of three, noted: "If you run out of diapers, they got you covered. If you need baby clothes, they got those. Baby food, formula, basically whatever you need to be a dad. If you need to know what to do with your child, like if your baby is crying or sick, they got 24/7 Dad classes." Tellingly, however, when I asked Keegan what was the most important thing he got from the program, he simply said, "that my kids know I'm coming back to them at night."

THE RADICAL ROLE OF FATHERING PROGRAMS

Policy discourses about marginalized fathers are rife with assumptions that they need to learn how to identify with the father role and accept their paternal responsibilities. Yet, according to the men I studied, the real identity task for poor fathers of color is developing a sense of self-worth in a society that stereotypically casts them as parenting failures. Discussions of what a father's "role" should be—breadwinning, caregiving, or a combination of the two—were less significant than the role of resources in allowing them to claim identities as responsible fathers who must parent in the context of poverty, racism, and the daily struggle to stay alive. Their rationales for enrolling in the program pointed to how both financial providing and caregiving assume access to resources—material, social, and symbolic—that marginalized fathers rarely have.

Many scholars argue that fatherhood policies and programs should focus as much on supporting men's nurturance of their children as they do on promoting fathers' abilities to provide financially.[22] Yet, as I have shown in this and the previous chapter, financial and emotional support are deeply interwoven in marginalized fathers' understandings of paternal provision. A primary reason for this is that opportunities for safe, legal employment are a necessary precondition for being a parent who can continuously provide both money and care. This is especially the case for fathers who do not live with their children and incur what are for them significant costs just to be in their children's presence. This includes travel expenses, the price of in-kind goods, and forgoing more lucrative money-making activities to stay alive and out of the purview of the criminal justice system.

From men's perspectives, teaching fathering skills and the importance of fathers is not the most crucial charge of parenting policies and programs. Their most powerful political potential rests in providing a structure of opportunity that promotes marginalized men's abilities to claim and enact responsible father identities and have others positively appraise them for doing so. All too often policies have tried to promote fathers' financial support of children and economic "self-sufficiency" at the expense of their self-worth and self-efficacy as parents. The DADS case showed how policies can do both, but only if they truly focus on the context of involvement and what that really looks like in the actual lives of socially and economically vulnerable men.

A greater focus on the context of fathering also means that policies need to do more than increase men's economic opportunities for minimum-wage, short-term employment. They also need to offer basic resources and spaces where poor fathers of color can identify as successful providers, broadly defined. Fatherhood programs may not be able to change the structural inequalities that undermine fathering in poor communities of color. But, as fathers' stories poignantly revealed, they have the radical potential to help individual men cope with the personal consequences of inequalities, especially poverty, racism, and the stigma of incarceration.

This focus on context illuminates the cultural and structural dimensions of fathering. Attention to both can boost the effectiveness of fathering interventions and challenge culture-of-poverty assumptions related to marginalized men's parenting.[23] DADS allowed men to engage in the active, rather than just aspirational, construction of a responsible father identity. This suggests that fatherhood programs work less by reshaping fathers' commitments to parenting than by providing a situated context where men can more successfully enact ideas of good fathering they already have.

Men's stories also help us understand how different means-tested programs can enhance or undermine feelings of social inclusion and parental self-efficacy. Sociologist Sarah Halpern-Meekin and colleagues found that recipients of the Earned Income Tax Credit described their refunds as earned rewards for hard work, not a stigmatizing handout.[24] Similarly, fathers saw DADS as an opportunity to prove their parenting and hard-worker status, despite the program's low wages and uncertain long-term impacts. Given the dark history of means-tested programs and the widespread stigma attached to welfare cash assistance and mandatory welfare-to-work programs, this perspective has vast social and policy implications.[25] It illuminates how anti-poverty policies and government transfers can be designed and implemented to valorize, rather than stigmatize, parents living in poverty.

Programs like DADS are likely to increase the salience of fathering and shape expectations of fatherhood marginalized men can attain. They are most radical not when they (re)shape fathers' meanings of "being there," but when they give them the means to be there in the variety of ways that already make sense to them, their children, and coparents. How fathers used the program to negotiate relationships with the latter is the topic I turn to next.

4 Making a Case to Mothers

"My main priority right now is my son. I'm here to show his mother that I'm trying," said DADS participant Alex, referring to his four-year-old, Fernando. Alex, twenty-four and Latino, quit school during his sophomore year to care for his three younger siblings after his father was incarcerated. Alex's mother left the house when he was nine to "run some errands" and never came back. This experience shaped what Alex wanted most for Fernando's childhood: a married two-parent home where the mom and dad lived together, loved one another, and got along. Guided by research finding that kids do better when they grow up with both married parents in the household, Alex's aspiration has been one of the primary aims of responsible fatherhood policy.

Yet it was not to be for Alex, Fernando, and Fernando's mother, Camille. Things had been tense between Alex and Camille for several years. They were dating when they unintentionally conceived Fernando. They stayed together through Camille's difficult pregnancy and two years of surgeries and hospitalizations for Fernando's severe cleft lip and palate. They broke up the week before Fernando was born, but they got back together eight days later after Alex rushed to the hospital in time to cut the umbilical cord and be the first to hold his newborn son. According to Alex, when Camille went back to work, he cared for the baby and did all the housework: "I did everything for her, made sure the house was clean, laundry was folded, and dinner was on the table when she got home. And, of course, I took care of [Fernando] because that's my son. . . . I was basically the stay-at-home mom. This was her house we were staying at because she got Section 8 to get her own spot. . . . She knows deep down inside I'm a good father. I've been to all his surgeries and his doctor's appointments. The first couple of years of his life were really devastating, and I was always there." Alex and Camille were under constant stress trying to live on one very low-wage income while managing Fernando's medical issues. Alex often looked for jobs, but could not find one with decent pay he was willing to keep. Because of this, Camille questioned Alex's commitment to her and Fernando. Alex wondered why taking care of the baby and household was not enough. This caused constant conflict, and they split up for good around Fernando's second birthday.

Since the breakup, Alex had a singular focus on his son, his future, and minimizing the tension with Camille that he believed kept him away from Fernando. Alex came to DADS hoping to complete the high school diploma he put on hold eight years earlier to support his siblings and to earn enough to afford being a "half-time single father." His coparenting aspirations, which started with dreams of raising his son in a happy two-parent married household, quickly morphed into more modest goals for regularly seeing Fernando and making mutual parenting decisions with Camille. Policy makers intended for programs like DADS to help families achieve the former. Yet, given the complex relationship and economic challenges of marginalized parents' lives, programs must focus more on the complicated realities of the latter.

The rest of Alex's story helps us understand why. Alex initially came to DADS at Camille's urging about a year before I met him. They constantly fought about why Alex was not providing more money for Fernando when Camille worked so hard to keep the two of them financially afloat as a single mother. Alex could only work part-time while going to school through DADS, and his $300 monthly earnings barely put a dent in his own living expenses. According to Alex, he simply could not afford to give Camille more, and because he could not pay, she would not let him see Fernando. He admittedly "partied and did drugs" to cope with the pain of missing his son, which reinforced Camille's decision to limit their contact. Disheartened, Alex quit DADS.

After the required six-month waiting period for reenrollment, Alex was determined to "prove that I'm committed because [Camille] probably thinks I'm a low-life, and I'm not going to amount to nothing." Although he was back in DADS and reportedly clean of drugs, Camille was reluctant to let him resume regular contact with Fernando. Alex stayed in the program because he saw it as the "price of admission" for seeing his son at all. That he could not do so more often was the crux of his most recent and frequent argument with Camille, who told him the last time he tried to visit that: "You're not the parent here. I am. You have no say because he lives with me, and I provide for him. You're not there. You're not really a father." Alex responded: "'I can't be because you won't let me be. If you would, things would be different.' To her, everything is about the money. She's mad because I don't buy him clothes. The thing is, I don't even know his clothes or shoe size because I haven't gotten to see him in so long." Alex started to cry as he told me, "My son knows more about her boyfriend. I can only see my son when she needs something from me."

Things got even worse. Four days before my interview with Alex, Camille called to tell him that she was moving out of state, and that he needed to come over immediately if he wanted to see Fernando one last time and say goodbye. Alex pleaded with her: "'You can't do that! You don't have full custody, and neither do I. How are you just going to take him? What, I get to see him for thirty minutes, and then you're gone?' She just said, 'Yeah, at least see him, and tell him you love him. We're going to be back, but I don't know when.'" Alex was unsure why Camille was moving so suddenly. She told him she needed to look into some "family problems," but all her family lived locally. Alex suspected the real reason was that Camille faced eviction and could save money by moving where her new boyfriend had a more lucrative job opportunity. Being the sole breadwinner had taken a toll that Camille could no longer bear.

Not knowing when he would next see Fernando, Alex cried himself to sleep each night since they left. He had resigned himself to the idea that school and work through DADS were the only ways for him to be there for his son until they were physically reunited. Alex deeply regretted how breaking up with Camille meant "losing my son as a family." Still, he concluded, "At least I'm here to make a case to her that I'm trying. I still consider [Camille] my family because she's my son's mom, and she does take care of him all the time." Reflecting on what he learned in DADS, Alex reasoned: "I know now just to tell her, 'I think it's best if we just talk about our son.' . . . I grew up without a mom, she grew up without a dad, and neither of us wanted that for him. I knew him growing up without both parents in the same house is going to affect him, but that I barely get to see my son is now my bigger worry."

Alex's situation goes deep to the heart of two key issues related to mothers and responsible fatherhood policy. The first involves marriage. Congress first committed public funding for fatherhood programming as part of the 1996 welfare reform law that promoted married families with the goal of reducing poverty.[1] Along with strengthening father-child relationships and improving fathers' economic opportunities, another major goal of fatherhood policy is to "foster responsible parenting and build healthy relationships (including couple and coparenting) and marriage."[2] Federal grantees like DADS were required to include activities that "promote or sustain marriage" by providing "information about the benefits of marriage and two-parent involvement for children," "enhancing relationship skills," and offering "education about how to control aggressive behavior."[3]

Fathers are more likely to stay involved in their children's lives if they are married or romantically linked to mothers. Moreover, coupled or not, how well parents cooperate when it comes to shared parenting decisions strongly influences how active dads are in their children's lives.[4] Fathers often cite contentious coparenting relationships as a main barrier to involvement.[5] Consequently, many have advocated that marriage—especially teaching about the benefits of two-parent families and the communication skills associated with happy marriages—should be a core component of fatherhood programs.[6]

Yet marginalized fathers with little education and low earnings are significantly less likely to marry their children's mothers.[7] Among men in fatherhood programs, many of their couple relationships are beyond repair once they enroll.[8] Some parents never have more than a short-term sexual connection leading to a child's unplanned conception. As sociologists Kathryn Edin and Timothy Nelson found, these unplanned routes to parenthood rarely lead to lasting relationships or marriage: "For these couples, children aren't the expression of commitment; they are the source."[9] In many cases, as with Alex and Camille, a difficult breakup is a primary motivating factor for enrollment, which likely explains why coparenting and mediation services are underutilized in programs like DADS.[10] With little hope for reconciliation, fathers likely sense that parenting and relationship classes that teach about marriage are not for them.

Alex's dilemma points to another reason this pro-marriage approach can be problematic. Middle-class fathers tend to experience parenting as part of a "package deal" of work, marriage, home, and children in which the spousal or partner relationship takes priority.[11] Marriage advocates argue that this links men's parenting to their partnerships in ways that promote commitments to work, children, and breadwinning.[12] However, economic obstacles make it harder for low-income fathers to follow this script. Many marginalized men like Alex experience relationships with mothers as secondary and as paths to primary relationships with their children.[13] Alex wanted Fernando to grow up in a two-parent family where he and Camille raised their son together in the same household. Yet trying to work things out only intensified their arguments, to which Fernando was often a witness. Alex understood how breaking up with Camille had severed his connection to his son, but he also knew the package deal was no longer a possibility for them. His plan B entailed proving his dedication to Fernando and developing a more cooperative coparenting relationship with Camille. This brought him back to DADS.

Alex and Camille's story, albeit from his perspective, exemplifies an important issue at stake in fatherhood programs: mothers' role in shaping how and how much fathers are involved with their children, especially among nonresidential dads. Mothers' views of fathers and how much mothers encourage or discourage fathers' involvement—often called "maternal gatekeeping"—can better predict fathers' involvement than men's own perceptions of their parenting.[14] It is therefore crucial to consider how fatherhood interventions like DADS can shape fathering by influencing mothers' attitudes and behaviors.

This chapter shows how Alex and others used DADS to help them navigate complex coparenting situations. As program staff acknowledged, marriage made little sense in most fathers' cases. DADS offered support for their more immediate family goals of having father-child contact and reducing coparenting conflict. Fathers wanted to prove their parenting to the mothers they believed controlled access to their children. Even men's one-sided narratives revealed that what they experienced as mothers' "gatekeeping" was a result of complicated social and economic factors that conspired to construct much more than a maternal barrier between them and their children. In this chapter, we see how men used DADS to manage coparenting challenges that largely emerged from shared financial and relational difficulties, challenges for which marriage would have offered little relief.

MISSING THE MARRIAGE MARK IN FATHERHOOD PROGRAMMING

For decades now, marriage promotion and responsible fatherhood have been companion policy provisions in political efforts to encourage two-parent families. However, marriage promotion does not align with the realities of low-income families' lives and complex parenting configurations. Parents are together as couples in four of five cases when children are born to unmarried families, but more than half of these romantic relationships end before their children turn five.[15] Understandably, many exes find it difficult to coparent amicably in the aftermath of difficult breakups, especially once new partners enter the picture. Coparenting conflict presents many practical challenges for low-income fathers' abilities to spend time with and support their children, including higher transaction costs, which can include time and money spent arranging for visitation, bargaining over access, and travel expenses.[16] Social scripts for how to be an involved father outside the package deal, especially for poor men who struggle to afford the costs of contact, are rare. Helping men navigate coparenting challenges is therefore a critical policy issue that directly affects children's access to parents and parental resources.

To be effective, parenting policy must reflect that marginalized fathers' financial struggles and relational challenges are entwined. Across all economic situations, fathers are more likely to provide formal and informal child support when they have cooperative coparenting relationships with mothers.[17] As coparenting worsens after a breakup, informal support from fathers tends to decrease, which often prompts mothers to file court orders, leading to further deterioration of the relationship.[18] Mothers are more likely than fathers to believe that fathers' visitation rights are conditional on fulfilling their child support obligations.[19] Mothers also perceive fathers as more competent parents when they make financial contributions to children.[20] Higher levels of mistrust and conflict in low-income men's romantic and coparenting relationships lead many fathers to feel that mothers "gatekeep" by blocking access to children in the aftermath of adversarial breakups and fathers' subsequent struggles to pay support.[21]

"Gatekeeping" is a controversial concept in families, family studies, and policy circles. It almost always refers to mothers' behaviors, and because it implies limiting access to children, it suggests that mothers are to blame when fathers are not involved. Yet mothers' gatekeeping is often a reaction to fathers' parenting, rather than a deliberate effort to restrict it. Psychologists Sarah Allen and Alan Hawkins proposed one of the earliest definitions of gatekeeping: "reluctance to relinquish responsibility for family matters by setting rigid standards, wanting to be ultimately accountable for domestic labor to confirm . . . a valued maternal identity, and expecting that family work is truly a women's domain."[22] These beliefs, Allen and Hawkins argued, build gates between fathers and children that reduces men's opportunities for childcare. In other words, women have more respectability, power, and privilege in the domestic domain. From this perspective, there is some ambivalence about fathers being more involved: Mothers want and need help with childcare and housework from fathers, but it means giving up some of their domestic authority to get it.

One of the problems with this understanding of gatekeeping is how it characterizes domestic power as deriving from women's insistence on maintaining parental authority, when in reality it mostly means mothers have more responsibility for devalued and unpaid family labor. Yet gatekeeping is not necessarily about mothers' desires to maintain domestic power, nor is it always unidirectional. Fathers play a significant role in gatekeeping, as do economic constraints. Psychologist Sarah Schoppe-Sullivan and colleagues found that perceptions of relationship instability and fathers' parenting efficacy, not traditional gendered views of who should do family labor, predicted maternal gatekeeping. The original definition of gatekeeping based primarily on married dual-earner, middle-class, residential parents has since been expanded to include things that mothers do to facilitate as well as restrict fathers' involvement.[23] Gatekeeping is not the same thing as "gate closing," which includes criticizing fathers' parenting, redoing childcare tasks, and taking control of parental decision-making; it also includes "gate opening" or encouraging behaviors, such as asking for fathers' opinions about childcare matters and arranging for father-child activities.[24] Mothers are more likely to close gates if they start to suspect that their own relationships with fathers are headed for breaking up or if they believe that men are not competent, committed parents.[25]

"Gatekeeping" is a concept that was developed to describe relatively privileged parents' conflicts over who does which aspects of housework and childcare. Its application to economically vulnerable complex families— especially those in which parents do not live in the same household and struggle with meeting children's basic needs—is severely limited. Gatekeeping also means something else entirely when it refers to poor, single mothers' efforts to secure resources for their children and protect them from the ramifications of intermittent contact with nonresidential fathers and exposure to violence and drug use. In these cases, mothers' "power" to control access to children results from their much greater responsibilities for feeding, clothing, housing, and protecting children—and usually with little public support.

When low-income couples with shared children break up, mothers are much more likely to shoulder primary financial and caregiving obligations for kids. Restricting contact with nonresidential fathers who try but are often unable to contribute more for shared children is an understandable response from custodial mothers. Single mothers do not have the luxury of claiming they are "doing the best" they can when they, too, struggle to support their children amid similarly dire financial constraints. In these situations, mothers' behaviors are less about maintaining authority through erecting a metaphorical gate between fathers and children and more about ensuring their children's needs are met. Poor mothers have little time to worry about "gatekeeping" when there is no literal house to which the gate leads.

Research specifically on low-income, unmarried parents enrolled in fatherhood programs also shows how coparenting relationships include both gate opening and closing among mothers. Family scholars Jay Fagan and Rebecca Kaufman found that nonresidential fathers reported experiencing mothers' undermining and gatekeeping, but also significant cooperation and support.[26] Mothers' undermining behaviors included making negative comments about fathers, being dismissive about fathers' parenting views or styles, and replacing fathers with other adults, like new boyfriends. Gatekeeping entailed mothers not allowing children to see their fathers and trying to keep fathers' new partners from being around children. However, it also involved gate opening, as sometimes mothers bent official custody and child support rules so that fathers could see children more.

We know that participation in fatherhood programs is associated with improvements in coparenting skills, especially communication, but we know less about other potential ways that fatherhood programs promote coparenting support and alliances.[27] This is crucial because there seems to be a causal and reciprocal relationship between maternal gatekeeping and fathers' involvement. That is, mothers' gatekeeping is as much a response to fathers' behavior as a regulator of it.[28] What fathers do (or don't) triggers mothers' gatekeeping, which in turn shapes fathers' future access (or lack thereof) to their children.

We saw this in Alex and Camille's situation. He believed that Camille was closing the gate on his relationship with Fernando. Yet her behavior was likely triggered by their shaky romantic relationship and Alex's self-admitted drug use, unemployment, and scant support for their son after they broke up. I did not interview mothers and therefore cannot speak to their experiences. The perspectives of the girlfriends, wives, and coparents of the sixty-four men I studied would likely have diverged from fathers' in significant ways. Nevertheless, as with Alex's description of Camille, embedded in fathers' accounts were crucial details hinting at mothers' sides of these stories.

Research on women who share children with fathers much like those in DADS also suggests that mothers would see these situations differently. Sociologists Kathryn Edin and Maria Kefalas found in their study of low-income, unmarried mothers that most couples fought frequently about money, but not because men were unemployed or made little money.[29] Money usually became an issue only when mothers thought that men were lazy, quit jobs for bad reasons, or spent too much on alcohol or drugs. When poor mothers work hard to provide for children and fathers apparently fail to do the same, money is not merely economic; it is symbolic of men's presumed lack of commitment to family. If fathers continue to struggle financially, most mothers feel they are better off on their own than with men who have questionable spending habits and may become drains on household resources. Mothers also point to men's problems with substance abuse, incarceration, cheating, and intimate violence as reasons why relationships with the fathers of their children do not last. In these unpredictable and difficult circumstances, mothers deem low-income men too risky, both when it comes to the money they need now and the long-term prosperity they desperately desire. As primary parents tasked with ultimate responsibility for raising shared children, mothers must figure out how to support their kids, or else risk losing them to state custody. Once babies come, mothers start to evaluate men's viability as partners and future husbands in terms of these goals. Many men come up short.

Fathers have a different perspective. They often see mothers' demands for financial support as women being money hungry and valuing men only for what they provide. Poor women mostly partner with poor men, which means that money is equally hard for fathers to get. As sociologists Kathryn Edin and Timothy Nelson put it, mothers' gatekeeping and fathers' mistrust both result from the "denominator problem," the disparity between what a man feels he should provide and the actual cost of raising a child.[30] That is a huge gap for many families, and mothers must make up the difference. Women struggle with the shortfall and may conclude that men are not worth the trouble. Men are left feeling that mothers see them as dispensable and easily replaceable, or if they have a formal child support order, as merely a paycheck.

Poor mothers and fathers face another slightly different denominator problem, which is the difference between what poor fathers can realistically provide and how much mothers need. Most noncustodial fathers pay little of what it really takes to raise a child, and when they contribute anything, they tend to expect some access to children in exchange for their hard-earned money. As Edin and Nelson explained, traditionally gendered family responsibilities have been reversed among many low-income, unmarried families.[31] Mothers end up being the main breadwinners as fathers fight for more access to the relational aspects of parenting. In a no-win situation shaped by poverty, fathers struggle to forge valued fathering identities beyond the breadwinner role, while mothers must pay the bills, balance the family budget, and provide the bulk of childcare without receiving much public recognition for any of it.

Fathers want to be more than just a paycheck, but many are barely able to be even that. In a desperate search for some help, mothers demand something—anything—when fathers show up for visits. If he cannot bring the diapers, clothes, or cash she needs, he may not be able to see his kids. From fathers' viewpoint, this not only erodes their parenting identities, it completely denies them one. Just as Alex recounted of his last fight with Camille, she reportedly said: "You're not the parent here. I am. You have no say because he lives with me, and I provide for him. You're not there. *You're not really a father.*" Alex saw it differently: "'I can't be a father because you won't let me be. If you would, things would be different.' To her, everything is about the money."

As mothers and fathers work, often unsuccessfully, to mitigate these denominator problems, child support policies and welfare bureaucracies tend to make them worse. They enforce fathers' financial obligations, but unless there is an existing visitation order, do little to ensure that fathers actually see their children. Courts are still inclined to award primary physical custody to mothers while garnishing formal monetary support from fathers' paychecks, which can feel disempowering to men who desire closer relationships with their kids.[32] To make matters worse, marginalized men rarely qualify for significant government assistance, giving them even less power in households where women and children are primary beneficiaries of state services, albeit limited. As Edin and Nelson put it: "At every turn an unmarried man who seeks to be a father, and not just a daddy, is rebuffed by a system that pushes him aside with one hand while reaching into his pocket with the other."[33] Put another way that would have resonated with Alex, when it comes to fathering, the state, too, makes everything about the money.

Just as mothers feel the pull to partner with someone new who can better fulfill the father role, when men feel they have failed with one mother and child, they often see a new partner and having children with them as an opportunity for another chance at fatherhood.[34] Due to closer physical proximity and better relationship quality, fathers tend to be more involved with the biological and social children with whom they live than they are with nonresidential children from previous romantic relation-ships.[35] "Serial, selective fatherhood," whereby men invest their limited means in a single household, gives them another opportunity to prove that they can be successful and responsible parents.[36] Unfortunately, it also means that children who do not live with fathers receive less, which further strains coparenting relationships with exes.

Encouraging marriage without addressing this family complexity—especially how mothers' and fathers' interests tend to conflict—may do more harm than good if it emphasizes responsibility only to current part-ners and residential children. Designing fatherhood programs around package deal assumptions could also backfire by reinforcing the idea that fathers' access to children depends on committed or marital relationships with mothers. Few fatherhood interventions focus on coparenting among unmarried parents who will likely never marry.[37] Even fewer target those who have never even been romantically involved.[38] Yet effective father-hood programming requires recognition that, for many coparents, mar-riage is neither feasible nor preferred.

However, programs can help fathers improve coparenting as the pri-mary end goal. In the Parents and Children Together (PACT) evaluation of responsible fatherhood programs, many fathers reported that mothers retaliated against them for highly conflictual breakups by blocking access to children or by demanding that fathers provide extra money or goods in exchange for visitation.[39] Still, many fathers in the PACT study noted a year after participation that programs helped them more effectively navi-gate coparenting challenges, an improvement most attributed to commu-nication skills they learned.[40]

The DADS case provides another important opportunity to understand how coparenting services help low-income fathers navigate and negotiate coparenting in poverty. Most fathers described experiencing significant coparenting challenges. Of the fifty fathers I interviewed individually,[41] eleven (22%) described having low-conflict, highly cooperative relation-ships with their children's mothers; seventeen (34%) reported moderately cooperative relationships; and twenty-two (44%) described experienc-ing high-conflict relationships or so much tension that they had resorted to having no contact with their children's other parents.[42] Eight (16%) fathers described having physically abusive relationships, with six of these disclosing that at least one of the mothers of their children had a current restraining order against them forbidding contact.

Men's commitments to being responsible fathers rarely translated into desires for romantic commitments to coparents. Most were motivated to enroll and stay in DADS in order to forge stronger father-child relationships that had been undermined by couple conflicts. Fathers used the program to create a sense of themselves as responsible parents outside the bounds of package deal understandings of family and fatherhood. They also developed strategies to circumvent what they experienced as mothers' gatekeeping, most notably by utilizing program services to prove their paternal commitments in the context of dire financial constraints.

Men's stories point to how fatherhood programs might help mothers and fathers, not aspire to marriage, but manage the denominator problems that keep many poor unmarried coparents locked in perpetual struggle. Just like with Alex and Camille, one of their most significant challenges is trying to coparent within a political and economic structure that pits their interests against one another's and keeps the numerator—what marginalized fathers like Alex can realistically provide—ever so low.

"THE MOTHER OF MY KIDS NO MATTER WHAT"

Most fathers described couple relationships with their children's mothers as nonexistent or irredeemable. Of the fifty interviewees, only fourteen (28%) were in ongoing romantic relationships with the mothers of all their children, and each described their coparenting relationships as low- or moderate-conflict. The other thirty-six (72%) were either single or romantically linked with women with whom they did not share all their children. Only fifteen (30%) interviewees described thinking about or desiring marriage in the future; these included the five who were already married (and feared they might not stay married to their current spouses) and another five who were open to marriage but adamant it would not be to their children's mothers. Rather than needing support with improving couple relationships based on package deal understandings, most wanted help with coparenting situations for which there were no hopes for romantic reconciliation.

When fathers talked about emotional connections to coparents, even in cases where they were coupled, they were more likely to talk about loving them as the mothers of their children than as romantic partners. Udell, a twenty-three-year-old Latino single father who shared two children with his ex-girlfriend, explained: "I'm still waiting to work things out with her, but I haven't seen my kids in three weeks. . . . I still love her. That's the mother of my kids no matter what. Hopefully, soon in the future, our kids will be all in one family. It's something I dream for. It's why I'm [in DADS]. I can't be happy without my kids around." Similarly, Arthur, a twenty-two-year-old Latino single father of one, told me that he was "middle school sweethearts" with his son's mother, an ex-girlfriend who was struggling with drug addiction and currently in a rehabilitation program: "I kicked her out. I couldn't deal with that around my son. He always wants to know when she's coming home. My mom is always telling me, 'She's trying to get better for you guys.' But I don't care. I don't want to get back with her. I don't want anything to do with her. . . . I love my baby mama on a certain level though. I will not give her another chance to be with me, but she is his mother." Tellingly, like Udell and Arthur, fathers were more likely to refer to their children's mothers as *baby mama, baby mother, the mother,* or [children's name] *mother,* instead of *wife, girlfriend,* or *ex-girlfriend,* even when the couple relationship existed long before children were conceived.

Many fathers described how focusing too much on their romantic relationships with mothers distracted them from providing and caring for their children, especially when persistent conflict over couple issues threatened to derail otherwise cooperative coparenting. Most of these men also noted how DADS helped them concentrate on parenting and learning to see their children's mothers, not as adversarial exes or potential girlfriends with whom they could reconnect, but as partners equally invested in the well-being of their shared children. Maxwell, a twenty-one-year-old Black single father of one, shared custody of his young son with his ex-girlfriend of five years:

I'm a single parent, but now I give her respect. She don't pick up her boyfriend in front of my son. She still takes care of him, and we still go on trips together, like to the fair or zoo. She also keeps me on track in [DADS]. She comes up here and visits me, keeps me up on my classes, pushes me to never give up, even though we're not talking [romantically] anymore. When we stopped talking, everything went down. I was slacking on my work and always worried about her. I couldn't focus. I've learned here to just shake my head and be like, "You've got to worry about yourself and your son. You can't dive in with this person." I still love her, but it's time to move on. . . . We always get along when it comes to my son. I know now everything isn't about us. It's about him.

Likewise, Ricky, a twenty-two-year-old Black single father of one, told me: "If we aren't together [as a couple], we don't get mad. When it's just about my son, we talk, and everything is really good. Like she told me, 'We got to get rid of whatever with you and me. It's about our son. That's it.' I'm single now because I got to have it be all about my son." Worrying about their couple relationship, and the inevitable fighting associated with getting back together, would have been diversions from his parenting.

Fathers also talked about the value of DADS parenting and relationship classes in terms of learning to communicate better and resolve conflict for the benefit of children rather than couple issues. They understood being amicable with partners and coparents as a way to improve their fathering rather than creating a larger family package. Rodrigo, a nineteen-year-old multiracial expectant father, lived with his unborn daughter's mother:

We do have our differences. We're not sitting there just talking to get our feelings out. We're talking to understand each other, and it really helped us a lot. We learned, basically, it's not about us. We're not sitting here to understand each other and make each other happy. Well that's for us, too. We're benefiting from it, but it's for my daughter. I really, really, really, I really don't want us to raise a daughter not together. I want us together in our own house so our daughter sees us together all the time. I've never had that. I really want it for my daughter. I want to be there all the time. I don't want to miss any moment of her life. I would just hate the thought of somebody else raising my kids or another man being around my daughter. If that's putting up with problems I don't like, then I'm going to swallow my pride and do it for my daughter.

Like Rodrigo, many fathers described how keeping mothers happy and keeping their fights to a minimum made it more likely they would be able to stay involved in their children's lives long term.

That is, fathers wanted to strengthen their coparenting relationships specifically to increase their odds of having consistent close father-child connections. Orlando, a thirty-five-year-old Latino married father of five, told me at the beginning of our interview that he enrolled in DADS as a fathering "refresher course." Yet, as he talked, it became clearer that he was dealing with a lot of relationship tension at home with his wife, the mother of his three youngest children. He admitted that he was in the program as a way of "doing everything in my power to make this work. . . . It's hard being a friend and a partner to my wife, not just a coworker kind of thing. If it doesn't work out, then it doesn't work out between us, but I'm never going to leave my children. . . . At least I know that I did everything humanly possible that I can to be with her, stay with her, but don't ask me to walk away from my kids." I eventually understood that DADS was not merely a "refresher course" for Orlando to sharpen his parenting skills. It helped him manage the fear that splitting up with his wife likely meant reduced contact with his children.

This common fear that breaking up with mothers would mean severing connections with kids was particularly strong among nonbiological fathers and those whose paternity was in question. Without a genetic or legal tie, they knew their relationships were especially tenuous and dependent on staying on good terms with mothers who mediated access to children, many of whom they had been raising since birth. Curtis, an eighteen-year-old Latino father of one, started dating his girlfriend, Camey, right around the time his stepson, Vincent, was born. He was committed to raising Vincent, but the relationship with Camey was shaky, which meant Curtis only saw his son when they were getting along. Although he loved them both, Curtis admitted that he was only "kind of in a relationship" with Camey as his link to Vincent. Curtis explained: "We don't really break up because we don't even really say we're together. Whenever we are at each other, we just stop talking for like two days. Then we're back to normal. . . . I need these classes to make us stronger, to where it's practically unbreakable, like nothing can come between us, so nothing can come between me and my son." Outside the frequent cooling-off periods when Curtis stayed away, he spent about five days each week with Vincent and Camey. To him, being relationally "unbreakable" meant seeing Vincent every day and admitting publicly that he and Camey were a couple, in large part so others would treat Curtis as Vincent's "real father."

Other fathers described breaking up or limiting contact with mothers specifically to improve their coparenting relationships. Jeremiah, a twenty-four-year-old Black single father who shared three children with two women, told me:

> Us around each other too much is causing unnecessary arguments, and that's not good for the kids to see. Before it got worse, I got my own place, and she got hers. We are a lot better now that we have space from each other. . . . I don't get how some people, they're not with their mate, so they don't be with their children. They're with somebody else and not paying much attention to the kids. They don't see them or talk to them over the phone. I would never do that. I want to be with the baby's mother, but it's harder being without the baby.

DADS helped Jeremiah and others understand that their best hope for cooperative coparenting was by separating their romantic entanglements from their fathering.

Harris, an eighteen-year-old Black single father of one, Amari, likewise explained how the program allowed him and his son's mother to see beyond their disagreements. Taking DADS relationship classes led them to make an informed decision that prioritizing their son meant ending their four-year relationship. "Now we talk about the kid, and that's it," Harris told me. "Before [DADS] we could never work together when it comes to [Amari]. I hated her. She hated me. We just had a baby together. [DADS] gave us the opportunity to understand that it's not about us and our needs. It's about taking care of [Amari] to make all that dysfunctional arguing not affect him in the future. Now we focus on the kid, which makes us better parents. To do that, I had to leave her." Like most of the thirty-six interviewees who were never or no longer romantically involved with at least one of their children's mothers, Harris had many negative things to say about his ex as a former girlfriend, but eagerly described her as a caring, competent parent. DADS helped him realize that, although he "hated her" as a romantic partner, he deeply respected her as a mother. Many men believed that they became better fathers when they stopped trying to date mothers and instead spent their time and energy on forming parenting alliances without romantic involvements.

Fathers were especially receptive to program messages that getting along with coparents was one of the best ways to care and role model for their children. James, a nineteen-year-old multiracial father of two, struggled to parent his girlfriend's oldest child who had a biological father he believed was a deadbeat. Classes on conflict resolution helped him manage the tension this created between James and his girlfriend. "We used to argue a lot about the little stupid stuff and not let it go," he said. "But we learned how your relationship affects your kids and how your kids sit there and watch and learn. If you're cussing your significant other and all that, your kids are going to do it and learn the bad way. They taught us to set a good model for them, and that's what I'm trying to do." Modeling positive relationships meant doing so as parenting collaborators outside the strictures of a dating situation. It was better, fathers reasoned, for children to "watch and learn" how parents can get along after a break-up than for them to see that fighting was an inevitable part of staying together for the sake of kids.

Alec, a twenty-one-year-old Black father of one, similarly described how the classes taught him to stop escalating arguments in front of his son. Incarcerated recently for a domestic violence dispute involving his girlfriend, Alec claimed he was arrested because she broke a window and blamed it on him. They started throwing rocks in each other's direction in her front yard one night during a heated argument over money. "Things are better with my girlfriend now," Alec said. "I used to raise my voice sometimes, but now I try not to because I see where it leads. We've learned about communication and time and effort. Mostly, we've learned that you got to worry about the kid too because if we're out fighting and throwing rocks and everything, the kid's in the middle, so they could take in some of that." Alec meant "throwing rocks" both literally and as a metaphor for their loud, violent confrontations. DADS taught him to keep his son out of the crossfire. Jimmy, a twenty-year-old multiracial father of two, likewise noted, "They taught us that, if you and your spouse got problems, don't let it out in front of the kids. Just walk away. Actually, go for a walk, cool down, and then come back. Kids watch everything you do and learn. Don't cuss, and use the class to get that stuff off your chest you've been holding in." Learning to get along for the sake of strengthening romantic relationships was useful for some, but constructive conflict resolution that made sustained paternal involvement more likely was the priority for most.

Staff also emphasized parenting effectively regardless of parents' relationship status. Their experience working with parents in high-conflict relationships compelled them to focus on families' more pressing needs over marriage. Amber, a program director, explained: "We're focused on helping parents raise children together. Whether you're with the other parent or not, it teaches men they are valid as fathers, and that we have services if you want to just be a father." Validating men as fathers—not financial providers or future husbands—entailed unpacking package deal assumptions that men are worthy parents only when married to mothers. As Samuel, the program's executive director, concluded: "That's one thing we try to get across, that even if they're not together with the child's other parent, they still need to be there, working together, not talking bad about each other in front of the child." For many in DADS, working together was only possible when their parenting was not part of a romantic partnership.

The emotional and practical separation between men's parenting and partnering—and especially the idea that focusing on the latter can undermine the former—is out of sync with how policy tends to frame the importance of marriage and couple relationships for paternal involvement. Whereas it is more common for privileged families to begin with parents' commitments as couples, often via marriage, lower-income families are more likely to begin as coparenting situations through which parents try to make couple relationships work for children's sake. Most parenting skills curricula, including the one used in DADS, assume ongoing romantic relationships between heterosexual parents. Cultural and political messages prioritize marriage as the best context for raising children and enabling dads to stay involved. Alas, when those relationships do not last, or never existed in the first place, parents have few social scripts for how to navigate non-coupled coparenting. Worse still are cultural messages that, if they cannot make romance or commitment work, exes naturally despise one another and should cut off all ties.

Men in DADS forged novel ideas of family more conducive to coparenting outside coupling. Despite all their challenges and conflicts, Alex said of Camille: "I still consider her my family because she's my son's mom. . . .

I know now to tell her . . . 'It's best if we just talk about our son.'" With mixed success, fathers learned to think of their children's mothers in less adversarial ex-girlfriend terms and more as cooperative business partners working together on behalf of their kids. Maintaining familial affection for mothers as fellow parents of their shared children helped fathers like Alex resolve any residual feelings they had from untenable romances that undermined otherwise supportive coparenting alliances.

DADS offered fathers a script for how to parent together without being together, one that did not assume marriage was the best way to keep men involved. Ultimately, Alex and many of his fellow participants realized that their kids were better off if they let go of the two-parent family ideal, which kept them tethered to conflict, hurt feelings, and power struggles that risked access to their children. Maintaining that access was their parenting priority, one that often came with a cost.

"YOU GOT TO PAY TO PLAY"

Messages that fathers should provide care and time motivated them to challenge the notion that mothers should dictate when and how they saw their children, especially when dads could not provide a lot of money or things. Udell, the father who had not seen his children in three weeks, described how their mother only allowed him to see them when he could show up with a certain amount of cash: "She uses my kids to get to me. She changed her number. She moved out of the apartment we had before. She says, 'If you want to see your kids, I need gas money. So that's the only way you're going to see the kids, if you give me gas so I can get to work tomorrow.'" Udell was learning in DADS how to talk about wanting to see his children in more empathic terms that acknowledged that his kids' mother was also parenting through significant constraints—and unlike him, on a full-time basis. It angered and saddened him that he had to bring money when visiting his kids, because he saw it as their mother using his "kindness as a weakness." Yet when I asked if it mattered that the money was for gas to get to the job she needed to support their children, Udell admitted, "Yeah, I guess she needs the help."

Other fathers described similarly tense coparenting situations in which mothers conditioned access to children on fathers giving money or in-kind goods, creating what some referred to as a "pay-to-play" system. This upset men, not only because it limited contact with their kids, but because it signaled that mothers primarily valued fathers for money while minimizing the importance of their emotional connections with the children. This conflicted with the messages they received from DADS about how fathers' time and care were as important as money for being a responsible father.

Fathers passionately discussed this during a focus group. Jayden, a twenty-four-year-old Black father of three, said to audible agreement from the others: "If you want to spend time with your kid, you got to pay to play. They just want the money. We get a lot of pressure from our baby mamas." Douglas, twenty-three, Black, and a father of one, added: "But they feel like the time is nothing. I just threw my baby a birthday party, cashed it out. That's more than the clothes or shoes I bought. I'm like, 'Damn, I don't have a job right now, and I just spent everything I got for my baby's birthday.' It still wasn't nothing." Cody, a twenty-four-year-old Black father of two, concluded: "Yep, my girl, she cares that I'm there in the house with my daughters, but she wants me there plus the money coming in every week. The love don't count."

Jayden's use of the phrase "pay to play" was especially apt because many fathers' descriptions of time spent with children entailed just that: the fun aspects of parenting such as "hanging out" in a leisurely way, playing games, shopping for toys, trips to the park, eating out, and birthday parties. One could understand why full-time custodial mothers responsible for the less fun but essential and more expensive aspects of childrearing—feeding, housing, clothing, diapering, childcare—would reasonably be frustrated with fathers who wanted to show up occasionally, offering little or nothing necessary to meet their children's basic needs.

However, even fathers like Cody who lived with and cared for children full-time shared that mothers still expected men to pay and saw them as lesser fathers when they could not provide significant financial support. Fathers felt that mothers put children in the middle of their conflicts when enforcing these transactional components of coparenting by, for example, demanding money or diapers in exchange for visitation or discounting the importance of dads' caregiving and housework in the absence of income.

What mothers likely saw as getting desperately needed resources fathers viewed as using children as pawns in a way that diminished their full value as parents. Program messages that fathers were important for reasons other than money and material goods resonated with men who had little of either to offer. They struggled to reconcile the idea that paternal love was valuable in itself with mothers' view that "the love don't count" without the money. Without interviewing mothers, it is uncertain if they actually said or thought this. What was verifiably true was that fathers *believed* that mothers valued their financial contributions most and conditioned access to their children on men's abilities to provide them.

Still, fathers rarely acknowledged that, in almost all cases, mothers bore greater financial and caregiving responsibilities for their shared children. Although more than what fathers could easily afford, the cost of a box of diapers or a tank of gas was a small fraction of the expenses associated with raising their kids, and mothers had to figure out how to make up the difference. Even fathers who made regular child support payments rarely paid more than $100 per month, an amount that barely covered the cost to feed one child. Many coparenting conflicts seemed to arise from mothers and fathers being differentially positioned while both struggled hard to parent in poverty. Fathers truly felt they paid what they could, but it was usually an amount that came up far short of what mothers needed. Men experienced a punitive "pay-to-play" arrangement, while mothers likely felt they were leveraging the little power they had to acquire something—anything—for their kids.

Melanie, a program manager, discussed how DADS tried to help fathers understand and manage this dilemma, especially when trust issues complicated coparents' financial challenges. Fathers often complained to her that mothers "played games" and "punished" them in negotiations over access to children:

Sometimes mom is making it difficult for dad because he wasn't there before. When they start trying to step up because they understand their value, the moms can be resistant, like "Don't think because you took a class all of a sudden you're a good father." They won't always trust them, and they'll say, "You're not really at school. You're not at work. I bet you're flirting with somebody [at DADS]." Then he'll say, "I'm not putting up with her. I'd rather not see my kid than have to put up with that." . . . Then later, "No, I

really do want to be the father of my kid, but she is not letting me see them."
. . . Many mothers are fed information that if he can't support the child
financially then you don't need him, you can do all that by yourself. . . . Even
if he gets a job, he's not going to earn enough to truly, realistically support a
family. [DADS] is about establishing what he can do until he can do better.

Melanie counseled fathers to see things from mothers' perspectives. She
wanted men to understand how most women did not intentionally close
fathers' gates to their kids, but rather wanted their children to have their
basic needs met and a father they could trust.

In particularly high-conflict cases, staff encouraged fathers to utilize
the court system to mediate these challenges. Many respondents perceived
"putting child support on" or "taking a father to court" as retaliatory, especially given fathers' common belief that the legal system was discriminatory against men in parenting cases and that government aid benefitted
women more. Gary, thirty-nine, Black, and a father of two living with his
youngest child's mother, explained:

Fathers who have [to pay] child support are treated the worst. The ones who
aren't paying, they're not even allowed to see their kids. . . . I'm getting taken
to court because my little girl's mom doesn't have a car to take her to the
doctor, even though my support is current. "What makes you think you're
better than me because the child stays with you?" It makes us look bad, like
"Oh, he doesn't really want his child, he doesn't care about his child." . . . Men
have to work harder to prove their parenting. They automatically discrimi-
nate against us because we're men. We have to do more to get them back
when they don't even have to try, and we still have to pay [child support]. . . .
You're doing all the things you're supposed to, being compliant, and they're
still giving her cash aid, food stamps. If you're getting your child, you've got
to pay back all this money. . . . It's like you all are making us stay in debt. . . .
At least here [at DADS] they will do the court things for you. They'll write
the documentation, go to court with you, help if you need a driver's license,
anything to do with a paralegal.

Gary's experience revealed another reason fathers felt locked in a pay-
to-play arrangement biased against men. Several talked about how the
child-support enforcement system mandated fathers' financial support
without ensuring visitation rights. Even if fathers paid, it did not guarantee time with their kids. Beyond this, because relatively few fathers

received means-tested assistance, some men saw child support as another source of aid women received. Although many rightly acknowledged that mothers received more aid as primary custodial parents who had greater responsibility for kids, others felt that the system was stacked against fathers who had fewer opportunities for public recognition and support as parents.

Some fathers also sought help with making decisions about pursuing legal custody. DADS encouraged them to prioritize what was best for children. His time in the program allowed Marcus, a twenty-one-year-old Black single father of one, to understand that his son's mother, Sheila, was currently better equipped to be the custodial parent. Since they split up over a year ago, Marcus felt torn between wanting to see his son, Brayden, more and the reality that Sheila offered a more stable environment. Marcus had neither a place to live nor a reliable form of transportation. His perspective shifted during his time in DADS, from seeing his relationship with her as one of fighting about control over Brayden to one of mutually committing to his security. Marcus confided:

> Whatever [Brayden] needs, she can call on me. I can come over and just see my son. As far as her letting me take him as I please, I can't. . . . She has a more secure situation, her own apartment, and she just fixed her car. She works two jobs. She's a good worker. That's why I made the decision not to fight custody because right now she is doing better than me. Even though I want to be there and see him more, it's looking at the bigger picture. She told me she would never put me on child support, but I told her I could if she wanted me to. It's for my son. She told me, "I wouldn't do that to you because I know the type of father you are." She knows that I'm trying to be there, trying to get my life together here at [DADS]. . . . At first, I really wanted to just lash out and take my son away from her. That's when [the DADS classes] came in. The choice not to tell her I want my kid more is because right now I'm not in a good financial position to take care of [Brayden] as he deserves.

Marcus realized that Sheila's intention was not to limit his contact with Brayden, but to offer their son stability. The program was helping him get his life in order so that he could afford an apartment where he could have partial custody. It also taught him that being a good provider was about providing Brayden with two parents who got along and loved him enough to put their wants aside in his best interests.

Marcus was one of the few fathers who told me they encouraged mothers to file for child support, something he felt better equipped to deliver while he was working and earning something through DADS. He was also among the men who seemed most sympathetic to mothers' struggles and concerns as primary custodial parents. Marcus's recounting of conversations with Sheila suggested that she, too, tried to understand the situation from his perspective with the reassurance of "I know what type of father you are." Marcus was confident that, as long as he progressed through DADS, Sheila was willing to give him the benefit of the doubt about his promise to secure a better job and reliable housing for Brayden's sake.

However, this strong sense of coparenting trust made possible by fathers' participation in the program was not warranted in all cases. For particularly high-conflict situations, DADS staff urged fathers to consider when legal intervention might be necessary to mediate destructive custody disputes. In extreme cases, DADS helped fathers acknowledge when their past abusive behavior meant that no contact with children or coparents was best for the time being.

While fathers like Marcus seemed sympathetic to mothers and willing to forgo more immediate time with children in hopes of a better family situation in the future, fathers like Nicholas fell on the other side of the spectrum. Nicholas, nineteen and Latino, was a single father who shared a young daughter with Alice. He claimed that Alice refused to list him on the birth certificate, filed a restraining order against him, and falsely reported a domestic violence dispute leading to his incarceration, all just to punish him for suspected infidelity. Although he admitted that they both had a history of drug use and hiding their daughter from the other, Nicholas insisted that Alice was unreasonably denying the child access to her father out of jealousy. This created a deep sense of mutual distrust that made it hard for them to speak to one another without physical anger, much less make an amicable joint parenting decision. In only interviewing Nicholas, I was unable to verify how much of his account reflected what really happened between him and Sheila. Yet, given Nicholas's own admission of jail time for physical abuse and the current restraining order, Sheila likely had reasonable grounds for limiting his contact with their daughter.

Staff provided a different kind of support for these situations by urging Nicholas to refrain from contact with Sheila and to provide some financial support for his daughter's household. Nicholas also learned in DADS that limited contact and legal intervention were better for his daughter than her being in the middle of an abusive relationship or having her father incarcerated again: "No matter what happens between you and your baby's mom, say nothing, don't be mean, get along. If she goes off on me, I'm not going to react, just say, 'Let's take it up with court.' Then you walk away."

DADS also helped fathers manage coparenting challenges related to family complexity, particularly in cases where maintaining contact with one child was contingent on minimizing it with others. Aaron, a twenty-one-year-old multiracial single father who shared three children with two women, noted that he was spending more time with his oldest child and communicating better with her mother since starting the program. Alas, this upset the mother of his two younger children who, Aaron said, "tried to have me choose between my daughter and my other kids. If she can't have me, she thinks no one else will. I had to take her to court. I didn't want my kids growing up hating each other because the boys' mother says I love my daughter more." The incessant conflict over his daughter eventually caused him to break up with his sons' mother. Aaron struggled with the financial, interpersonal, and emotional turmoil of trying to raise three kids with two women who each wanted him to have little to do with the other family. Worried that a judge would not see him as a fit parent due to his gender, he enrolled in DADS to make a stronger case for his fathering abilities in the custody disputes. In the meantime, he wanted to be in the program because it was a "peaceful space" that helped him "control my anger in middle of all this personal chaos."

Others similarly described using DADS to cope with the fallout of coparenting challenges involving new partners. Both Peter, a twenty-three-year-old Black father of two, and the mother of his children started dating other people after breaking up the year before. The biggest obstacle to seeing his toddler son and infant daughter was his ex-girlfriend's new boyfriend, who now claimed the children as his own:

> Her boyfriend don't want me seeing my kids. . . . She moved out of her house to go move in with him. I barely see them, and the guy makes it worse because he don't want me to see her and tells me, "You'll never see the kids. Your kids is my kids now." The kids' last name is not even mine anymore. I'm like, "OK, this matter gotta go to court," but I'm trying not to take [children's

mother] to court because I've been knowing her forever. Can't we at least be friends and coparents, for our children? But she wants to be on his side, to get back at me.

Peter last saw his children a month before our interview and had no idea when he would see them again. Harder still was that he could not afford a car and was allowed to see the children only at their maternal grandmother's house, and only when he brought diapers. Peter found the classes useful for dealing with this complicated situation: "It's not the relationship stuff Oprah talks about. They talk about real shit. It's got me thinking, 'What I gotta do for her to see that I'm committed to those kids?' At least with [DADS] my baby mama knows I can give diapers."

Like Peter, most men saw DADS as their only chance to cope with how relational and financial challenges intersected to shape coparenting struggles. Many fathers felt that seeing their children came with a price, whether it was literal money, changing their behaviors, or cutting off contact with others. DADS intervened by helping fathers understand why mothers would make demands for more financial help and why it was not always in children's best interests to maintain relationships or contact with coparents. Just as the program taught fathers to embrace their noneconomic responsibilities as parents, it also helped them resolve what they experienced as the pay-to-play dilemma by giving them the means to pay for more of what their children needed. In doing so, DADS gave men a rare opportunity to prove their parenting as they coped with significant financial and social constraints.

"TRYING TO DO SOMETHING RIGHT BY BEING HERE"

Many fathers felt that children's mothers did not see them as reliable partners or parents because of their struggles to provide financially. For most, their biggest coparenting obstacle was managing constantly shifting partner relationships in the context of highly insecure economic conditions. Of the fifty interviewees, forty found themselves in one or more of the following complicated coparenting situations: sharing children with more than one partner; parenting partners' children from the partners' previous relationships; and coparenting without being romantically involved with at least one of their children's mothers. Almost all fathers made far less than $1,000 per month, and many struggled with housing insecurity and lacked transportation. This made it difficult to house residential children and travel to see nonresidential children, an important consideration given that most (thirty-seven) interviewees did not live full-time with all their kids. Being in DADS was something proactive they could do to help them manage how poverty further complicated complex family arrangements.

Economic constraints seemed to have a particularly difficult impact on families in which fathers shared children with multiple partners. Not only did fathers feel responsible for contributing something to multiple households, thereby stretching meager means even thinner, but managing conflict also entailed negotiating multiple relational challenges without being able to use money to assuage the problems. Given the tendency for both fathers and mothers to repartner after breakups, and often with new partners who themselves had children from previous relationships, "coparents" often included a much broader array of people and networks than just biological parents. It was common for men to need support with coparenting among multiple mothers and fathers, including new partners of exes and even exes of exes.

DADS helped men navigate this tricky complex coparenting terrain. Facundo, a nineteen-year-old Latino father of one, shared: "The program is keeping me straight, busy, not home fucking around with my friends on the streets. I'm learning to negotiate all this with [my son's mom], her boyfriend, and my girlfriend." The way Facundo saw it, his son now had four coparents: him, the boy's mother, and their respective new partners. Making shared parenting decisions as part of this foursome was not always easy and required careful cooperation, but Facundo was grateful his son now had "twice the parents' love."

Several fathers noted that DADS helped them handle being on the other side of a blended family arrangement and effectively parent their partners' children. Martin, a forty-year-old Latino father of five, was a stepfather to his wife's four kids. They took DADS relationship classes together because:

We're supposed to be one, a team, to learn together how to communicate with each other and with the kids, being that we're a blended family. . . . In the beginning when I came into the relationship, she gave me all the rights to discipline, but I didn't feel right because I'm just barely coming into the house. I'm not their father. I wouldn't want nobody coming into my home and trying to bully me or tell me what to do or not, or think that they're my father. I didn't tell her, but I wanted them to see who I was, get to know me. My biggest fear was their not liking me. The classes helped because I'm not a new face no more. I'm their stepfather. Now I know how to communicate with them, to explain myself.

Through classes, Martin and his wife developed a greater sense of cohesion as a blended family unit. He learned to trust himself as a stepfather who was not overstepping his bounds, but guiding and disciplining "his children." Classes on communication, discipline, and the father's role provided a script of social fatherhood that many were previously lacking.

For the few who did have marriage as a near-term goal, DADS offered relational support and, as importantly, economic opportunities men believed they needed to prove they were worthy future husbands. Keegan, a twenty-one-year-old Black father of three, lived with his girlfriend of four years and was one of ten interviewees in a committed relationship with the mother of all his children. Of these, Keegan was the only one who explicitly described using DADS to prepare for marriage, specifically to become more economically stable before making his vows: "We've been thinking about getting married. I feel alright about it, but then at the same time I don't think we should have to get married just to be living right. It is the right thing to do to get married. She wants to marry me. I want to marry her. I have no problem with getting married. We can get married today, but she wants to have the big wedding. Financially it just isn't in the cards right now, but she feels better that I'm trying to do something right by being here." Other fathers who mentioned marriage shared children with multiple women. They focused more on ways the program helped them navigate how commitment to one mother would affect their relationships with children in other households. Otherwise, few fathers saw marriage as feasible or a priority given their economic circumstances.[43] They instead emphasized how DADS helped them address their more immediate relational concerns, like affording the gas and diapers needed to travel to and see their children.

Acquiring other necessities for coparenting and custody, such as shared housing where fathers could live with children, frequently drove men to the program. Elias, twenty-one and Latino, was one of many fathers for whom the stresses of finding and keeping affordable housing created coparenting challenges. He was homeless and expecting a child with Cora, who was eight-months pregnant with a baby they planned to name Eli. Elias had "fallen in love with" Cora's older son, Marco. Yet Cora was living across the country with her mother because she could no longer afford to live near Elias. In describing what motivated him to enroll, he confided: "I'm trying to get my place so she can come back with my boys. . . . The day they left it killed me. When I found out she was pregnant, it was the first time in my life I was scared." Recalling that Elias had told me earlier how he had been shot several times while in a gang, I asked why the pregnancy was his bigger fear. He replied: "When I got shot, I was pissed. When I found out I was going to become a father, I didn't want to fail. I was more scared of getting locked up or shot again. I'm trying to finish school here so they can have a good life financially, somewhere away from this life to get the boys into a nice private school away from the gangs. Right now, that means getting my own place because [Cora] told me, 'Make sure you got some stable income coming in, and we'll come back.'" In the meantime, Cora sent him daily pictures of her growing belly, and Elias kept the sonogram image in his wallet. The dream of having everyone under the same roof before Eli's birth kept him working and going to school through DADS.

Christian, a twenty-two-year-old Black father of one, similarly explained how housing constraints complicated coparenting and often prevented him from seeing his son, Julian. He was thinking about marrying Julian's mother, Julie. They were holding off until they could afford housing for the entire family and go longer without having a major fight that prompted Julie to, yet again, kick Christian out of her apartment. On days when Christian and Julie fought, he had to find another place to stay:

Me and his mom have separated several times. I absolutely love her to death. I've been asking her to marry me lately, but she just wants to make sure that everything is together before we try to take that extra step, to make sure we're stable. We spend a lot of time together, but I have to float around. I don't have a place to live right now. You just kind of work it out with what you've got going on the next day, and that tends to influence where you're going to stay. If things are going well with her, I have a place to live that day, and I get to see my son. One time they left me, and she would not deal with me until I tried to better myself. She wouldn't talk to me, so I went back to the streets and eventually went to jail. I was making more money, but I realized, "Hey, I do want to be with this woman." I agreed with her, so I came here. It's keeping me straight.

Christian saw DADS as his only chance to start a positive domino effect whereby he could make legal money, stay out of jail, afford stable housing, get his girlfriend to commit, and therefore regularly see Julian. For fathers like Christian, their relationship situation on any given day determined whether they had a place to live and could see their kids.

For others, the need for housing kept them together when they otherwise would have split and gone their separate ways. In one particularly complex arrangement, Owen, a twenty-year-old multiracial father of three, was romantically involved with one of his children's mothers while living with another, the only roommate he could afford. This was an ongoing source of conflict with his current girlfriend, who was considering moving in with them to avoid homelessness for her daughter. Owen stayed in DADS to work and earn a scholarship that would cover the full costs of attending the local community college. If he could get a degree and a better job, Owen reasoned, he could afford housing that would enable him to live with his girlfriend, spend time with all his children, and not sleep in the same room with an ex. For the time being, this complicated living situation was the only way to keep a roof over his head and see all of his kids.

Almost all fathers saw being in DADS as their primary way of working on their relationships with children's mothers as partners, coparents, or both. Given men's struggles to provide money, they believed contact with their children was directly or indirectly contingent on their continuation in the program. Those who relied on the court system to decide custody and visitation arrangements cited their progress as primary evidence of their paternal commitments. David, twenty-two and Black, had a complicated relationship with his only child's mother, Maggie, who was mad that David moved three hundred miles away earlier that year. He did not see his daughter, Aubrey, for the three months he was gone. Justifying the move as an attempt to find better-paying work so he could afford his child support payments, David was back in town, had Aubrey every other weekend, and admitted that the move was also a way of "escaping all the drama with [Maggie]." According to David, in retaliation for their breakup, Maggie told the judge overseeing their custody case that David was unfit to care for Aubrey and required supervised visitation. David was in DADS to "prove to myself, the courts, and [Maggie] that I was capable of watching [Aubrey]. . . . I admit that before I was partying. I wasn't stepping up as a parent or husband. I had to be more responsible, keep a job. . . . I now pay $96 in child support a month. Before when I just quit jobs, that caused a lot of argument. Now I know that if I lost this job at [DADS] it would matter. I've stepped up."

David's classmate, Arthur, similarly described how the program allowed him to "move forward" with his life in a less-than-optimal coparenting situation. Learning that he was a father around the time of his daughter's first birthday triggered a reevaluation of his life circumstances: "I became a dad in a week. It hit me hard like a train. Being here is about hitting back harder. I got to make sure I do something that's going to make an impact and actually get me somewhere instead of just not moving at all. I've gained a lot of steps from being here. I've stayed in school for a month. I've never done that before." As long as he was in DADS, he could maintain contact with his daughter, Ashley, and cope with the tremendous emotional and economic impact of sudden fatherhood.

Fathers were a key source of support and accountability for one another through these different coparenting dilemmas. The program was a space where they could commiserate about their children's mothers, vent frustrations, and calm down to avoid doing things they might later regret. Fellow participants and staff provided a more objective perspective about why children's mothers would reasonably expect financial support and get upset when they did not get it. Time spent in program activities was a respite from the constant tension at home for many. Men in the first focus group discussed how other fathers in DADS helped them manage strained coparenting relationships after Jayden, a twenty-four-year-old Black father of three, received a call from his children's mother on his cell phone.

KEEGAN (twenty-one, Black, father of three): When you go home, and she gets to yelling at you, you just walk out the door. [Turning to me]

With the classes, we give each other a lot of advice, especially about baby mamas.

JONATHAN (twenty-three, Latino, father of two): That's like one of my homies here. Today he was talking about some issue going on between him and another dude about his baby mama. He wanted to address the situation. I told him he could go after him, and the other guy could take it to another level because he ain't got nothing to lose. He ain't got no job, he ain't working for nothing. "But you got a job, you got a kid. He could get all loud and arguing, and that could be the end of your job. That could be your money you're taking off your kids. Man, don't do it. You got to feed your kids." I gave him that advice, and later he was like, "I'm glad you reminded me because that could have went a whole different way."

DOUGLAS (twenty-three, Black, father of one): It's for the other men that I even come to school. My homies, we all like brothers basically.

JESSE (twenty-two, Black, father of two): It feels better if you have someone around who knows what you're going through.

KEEGAN: If you get mad at your baby mama, . . . one of the guys in this class, I guarantee they'll talk you out of it.

JONATHAN: Yeah, we don't get as mad. We are able to handle the situation because we'd been taking them positive communication classes. I go to them and talk it out instead of doing what I was going to do. That woman get me in trouble. I'm at the point I ain't going to put my hands on nobody. I ain't got time to go to jail. I got to be a father.

KEEGAN: Right, before I'd be with three or four girls at one time. I wasn't really tripping about coming to school. I wasn't enjoying my son, not being around him because I was doing my own thing. But then I come to this class, they taught me how to be a father. Without this class, I don't think me and my baby mama would last in the house by ourselves. We would have broken up.

Fathers told me that classes worked much like this, as a support group for sharing and seeking advice about how to temper arguments and avoid making life-altering choices that would jeopardize coparenting relationships and connections to children. In DADS, fathers could vocalize the strains of fighting and feeling like mothers valued them mostly for providing and much less so for their parenting. Along with being able to commiserate, men received valuable advice about how to de-escalate arguments and ideas for how to navigate the daily realities of complex family life in poverty. This kind of accountability and support meant more coming from others who had lived through those same struggles and truly empathized with their coparenting challenges.

"IT'S NOT ABOUT THE MONEY, BUT I DO NEED HELP"

Legislators created responsible fatherhood policy with package deal ideas of family in mind. Yet DADS proved just as useful for men's efforts to navigate complex and contentious coparenting arrangements absent romantic commitment and marriage. Most men I studied had somewhat strained relationships with at least one of their children's other parents, and in many cases, these conflicts were a primary barrier to fathers' involvement in their kids' lives. Fully cognizant that tenuous and conflicted relationships with children's mothers prevented their involvement, fathers sought support for overcoming the relational and economic obstacles to cooperative coparenting. They especially hoped mothers would see their time in DADS as evidence of their commitment to reunification or sustained contact with their shared children.

If a goal at all, marriage was a far-off aspiration of the fathers I interviewed. They had more pressing and immediate family aims, including consistent contact with children, making joint parenting decisions, or being amicable with children's mothers. Many fathers described their couple relationships with coparents as irredeemable. Most did not want to get back together; they wanted to improve their status as responsible fathers in the eyes of those who mediated access to their children. This calls into question the feasibility and desirability of integrating marriage activities into responsible fatherhood services. Focusing on the father-child relationship in ways that mirror how fathers prioritize bonds with kids and seek avenues to prove their parenting, as DADS did, aligns more closely with fathers' lived experiences.

Policies and programs must address families as they really are, not as policy makers and practitioners wish for them to be. The reality is that many fathers are compelled to enroll in responsible fatherhood programs due to conflicted coparenting relationships exacerbated by deeply entrenched inequalities, including poverty, homelessness, and unemployment. Although DADS did not emphasize marriage, implicit in the curriculum and responsible fatherhood policy more generally was the idea that two-parent families and marriage are primary ways to help fathers be more involved. For some, this makes sense given that fathers who live, couple with, and stay on good terms with mothers are more likely to be involved. Yet for others, couple bridges have been burned, and families suffer trying to forge coparenting relationships out of the ashes.[44]

Even without interviewing mothers, it became clear from fathers' stories that many couples fought or broke up over the same issues identified in previous research: drug and alcohol abuse, crime and incarceration, infidelity, intimate violence, and especially spending habits that caused mothers to question men's family commitments.[45] Fathers believed they were providing what they could, and when that came up short, they felt that mothers ascribed little value to anything else they did or gave. In DADS, men learned that their time and care were as important as money for their children. Nevertheless, by fathers' own admissions, in many cases mothers were providing most of all three for their children, and often while parenting under the same socioeconomic constraints. These constraints impose impossible, no-win situations on poor parents who end up blaming each other for what are largely, though not entirely, structural problems. Mothers question fathers' commitments when men cannot provide more money, while fathers doubt mothers' intentions when they demand it.

DADS helped fathers navigate this dilemma that all too often characterizes coparenting conflicts among poor families. Fathers started to understand that mothers' requests for more financial support were not because women were money hungry or only saw fathers as paychecks, but because they legitimately and desperately needed more resources to raise their shared children. The program also gave fathers the language and confidence to push back against mothers' claims that they were deadbeats if they could not offer a lot. Melanie, a program director, captured this well when she told me, "It's rare that any man here qualifies as a deadbeat dad. Most have that desire to be part of their child's life. They just don't know how to go about mending that relationship to the point where they can be involved. . . . Not having money doesn't make him any less significant in that child's life. . . . He could provide a lot of money and still not be a good dad. Mothers just need to let fathers know, 'It's not only about the money, but I do need help.'" In emphasizing these messages over marriage, DADS helped men address both sides of the denominator problem. Fathers were in the program to make a case to mothers that they mattered far beyond money in their children's lives. As importantly, DADS gave men opportunities to provide more of what mothers needed. Making regular, albeit small, child support payments enabled by men's jobs through DADS helped smooth over some coparenting conflicts. Showing up with diapers or a loaf of bread earned as program incentives also often meant the difference between a father seeing his child or not.

Fatherhood programs likely miss the marriage mark given the complex families they serve. In spite of this, they can still open gates for fathers to coparent their children, which is really the intended outcome of integrating marriage and relationship services with fatherhood programming. DADS helped men understand that some mothers put gates in place to protect their children from real threats to their safety and security. It also allowed fathers to realize how poverty, not just mothers, erected some of the biggest barriers to paternal involvement. Fathers felt they could prove their parenting to mothers who seemed to care about money as much for meeting their children's needs as for its symbolic import as evidence of men's fatherly devotion. Research on maternal gatekeeping reveals that mothers are more likely to restrict fathers' access when they doubt fathers' parenting abilities and dedication.[46] DADS' greatest coparenting intervention was that it gave men the opportunity to develop and prove both. Being in the program rarely resolved men's denominator problems, but to quote Alex, it helped them make a case that they were trying.

DADS was a way for men to signal that they had more than just an abstract, optional commitment to fathering, which likely meant something to mothers who were doing the obligatory day-to-day raising of children. Rather than understand involvement as either an entitlement or something they must earn, DADS encouraged fathers to provide and do more to help ease mothers' burdens. Yet, as we will see next, DADS still endorsed a limited view of what men must do to be responsible parents.

5 New Fathers and Old Ideas

While waiting to meet Manesh for an interview, I spotted a poster hanging prominently in the lobby of the DADS main building. It showed a Black man and his young son lovingly looking at one another as the father pushed the child on a playground swing. The tagline read: "Take time to be a dad today." I asked Manesh, a DADS case manager and instructor, about the poster. As a proud father to three-year-old Zachary, Manesh, thirty-nine and Asian American, excitedly explained to me how the image represented one of his favorite topics to teach—the difference between "yesterday's fathers" and the "fathers of today":

> The father of yesteryear was supposed to be a breadwinner, earn the income, and work hard. When he did have time off, then came maybe sports or hanging out with his buddies. There was little involvement in the child's life. I notice that today's father, it's all about involvement with school, knowing the teachers, playing the sports. There's a big difference. Back in the day, fathers were typically working in factories. They went to work, and as long as they got food on the table and created shelter, that was good enough. You didn't necessarily have to have a relationship with your child.

The biggest generational change, Manesh reasoned, was that today's fathers want emotionally close relationships with their children.

Manesh also told me that only about one in ten men he taught through DADS had strong positive relationships with their own fathers. For many of the others, estranged relationships with their dads had little to do with family instability or their fathers living elsewhere. Although they lived together, some sons felt that their fathers focused more on work and financial providing than emotional engagement and building a trusting father-son relationship. The latter is what Manesh really meant by "involvement." It was the kind of relationship implied by the poster image of the father pushing his son on the swing.

DADS classes served a unique purpose for men according to Manesh: "It's not every day that we get a group of fathers just to talk about their relationships with their dads, the good and bad and otherwise of it, and to learn to appreciate new fatherhood. This is a rare space, a kind of sorority, if you will. Where else do fathers get a chance to talk to other fathers about being a father?" Noting that most social programs justifiably "cater to women and children," Manesh was proud that DADS specifically served men, especially by helping them understand their parental responsibilities in a rapidly changing society where dads "must now play all the roles. You have to be the loving father, the fun guy, the disciplinarian. You have to show affection, comfort, and especially be involved."

When I asked him to elaborate on what he meant by "new fatherhood," Manesh explained: "It's called 24/7 Dad for a reason. If little ones have a nightmare, you're there to hug, kiss, and hold them. Every waking hour, you're still practicing fatherhood. It's not just being there, because you can be there and be watching TV, watching football all day. Being involved is actually paying attention to your children." Even so, Manesh admitted that he walked a fine line between encouraging fathers to define involvement beyond money while acknowledging that many struggled with feelings of inadequacy around providing: "A lot of the fathers I reach worry more about basic needs in life—shelter, food, paying the bills— more than anything else. They say, 'I don't have my job right now. What am I going to do for food and shelter? How am I going to get something for their birthday?' I stress that involvement is about how some of the nicest things in life, the nicest times, are going to be stuff we do for free, having fun with our children. It's free to be involved with our children." Manesh recognized that fears of falling short as providers were central to many fathers' experiences, no matter how much he talked about involvement as "free."

Still, Manesh reasoned, DADS was one of the only social spaces where marginalized men could open up about these insecurities and develop different understandings of involvement. "It's tough being a father. It's tough being a man. It's tough being a rock all the time." To help men open up about these persistent pressures, Manesh asked fathers if they would be willing to talk about the last time they cried. He was pleasantly surprised with each group by how eager most were to share: "You will never tell your friend, your buddy, the one you're watching football with or working on a car with, the last time you cried. You just don't do that. But I remind them, 'We're all dads here. It's healthy for you to cry. You're OK. If you didn't cry, there's probably something wrong with you. You need that.' . . . Society shapes us, but we don't necessarily just have to be the hardworking, non-talking guy." The ability to have a good cry and not feel ashamed about it is part of being a responsible father, Manesh concluded, as men must model and validate the full range of emotions for their children. "When our kids cry, do we say, 'Man up, you're a big boy. You're not supposed to cry?' No, we say, 'It's OK, Dad cries too.' Let them know the last time you cried. Was it the playoff game when the 49ers lost, and you cried?"

Through lessons about manhood, feelings, and different kinds of involvement, DADS taught men that emotional expression is a key feature of "today's father," a dad who wants to be more nurturing and affectionate. One of the program's primary goals was supporting fathers in this rethinking of paternal responsibility by helping them see involvement as the provision of love, not just money. Beyond this, as Manesh described it, DADS was a "once in a lifetime opportunity to talk about what it means to be fathers, as men, in a group." I learned that DADS was as much about offering men material support for parenting as it was about providing them a space for parsing the meanings of manhood, fatherhood, and the intricate connection between them. Contrasting the "father of yesteryear" with "today's father" was not just an invitation to broaden definitions of responsible fathering. It was also a call to reconsider masculinity.

Yet these "newer" ideas of fathering are not actually new. For decades they have dominated cultural discourses of parenting for privileged men. That they are now central to responsible fatherhood programming represents an important shift in how U.S. social policy targets fathers and poverty. When poor fathers of color have limited involvement in their children's lives, it is often framed as a crisis of masculinity, an unwillingness among marginalized men to accept their gendered parental responsibilities.[1] This troubled masculinity narrative casts the family provider-protector as the emblem of "real" manhood. Fathers who deviate from this model, for reasons of economic circumstance or otherwise, are deemed not only inferior parents, but also insufficiently masculine men. DADS challenged this logic by redefining parental masculinity in noneconomic terms to be more nurturing and expressive. It taught participants that relational involvement with children, not just moneymaking, is a legitimate and valued way of being both a good father and a fully masculine man.

This is a significant and positive departure from how the U.S. welfare state has targeted fathers primarily as wageworkers with monetary obligations for children.[2] It sidesteps still-dominant and limiting ideas that equate manliness with well-paid work and family breadwinning, a form of "hegemonic masculinity," which refers to culturally idealized definitions of manhood.[3] Previous studies of fatherhood programs have analyzed how they sought to reshape men's gender identities in line with hegemonic ideas of masculinity.[4] DADS did something different. It promoted a nurturing paternal style that ostensibly challenged this hegemonic idea of fathering focused on men's breadwinning. Put another way, it redefined fathering by refusing to reduce men to wage earners. In doing so, it dispensed with the related idea that poor men are automatically failed fathers.

However, this seemingly progressive revision of fatherhood also subtly sustains gender, race, and class inequalities. DADS encouraged poor fathers of color to "man up" as emotionally involved parents who uniquely benefit children, reaffirming essentialist ideas that fathers are valuable parents because they are men. In this chapter, I call on sociological ideas of masculinity to make sense of this strategy. Hegemonic ideas of gender mutate and adapt over time in response to resistance and social change.[5] Much of the power of hegemonic masculinity and patriarchy derive from their flexibility and ability to adapt to these changes.[6] As sociologists Tristan Bridges and C. J. Pascoe argued, one way that hegemonic masculinity persists is through the development of "hybrid masculinities," which covertly reproduce gender inequalities by shifting, rather than dismantling, normative understandings of proper manhood.[7] Hybrid masculinities work by co-opting elements of identity associated with femininity or other types of masculinity deemed inferior. The nurturing style of fathering promoted by DADS is a compelling case of how hybrid ideas of masculinity can paradoxically upend some gender stereotypes while fortifying others.

HYBRID FATHERHOOD AND THE DURABILITY OF FAMILY INEQUALITIES

Fatherhood initiatives have historically focused on promoting marriage or employability over an emotionally close father-child relationship.[8] That DADS emphasized the latter is a huge step in the right direction for promoting more egalitarian parenting. However, the DADS case also shows how even a focus on fathers' nurturance can covertly reproduce family inequalities.

Prior research on services like DADS found that men used the programs to develop attainable ideas of successful fatherhood and manhood and to challenge racist and classist stereotypes that they are marginal to families.[9] DADS promoted a specific gendered paternal identity for marginalized men by teaching them to "man up" as fathers who nurture their children in masculine ways. I call this view of fathering *hybrid fatherhood* because it combines elements of parenting long associated with women— nurturance, care, emotionality—with those traditionally associated with men's parenting, including playfulness, discipline, and breadwinning.

Hybrid fatherhood is the parenting style exemplified in the playground poster that hung in the lobby of the DADS building. The poster was part of a government media campaign advertising the importance of fathers' involvement in their children's lives. In addition to "Take time to be a dad today," other ads in the campaign reminded fathers that: "The smallest moments can have the biggest impact on a child's life," and "It only takes a moment to make a moment." They showed racially diverse fathers reading with kids, teaching them to surf, eating cereal in bed, and playing cards and tea party.[10] What could possibly be wrong with images of men in moments of loving, playful connection with their children? Ironically, they can perpetuate inequalities.

On the surface, these touching images seem to illustrate a progressive idea of fatherhood, one with the potential to promote egalitarian parenting across lines of gender, race, and class. Many of the fathers I studied proudly showed me pictures of themselves and their children engaged in similar activities—hugging, dancing, playing sports, sharing a meal. Depictions of these dads—those typecast as our society's least responsible and involved fathers—directly defying race and class stereotypes of men's parenting were politically potent.

Yet, there is a problem with how the ads and DADS emphasized quality time, special outings, and play as central to father-child relationships. These depictions of responsible fatherhood exist as part of a social structure in which women still provide most of the day-to-day care labor for children. A similar ad with an image of a woman playing with her children that read "Take time to be a mom today" would not resonate in the same way. In a society where most mothers spend hours per day cleaning, cooking, and caring for children, it is important to contemplate the gender implications of publicly encouraging men to momentarily "take time" to be dads.

These messages conceal gender and racial differences in who actually does the less fun aspects of parenting labor. Affluent white fathers' involvement still focuses mostly on being breadwinners and part-time, secondary "helpers" when it comes to caregiving and housework.[11] The household, emotional, and mental labor involved in childrearing remains peripheral to social and political constructions of "involved" fatherhood.[12] Hence those government "Take Time" ads show one dad eating cereal with his son but not washing the cereal bowl, another surfing with his daughter rather than laundering the wet suits, and others playing with and reading to kids instead of picking up the toys and books after playtime is over. They certainly do not capture the cognitive work of knowing when it is time to buy more cereal or wash the suits before the next beach trip. Studies rarely even measure these components of parenting labor as part of paternal involvement. Research on how often men do the activities depicted in the ads reveals that residential fathers are more likely to play, eat meals, and talk about their day with children than they are to bathe, dress, and diaper them; they are even less likely to read to children, help them with homework, and take them to and from activities.[13]

Moreover, defying racist stereotypes of "deadbeat" fatherhood, residential fathers of color do more caregiving labor for their children than white fathers, including dressing, bathing, diapering, chauffeuring, and helping with schoolwork.[14] The "Take Time" ad campaign was a well-intended effort to portray diverse men of many racial and ethnic backgrounds engaged with kids. Shaped by a long history of racialized political discourses about irresponsible fathers, there is still an implicit directive aimed at men of color to spend more time with their children. Yet Black fathers are already the most likely to take time to perform the less playful aspects of parenthood.

In short, the "new" ideas of fathering described by Manesh have not translated into equitable parenting. They merely reflect what sociologist Ralph LaRossa described decades ago as the "culture of daddyhood," which endorses softer, more sensitive styles of fathering focused on play and emotional engagement with children.[15] The historical record reveals campaigns going back over a hundred years to promote nurturing ideas of fathering when men's breadwinning abilities have faltered.[16] Affluent white fathers have always had the most leeway to push back against perceived crises of manhood when market and policy changes undermined men's abilities to earn a family wage.[17] Long-standing stereotypes of bad dads have bolstered cultural images of good ones, and poor fathers of color have carried the stigma of irresponsibility necessary for the contrast. Hybrid constructions of fatherhood embedded in the trope of "today's father" idealize responsible dads as nurturing "new men," as opposed to stoic "traditional men" who are emotionally and/or physically absent from their children's lives. Yet, as sociologists Pierrette Hondagneu-Sotelo and Michael Messner argued, the idea of "new manhood" stigmatizes less privileged men who are assumed to be overtly dominant, emotionally stunted, uninvolved fathers.[18]

The notion that low-income fathers of color should embrace nurturance as central to an alternative masculinity reflects a sexist and racist history of poor men and men of color—along with care and emotionality—falling outside the boundaries of "proper" manhood. Although marketed as new during the latter part of the twentieth century, involved fatherhood, the idea that the father is one of children's primary caregivers, custodians, and teachers, was the dominant idea of paternal responsibility going back to the 1600s.[19] Only when industrialization pulled men into the market economy did domesticity and the direct care of children become feminized. "Marketplace masculinity" came to define successful fathering as emotionally distant breadwinning, and any dad who struggled to be a financial provider due to class or race was deemed both a fathering failure and a lesser man.[20]

Based on this history, men have a hard time relinquishing earning as central to their parental identities, and in doing so, many fathers distinguish the care they provide from "mothering."[21] Attempts to masculinize care leave intact two primary ideologies supporting the gendered division of family labor: the idea that certain tasks are either "men's work" or "women's work" and the assumption that tasks have a different value when men perform them. This explains how a key aspect of gender inequality—the durability of gendered parenting arrangements—is reproduced despite a growing cultural emphasis on fathers' caregiving.

Underscoring men's abilities to nurture while retaining the idea that parental roles are gendered and distinct is what sociologists Tristan Bridges and Michael Kimmel called "soft essentialism."[22] Less common now are hard essentialist ideas of women as naturally better caretakers due to innate biological qualities. In DADS, messages about men's parenting responsibilities relied on these softer ways to make old arguments about "new" men and fathers. Claims about hard essentialism—that mothers and fathers fundamentally differ because of sex-based distinctions—obviously reflect binary and biased understandings of gender. Essentialism, in its softer, subtler forms, alters the rhetoric of gender difference just enough to obscure these biases and leave the binary intact. Much of the power of patriarchy is its ability to adapt in barely perceptible ways that co-opt challenges from critics. Hybrid fatherhood does just that by carving out particularly masculine versions of parenting. Political efforts to promote responsible fatherhood focus on messages about "real" manhood and the indispensable contributions of fathers. A primary reason for this, according to political scientist Drucilla Cornell, is that "the father's role [must be seen as] manly and dominant enough for men to want to play it."[23]

In this chapter, I show how Manesh and other DADS staff transmitted this discourse of hybrid fatherhood and how fathers made sense of it. I had limited access to DADS fathering classes, in part because staff understandably wanted to protect men's privacy and not inhibit their comfort in sharing about their concerns and insecurities. More than that, I suspect, it was because I am a woman. During my time studying the program, there were no women 24/7 Dad instructors. This was deliberate. The two program directors, both women of color, developed close, trusting relationships with fathers. Yet the classes themselves were considered a "man's space" where fathers could open up, share their struggles, and be vulnerable. It was the rare context where they were encouraged, expected even, to cry. Women's exclusion from these spaces revealed assumptions that women and men would have different parenting concerns and modes of coping with them. It also reflected how emotionality in general, and crying in particular, touch on one of the few ways in which manhood is not privileged.

Fatherhood programs deliberately create a space where our society's most economically and socially vulnerable men are encouraged to be emotionally vulnerable, especially about how their socioeconomic marginalization shapes their fathering experiences. On one hand, valorizing men's caregiving is a powerful way of undermining very old classist and racist stereotypes about what makes a good man and father. But on the other, expectations of men as manly and caring "new" fathers can recreate gender asymmetry in families when they involve drawing boundaries around distinctly masculine ways of being a loving, involved parent.

THE MEANING OF "REAL" MANHOOD

It was telling that the first lesson in 24/7 Dad classes was about "What It Means to Be a Man" and how the "Roles of Dad and Mom" differ.[24] According to the curriculum, fathers need to understand what their unique role in the family is, how women and men confer different advantages to children, and that the ability to model healthy masculinity is central to being a skilled father. The *24/7 Dad Fathering Handbook* noted that a good dad:

Knows he is a model for his sons on how to be a good man and father and
for his daughters on what they should look for in a husband and father for
their children. He knows that, if possible, he should be involved in the daily
life of his children: from getting them up, dressed and fed in the mornings
to attending parent-teacher conferences, to supporting them in sports and
other interests and activities, to helping them with their homework, to tuck-
ing them in at night. The 24/7 Dad uses his knowledge of the unique skills
he and his wife/the mother of his children bring to raising his children. In
other words, he knows the difference between "fathering" and "mothering."[25]

This prescription for responsible fatherhood emphasized men's involvement in their children's day-to-day lives. It did not suggest that some
aspects of childrearing were more appropriate for men. However, the
overarching message was that fathers, by virtue of their manhood, perform
childrearing tasks in ways that benefit children beyond what mothers provide. The implication was that children specifically benefit when fathers—
as men—take on a caretaking role.

Lessons on the meaning of manhood also taught that an authoritar-
ian fathering style focused on patriarchal control and emotionally distant
breadwinning is outdated and less effective for raising healthy, happy children. The class exercise Manesh described at the beginning of this chapter, titled "Today's Man," listed seven traits that define "Yesterday's Man"
of the 1980s—self-confident, courageous, a leader, dependable, successful,
self-reliant, and controlling—and asked fathers to rate themselves on a
scale from 0 to 3 to indicate how much they identified with these characteristics. Next, they were supposed to list seven traits they believed define
the successful men of today. "Yesterday's Man" and "Today's Man" represent different forms of masculinity, and traits like self-confidence and
being controlling are apparently no longer defining features of successful
manhood.

One of the program directors, Amber, explained to me why it was necessary to begin with this lesson about manhood:

The first topic is what it means to be a man because you see yourself and
identify as a man before you step into the role of father. You have to understand what your role as a man is in the lives of your kids and what you bring
with you. Many dads say: "Mom can take care of you while I do what I need
to do. I don't feel confident as a father. . . . I don't know what that looks like,

or maybe I do because my dad was great, but I don't know how I can fulfill that role because I haven't gotten a job."

Amber decided to "take a step back" by not attending the classes because "fathers really need that space to bond with each other. Sometimes a woman coming is a distraction." She reasoned that men would be more reluctant to talk about masculinity and its connection to the father's role if classes involved mothers or women staff. It was socially acceptable for women, she claimed, to talk about the expectations and challenges of motherhood, but there were relatively few opportunities for men to discuss and develop their confidence as competent parents. As Amber elaborated, it became clear that the focus on gender—especially how men make distinctive contributions to parenting—was intended to help marginalized fathers overcome insecurities about being unworthy parents with little to offer children. The curriculum noted, "The 24/7 Dad is aware of himself as a man and aware of how important he is to his family."[26] The intended lesson was clear: Masculinity is fundamental to fathers' significance.

Samuel, the fifty-year-old Black executive director, explained why he believed it was necessary to address masculinity in a program designed to serve low-income fathers: "As men, if you cannot provide for your family, you don't feel like a man, so you have to offer job skills and a place where they can go. You also have to talk about being a man. When you feel like you're contributing to the family and can bring home the bacon, that makes you fulfilled as a man. It's just something within us, that we have to be able to provide, or we don't feel like we're enough." As was true of most DADS staff, Samuel had many years' experience working with low-income men of color through social service organizations. He had grown up and lived his entire life in the predominantly Black and Latinx high-poverty community where DADS was located. Staff members' professional and personal backgrounds sensitized them to how fathers' class and race marginalization made it difficult to live up to dominant ideals of fatherhood and manhood still focused on providing financially.

Samuel described how DADS tried to redefine responsible fatherhood and successful manhood by teaching that "a successful man is any man who realizes he needs to be there for his child and makes efforts to do that. He may not be successful by society's rules, but if he recognizes he needs to be there, and at least he's trying to do something and taking classes, to me that's a success." A major goal of DADS was to challenge societal expectations that being a good man and father meant making a lot of money. Samuel also noted, however, that the program prioritized helping fathers improve their employment prospects because men feel inadequate if they cannot provide. He reasoned that jobs were necessary for practical reasons—after all, fathers need to secure their own livelihood, and children require financial support from both parents—and because men are still accountable to breadwinner norms of masculinity. If they do not bring in at least some money, he added, it puts even more pressure on mothers, and their children often have to do without. Beyond this, Samuel concluded, it undercuts their self-efficacy as both fathers and men, perhaps ultimately preventing paternal involvement. In short, he believed DADS must address fathers' gender identities because they would be less likely to stay involved with their children if they felt like inferior men.

Jackson, the fifty-nine-year-old Black director of employment services, explained how this feeling of inadequacy was particularly acute for Black men. He discussed the emasculating effects of our country's historical legacy of slavery and current racist norms and practices, which push men of color into poverty and make them feel unworthy as parents and partners for being poor:

> These men are made to feel less than adequate as a man, whether it's true or not, because it's inherent to our culture. If your significant other is basically taking care of you, what does that say about you as a man? Men are embarrassed to be around their children if they don't have a job. . . . There's this discussion of slave mentality, based on what our ancestors went through, . . . meaning you don't want to show fear, that a man doesn't show fear. Under no circumstances should you be in that house taking food out of that baby's mouth. Whether that's true or not, this idea, it's part of your upbringing over generations, to be made to feel embarrassed in the home if they're not bringing anything into that household. . . . It's not malicious, but it happens, not just from the mother of the child, but from the family, from everyone. "What is he doing in the house if he's not contributing to it? I don't think he's trying. He doesn't have a job."

Jackson attributed behaviors that risked incarceration—selling drugs, theft, gang involvement—to internalized racist stereotypes of masculinity and fears that others would view them as failed breadwinners, unworthy fathers, and lesser men. He explained:

> They're faced with trying to supplement with what they don't have to give. So they say, "Yeah, I've got to do something because if I don't, I'm going to be forced to leave. I'm going to force myself to leave. So, guess what, here's three hundred dollars." Does anybody ask where he got the money? In some cases they do, but they're just appreciative that you're contributing, helping the household. They get a sense of reward from that, so they continue to do it. They don't perceive that they can do anything else. It becomes a way of life, the only thing [they] know.

Men are willing to engage in just about any moneymaking activity, Jackson reasoned, when demoralizing poverty and racism deny them dignity as fathers who simply want to provide for their children.

Although the curriculum did not directly address the racist history and dynamics of poor Black and Brown men's economic subjugation, it did include a lesson on "Dads and Work" that prompted fathers to discuss feelings of financial inadequacy and their social origins. Participants defined what "providing" meant to them and listed noneconomic ways of supporting children. The text noted that many fathers "allow work to control their lives so much that they lose sight of how much they value family. . . . They think of themselves as only providers of money or that providing money is so important that it's okay to not provide in other ways."[27] The *24/7 Dad Fathering Handbook* also underscored how finding the right work-family balance is not just a matter of spending more or enough time with family; it is about valuing work as a way of supporting one's family and using family commitments to motivate better work habits. The curriculum concluded that fathers should consider using family-friendly workplace benefits, such as flextime, paternity leave, and telecommuting, to spend more time with their children.

However, as Samuel and Jackson made clear, fathers in the DADS program did not typically struggle with letting too much work control their lives or overtake family time. What overwhelmed their lives, and their paternal identities, was how blocked access to well-paid job opportunities prevented them from securing a status as manly family providers. As Jackson put it, to the extent that fathers experienced a work-family conflict, it was in struggling to contribute enough financially—especially through legal and legitimate means—to feel like responsible dads.

The phrases staff and fathers commonly used to describe becoming a responsible father—*manning up, stepping up, growing up, being on the up and up*—rhetorically connected being a better or higher man and upward mobility for oneself and one's children. The most common, *manning up*, did not necessarily refer to anything particularly unique about men or manhood; it was merely a gendered referent for being a good parent. It implied not that irresponsible fathers have a troubled masculinity, but rather that they are not masculine at all. Staff and fathers' use of these masculine tropes to describe why and how men should increase their parental involvement reflected their understandings of how gender identity shapes fathers' behaviors. In this context, masculinity is not something that must be domesticated; it is a core part of a man's identity that can only be fully realized through paternal accountability.

Many fathers used *manning up* as a term to describe this sense of being "real" men who accepted their family responsibilities by financially supporting women and children. As the program taught, participants' identities as men and fathers were so entwined that many defined being a "good man" and a "good father" only by referencing the other. To Christopher, a twenty-two-year-old Black father of one, being a good dad is to be "just a man, get it together, to be taking care of my family, to be able to support my family like a man should. I feel good being able to provide, and that's all I ever think about at the end of the day. As long as I brought [my son] something, I don't care what I have to do to get it, as long as I get him taken care of." Other fathers used phrases like *stepping up* and *taking care of responsibilities* to describe their manly obligations to protect and provide for their children. Aaron, twenty-one, multiracial, and a father of three, said that being in the program meant: "I stepped up to the plate. I became a man and really raised my child instead of letting somebody else do it. . . . Being a man is someone that really takes care of their responsibilities at home with their children, at school, business-wise."

Consequently, many participants described how the program helped them be better fathers, as well as truer, more masculine men. Dustin, a twenty-two-year-old Black father of one, said DADS was about "making a big change, becoming more of a man for yourself and your family, which means being able to take care of your family. You weren't taking care of your family at first. Your girlfriend was doing most of the stuff, paying the bills. How is that being the man of your household, *your* household? . . . I'm not going to say I was a man to her before then because I wasn't. I'm learning to become a father, not only a father, but a real man for my family." Harris, eighteen, Black, and a father of one, described what he learned from DADS in similar terms: "I had to man up, swallow my pride, and just do what I had to do. That meant I had to stop procrastinating going to work. . . . A great dad admits when he's being wrong. He just stands up and becomes a man. In other words, there are no excuses for why I couldn't do this or that. It's owning up to your mistakes, what you did wrong in the past." Randall, a twenty-three-year-old Black father of two, also learned to "step up, be a man, stop being a boy. It's about taking care of my responsibilities, making sure they have everything they need." Fathers struggled to define *man, father*, and *responsibility* without circling back to the others.

Although jobs and money were central to dads' definitions of proper manhood and fatherhood, *manning up* also meant embracing broader definitions of parenthood and masculinity in the face of economic constraints. Marcus, twenty-one, Black, and a father of one, told me that being a real man means: "to have a job, a stable home, provide for your family by any means, being there for your kid, a role model. I do feel like less of a man when there are other dudes out here got more. Makes me feel real low sometimes, . . . but the program showed me how important I am to my child without all that, that being a man is about 24/7 choices, making that choice to be there with my son instead of making the choice to be with my homies when things are hard." Participants described how they learned that admitting insecurities and past mistakes was fundamental to responsible fathering founded in "real" manhood. As Tanner, a thirty-seven-year-old multiracial father of two, similarly explained:

> Being a man as far as fatherhood is heading up to what you're doing wrong, like when I spent time in jail for drugs. This last time I stepped up, I was a man about my consequences and got tired of being tired. Seeing myself on this side of the glass and my girl and my kids coming to visit, or my kids not wanting to come and visit. I think my responsibility to them is being that man God made me to be, . . . being structured, being a provider of protection, emotional support, guidance, living up to the whole statement of the

difference between right and wrong, having honor and pride. . . . Anyone can be a dad by producing that offspring, but it takes a real man to be a father.

For Tanner, a man's responsibility to protect women and children entailed keeping them safe from physical harm, along with shielding them from the pressures of poverty.

Not showing fear or anxiety in the face of economic distress was another way fathers were supposed to "man up." Many recounted stories of taking financial responsibility for siblings or other family members at young ages as their initiation into manhood. Udell, a twenty-three-year-old Latino father of two, remembered how he "had to become a man, raise my little brother and sister. . . . Being a man, we're brought into the world to be strong, to hold it down for the little ones." His classmate Lee, a twenty-one-year-old Black father of two, recalled learning from his grandmother that, "If a man don't work, a man don't eat. He never eats before women and kids do." Most fathers had early childhood memories like these of learning that real men sacrificed for their families, even if they were actually still boys.

Program messages about the meanings of manhood revealed that marginalized fathers' gendered paternal identities, that is, how they think and feel about themselves as men and dads, have become a primary aim of parenting policy. These meanings and messages also reflect how patriarchy—a social system in which men hold more power, garner more resources, and enjoy a higher status—looks very different from the vantage point of marginalized fathers. Inequitable access to steady and well-paid work resulting from race and class inequalities erodes the status of poor fathers of color; women's relatively greater economic contributions to low-income families of color further erodes it within families.[28]

All men, however, regardless of their position on the socioeconomic ladder, benefit in some ways from what sociologist Raewyn Connell termed the "patriarchal dividend," or the privileges that accrue to males, men, and masculinity.[29] DADS taught and fathers internalized the message that manning up as responsible fathers meant knowing the "difference between 'fathering' and 'mothering'" and enacting gender differences in how they parent and provide for their children. DADS tried to help men overcome their parenting insecurities, especially those rooted in race- and class-based inequities, by convincing them of their gendered value to children.

The problem with this approach is that, in trying to overcome the demoralizing effects of racism and economic oppression on fathers' parental identities, the program reinforced sexist ideas of what parents offer to children by virtue of gender alone. As dads talked about how their struggles with unemployment and poverty brought up fears of being failed providers and weak men, they were quick to add that making money was not enough to "man up" as a responsible father. They also learned from the program that being real men meant taking care of their children as masculine parents.

BREAKING OUT OF THE BREADWINNER BOX

Classes were not particularly prescriptive about what kind of masculinity was required to "man up" as responsible fathers. Staff talked more about challenging stereotypes of how men should think, feel, and act. Fathers learned that being real men involved doing some, if not necessarily equal, childcare. The 24/7 Dad lesson on "Getting Involved" included a section entitled "Don't Let Mom Do All the Work," which explained, "Helping with school work, meetings, and events gives mom a break. Getting involved will help your child and your marriage. It takes the pressure off mom and shows your wife and child that you respect her."[30]

Another lesson on the importance of special daily moments urged fathers to "spend time every day with your children and, if married, with your wife. . . . Tuck your kids into bed, take an evening walk, or simply have dinner or breakfast together."[31] These messages implied that mothers are mostly responsible for the daily labor of childcare and that fathers' "helping" gives mothers a much-appreciated respite from care work. In addition to the problem of assuming, in most cases erroneously, that fathers coparent with mothers to whom they are married, this encouragement to assist moms and spend quality time with children presented a limited view of fathers' day-to-day care responsibilities.

The director Samuel's description of why fathers needed to be involved in the daily care of their children suggested a more equitable division of labor necessitated by the economic realities of modern family life: "We really try to stress that both units should be handling the business of both ways. We all know that we're not the traditional 1950s setup anymore, where the man is the breadwinner and the mom stays at home. For a lot of families to function, two parents need to be out there doing the job and also taking care of the kids." Unfortunately, in doing both, Samuel explained, fathers often find themselves in a dilemma. Despite a growing expectation for fathers to take on a caretaking role, they receive little social support and face stigma when they do:

> Traditionally, men have been the second thought. There's always been resources for women, but men have not always had these resources. . . . Look at any commercial. The male is always looked at as the stupid part of the family and in this joking manner where it's almost like men don't matter anymore. Traditionally, the male dominated in this society, but when it comes to parenting, we're constantly bombarded by messages that we're not as important, that we can't show the same affection that women can. Even today, where both will be doing equal things in the home, people still chuckle if they hear that a man is a stay-at-home father and that the mother's out [working] making the bread. In some circles, he'll be looked at as a weak person. . . . Men play an important part, and we shouldn't be marking lines.

For Samuel, those "Take Time" ads were not just about encouraging fathers to spend time with their children. They were about positively portraying men as competent, loving, and significant parents.

Fathers were especially receptive to messages that, in addition to breadwinning, real men care for their children. Arturo, a twenty-two-year-old Latino father of one, described how DADS taught him that being a good man and father involved doing both paid work and unpaid care for his daughter:

> A good father would be loving, caring. He would be there for his child and the mother of his child. He would be willing to protect them against anything that would come through the door. . . . I tell myself, "OK, if I'm going to be a man, a grown man has to make sure they're at work on time every day." I got to make sure I pick up my daughter, to make sure she has something to eat, take her bath, change her clothes. Then we watch a movie and lay down for the night. Being a man is in these choices that you make.

Arturo defined a real man as someone who is personally accountable for doing everything for his child. Alas, he was the exception in how he talked about being equally responsible for making money and doing all aspects of childcare.

Other fathers described how they learned from DADS that manning up meant not assuming that caring for kids is only women's work. Yet most fathers talked about this as a way of "helping" mothers. David, a twenty-two-year-old Black father of one, explained: "I've sort of stepped up to be the man of the household, and we both can work. I'm not just going to leave it up to one person." I asked, "What does 'stepping up' mean?" David said, "Just taking the initiative, just help out around the house as much as I can, whether it be cooking or cleaning, or bills, or fixing things. Don't just sit down all day and think it's going to get fixed on its own. . . . Stepping up means not assuming something isn't my job because I'm a man." Likewise, Tomas, a thirty-three-year-old Latino father of three, similarly described what he learned about manhood from DADS:

> If you're going to say something, do it. Don't be afraid and say, "No, I can't." In class, [the instructor] talked about how being a man is going to work, come home, have your self time, which means anywhere from ten to twenty minutes to just be like, "OK, I just got home, let me get refocused." . . . If you have a wife, help make dinner, help do chores, pitch in. Don't just come home and think you're king of the castle and try to say, "I worked hard, and I want this done in a certain way." Help out with the chores and the household, help with homework. A lot of guys don't. I admit I didn't. When it came to that, I was like, "Well, I'm not good at math. Have your mom do it." Now I know that is wrong. . . . Even the minutest thing, like folding the laundry. It may not be minute to somebody else. It could ease her workload or tension. Help out, fix a bike tire. I may not have time for it, but that may be the one thing my kids really want, and they'll see in the long run that, "You know what? Dad does a lot."

Very few fathers spoke, as Arturo did, about doing an equal share of housework or childcare as part of manning up. Many more talked instead like David and Tomas about "helping out" or "pitching in" around the house to ease mothers' workload.

This larger group of "helpers" maintained a sense that "stepping up" as fathers meant choosing of their own volition to take some of the burden off moms, as if any sporadic and discretionary effort to care for their kids was going above and beyond what men were obligated to do. According to Jesse, a twenty-year-old Black father of two, men who step up "don't have the mother do everything when they can choose to play a part too. I can change a diaper, give my kids a bath, and take time to play with them."

DADS did address how gender stereotypes limited men's comfort with doing more family labor. Staff encouraged fathers to question rigid definitions of masculinity that equated care work with being unmanly. Karen, fifty-eight and white, taught an exercise called the "Man Box" as part of the program's relationship classes:

> You put "What is a man?" and the box [on the board.] They tell you "strong, provider, fighter, lover," and so I say, "Now, you're a gay man. Where are you in the box? You're not in the box." Some will say they can barbeque, but they never say "cook." They don't say they clean well. We talk about the stereotypes and if you're out. "Who here hasn't done anything outside this box? Any of you wear pink?" They learn that it's OK to be outside the box. "If you cry, where are you at?" They say, "I'm out of the box." Those are the types of things we work with, on understanding that society has put you in this box.

Karen explained how gendered expectations circumscribed men's family responsibilities to include only making and providing money, not care labor. Struggling to be successful breadwinners meant that men did not fit in the metaphorical box, and a big part of DADS was helping fathers reconceptualize their parenting identities and roles outside its stereotypical confines.

Joe, a fifty-year-old white 24/7 Dad instructor, also urged fathers to question how they were socialized to think of housework and childcare as women's domain. Expanding fathers' ideas of acceptable household tasks for men was one of his main teaching goals: "We look past traditional roles and at roles today, how they're kind of merged, sharing duties, cooking, hygiene, getting the car fixed, whatever it might be. We make a list, and we also do Mom's roles and traits to see which ones are more traditional to see that we've been placed in them by our culture. Then we also see how they're shared. I challenge them, 'Why can't Mom do it? Why can't you do that one?' A lot agree. Some still have those set ways, that Dad needs to work and bring home the money." When discussing "not marking lines," being "outside the box," and looking "past traditional roles," respectively, Samuel, Katie, and Joe all noted the importance of teaching fathers to rethink how they have been boxed in by socially acceptable boundaries of masculinity. A significant part of this rethinking of manhood involved advising fathers to embrace "newer" ideas of paternal involvement focused on being self-aware, emotionally expressive coparents who get in touch with their feelings and encourage their children to do the same.

SHARING FEELINGS AS FATHERS

The 24/7 Dad curriculum noted that a responsible father "knows his moods, feelings, emotions [and] capabilities, strengths, and challenges. He is responsible for his behavior and knows that his growth depends on how well he knows and accepts himself."[32] The lesson on "Showing and Handling Feelings" described "men['s tendency] to better control their feelings than women" as a detriment; it cautioned that "men tend to not take care of their emotions when they grieve" and are more likely to "show anger . . . rather than sadness."[33] Tips for how fathers could counter these tendencies included self-care, reflection on the causes of grief and sadness, staying connected to friends, working out, and crying when necessary. As Manesh explained, it was crucial for men to talk in the company of other men about what they learned as boys about crying and what they wanted to teach their own kids about openly expressing emotions and grieving loss. Lessons on effective discipline and communication similarly advised fathers to guide children gently rather than control them through fear, and to seek empathic understanding rather than engage in fight-or-flight behaviors motivated by aggression and contempt.

Breaking the emotional boundaries that kept men boxed in required a safe space where they could talk freely about their feelings, especially those related to the challenges of living up to breadwinning expectations as low-income men of color. Classes and other program activities addressed how it was acceptable, desirable even, for men to admit fear and self-doubt, especially to other men who empathized with their feelings of inadequacy. Staff encouraged fathers to cope with stress and trauma through emotional expression and counseling, rather than anger or violence. Like Manesh, Joe talked with his classes about where, when, and how much it was appropriate for men to cry: "Some of them say, 'We don't cry, right? Don't be a girl,' things like that. Some of them share that it was OK for them to cry at home. Others say, 'There's a time and place for everything. You can cry at home, but not out there.'"

Fathers appreciated how staff taught about emotionality and support seeking as reflections of masculine strength, rather than weaknesses that undercut their manliness. Men described how they learned that crying and asking for help are fathering skills, not liabilities. Rodrigo, a nineteen-year-old multiracial expectant father, told me:

> A man can let his pride get in the way and won't open himself up to these opportunities like this program, like it's belittling to accept help from someone else. Women don't feel that way. . . . Being here helped me put pride aside and realize I'm not just living for myself. I got a daughter and woman to keep happy. I have to be a man to be able to provide. . . . Coming to a place like this, asking for help, swallowing your pride, admitting your flaws, expressing your emotions, that's being a man. You're making your daughter's and your woman's life right, and now you can really label yourself as a man. . . . Being a real man is knowing what's more important than your pride.

Men learned to open up and not let their egos get in the way of seeking help on behalf of their children.

Dads also described the classes as a rare space where they could discuss how intersecting race, class, and gender inequalities resulted in fears of inadequacy as men and fathers. Caleb, a forty-year-old Native American father of three, explained:

> I like the idea of men fellowshipping about things. Usually we're locked up. We're isolated. We isolate ourselves as men, and we feel like we're the only ones screwing up. Like we're the only ones who did something bad and that we must be really bad people. Hearing stories other people went through, the abuse in their childhood and what not, and how they became the parents they were. . . . It's a bunch of dudes sitting around telling their feelings and shit. Some men take a while to warm up. I don't know why. It's inside, but it's like a brick wall. It's like an unknowing how to let out. . . . It was really helpful getting confirmation that all dads think the same way. We get with a lady, we have kids, and then it's all about them and work. Them and work.

Them and work. People like to say we're all about elbows and shoulders and football games and chips and stuff. We're so much more than that.

The "unknowing how to let out" feelings that Caleb described meant unlearning masculine norms of emotional constraint and breaking down the "brick wall" of stoicism that kept fathers tethered to trauma and feelings of deficiency.

Fathers in the first focus group echoed Caleb's sentiment when they discussed how mainstream portrayals of family life rarely acknowledge men's parenting perspectives and feelings. They collectively lamented that, because men were expected to suppress their emotions, people assumed they did not feel them as strongly as women. Keegan, a twenty-one-year-old Black father of three, said: "Mothers should know everything that we know, but we don't know what women know because women don't know what men know. They don't know how we feel or nothing." His classmate Saul, twenty-two, Latino, and a father of one, added: "Right, it's just two different perspectives, but our side really doesn't ever get seen because it's not really talked about. For me, we don't really share our feelings. That's something we're able to do here."

Much of what fathers shared during these discussions about feelings and crying were childhood memories of ridicule and punishment for showing emotions or fear. The classes helped Daniel, a twenty-six-year-old Black father of five, recall: "If I was about to get spanked, and that switch came out, I shouldn't cry. I was supposed to be, I don't know how to put it, a punk. Yeah, I'm not supposed to show emotions. But in those classes, they said that's a healthy way of letting it out. Be open and talk to someone, like a support group here." After fathers shared about formative emotional experiences like Daniel's, they discussed how they wanted to pass on different messages about fathering and feelings to their own children. Hank, a forty-four-year-old Latino father of four, estimated that he had only seen his own father cry three times. It was even rarer for his dad to tell him "I love you." Hank strove to be much more physically and emotionally affectionate with his kids:

I'm not embarrassed to hug them or tell them that I love them. Even my sons, I'll give them a little peck on the cheek. . . . I don't do it if I know it's going to embarrass them, but I'll give them a strong hug, not a buddy hug, a lovable hug. I do that with my daughter and my son now, too. . . . [My dad] told me men shouldn't cry and things like that. I guess to him it would show weakness. . . . But it's just too much toughness there. I just don't think it's healthy for anybody, whether you're male or female. I don't want my son to have to hold that all in like I did.

In addition to modeling hard work, fathers like Hank wanted to become better emotional role models for children as men who demonstrated love and self-compassion.

Some fathers described learning at a young age that boys and men should experience and display the full range of human emotion. They appreciated the opportunity to connect with and support other fathers who sought validation from fellow men that this was acceptable. Nicholas, a nineteen-year-old Latino father of one, said:

> I was raised by my mom. She taught me how to feel. It was never like, "Oh, you're weak if you cry." I'm going to cry. I already agreed with that. They said it was OK, you know. Sometimes a lot of guys have a hard time doing that. There's a time and place for everything though. It's a very good program for fathers because, in a lot of situations, they don't really have no one to talk to about how to be a father or a man. I've seen men here who are really hard, like, "I'm not going to cry. I don't care what you say." They hear somebody else talk about it, and then they really look at it differently.

An advantage of being in the program with similarly situated men, Nicholas noted, was that they could model for one another a more emotional and empathic masculinity.

Emmett, twenty-four and Black, was one Nicholas's classmates who benefitted from DADS in this way. After the death of his infant daughter, Shannon, the program became an emotional refuge, the only place where Emmett felt comfortable enough to be open about the trauma he was living through. Losing Shannon forced him to "break open" after a lifetime of stoic suffering. Although he did not worry that others would judge him for crying, especially over one of the most tragic experiences one could endure, he still struggled not to cry and emote "too much" as a "real" man:

> I was taught a man doesn't cry. . . . "Shut up, why are you crying? Are you a girly? Are you a little girl?" . . . People picked on me to get me to stop. After a while it worked, and I didn't like crying. When I do cry, it's because, yeah,

I've held back crying for so many years, so it just comes out and breaks out. . . . A real man knows when to cry and when not to cry. What makes a man is he's aware of his emotions, he is in control, and he is self-aware. What makes a good dad is a good man. The man makes a good father. I learned that in [DADS]. . . . A good man is someone who is considerate, not selfish. I was very selfish, and that's what kept me from being a good man for many years. Now I have to be aware and in control. I have to say "I'm sorry," too.

All of this came to the fore in our interview. Emmett apologized in advance for any tears that "might slip out" and again five more times for "being so emotional" as he cried during the interview. He guessed that it would be a long time before he did not feel the need to apologize for his feelings. In the meantime, DADS was a source of solace, a place where he could cope with his loss while finding the level of emotional control that felt right to him. This would be especially useful, he concluded, for teaching his future children that all their feelings were valid. He did not want them to learn, as he so painfully had, that men should suppress and hide their emotions.

DADS taught men that they could be responsible fathers—and fully masculine "real" men—through caregiving and emotional expression. Fathers learned to develop a greater sense of themselves as good dads despite their limited earning capacities. Yet these ideas also allowed marginalized men to capitalize on the "patriarchal dividend" associated with the valorization of masculinity, thereby reinforcing patriarchy in subtle and significant ways.

THE PARADOX OF PROMOTING HYBRID FATHERHOOD

DADS's emphasis on men as emotionally engaged parents reflected a gendered restyling of fathering that, in many ways, challenged patriarchal ideas in families and in policy making. The program underscored men's abilities to be affectionate parents with a nurturant masculine style that wove together traditional elements of fathering—namely, protection and providing—with the caregiving and tenderness typically associated with mothering. The goal was to help fathers overcome their fears of emasculation rooted in anxieties about being failed providers and expendable parents.

Amber found that, once fathers understood their "unique role," the program's education and work components allowed them to "feel they deserved to be involved" and live up to the "breadwinner mentality." Melanie, another program director, forty-one and Black, believed that the primary purpose of DADS, and her role specifically, was to "empower fathers by letting them know from a woman's perspective, which they don't really get a lot, that I'm valuing them as men." The DADS staff deeply understood the significance of validating fathers—as both men and parents—given that their social and economic constraints made living up to the breadwinner ideology exceedingly difficult.

DADS taught that men's nurturance is uniquely valuable for children. Caring, loving fathers, staff reasoned, offer children two valuable life lessons women cannot impart: that care is a legitimately masculine activity and that they are worthy of love from men. A relationship class instructor, Darren, eighty-five and Black, guided fathers through discussions about this:

> We connect to manhood categories, healthy and unhealthy. They always want to talk about what is unhealthy. . . . After we talk about baggage, about not having a father, about having gone to jail, we talk about hanging out with people who smoke weed, get drunk, party, calls his woman a "bitch." We talk about how to become a good man despite all that. The key is to risk love, and it's helpful for a man to talk about it. . . . It's not easy for a man to look at himself, but you've got to do that to . . . model for that child how to risk love. All men want fathers because that's who you feel comfortable with. Children think, "He cares about me. He legitimates me."

This notion that fathers provide unique emotional benefits for children is rooted in a particular understanding of gendered parenting. It does not assume hard essentialist ideas that women and men parent differently due to sex-based differences or that women are naturally better caregivers. Rather, it reflects a kind of soft essentialism that fathering is categorically distinct from mothering because men's emotional engagement with children provides them with a certain confidence and validation that women's parenting cannot.

Many program messages about manhood challenged ideologies of patriarchal control based on dominance, aggression, and money. By encouraging introspection, connection, and vulnerability, this "healthier" category of manhood rejects toxic forms of masculinity that engender violence and oppression. Channeling these ideas in the service of supporting marginalized men as they developed more nurturing ideas of masculinity and parenting is a progressive turn in the gender politics of family policy. DADS addressed men as caregivers and coparents, not just as workers, wage earners, or potential husbands. It taught participants that they do not have to be financial providers to be responsible fathers, which is an identity and social status often denied to poor men of color. By affirming that affectionate fathers who care for children are truly masculine, messages based in hybrid ideas of fatherhood can help men resolve the gender tension associated with growing norms of emotionally engaged fathering.

These lessons about manhood challenged key aspects of patriarchy, but reinforced others. The softer style of masculinity that DADS advocated still assumed gender difference and hierarchy and that men hold exclusive power to make children feel fully acknowledged, valued, and loved. These assumptions were based on gender stereotypes that "fathering" is separate from "mothering" and that there are distinctly masculine ways to provide love for children. Although it broadens definitions of paternal responsibility to include care, the discourse of hybrid fatherhood does not appeal to men to do equal childcare or household labor. Rather than dismantling gender ideologies of family roles, it merely reconstitutes them by casting responsible fathers as helpers who take some of the care labor burden off women.

Hybrid views of fatherhood position "new" fathers and "real" men as superior to those who are not involved in their children's lives. The directive for fathers to "man up" relies on ideologies that cast uninvolved fathers as lesser, emasculated men who have failed at both parenthood and gender. The problem with the "real manhood" discourse in this case is not necessarily the qualities or behaviors associated with it. There is certainly no fault in the idea of loving, engaged fathers who take pride in being with and caring for their children. Nevertheless, these expectations prescribe parenting behaviors that risk making fathers who fall short feel inferior and shameful. This strategy counters limiting definitions of masculinity and fatherhood, but only through a contrast to women and "other" lesser men and fathers.

As the newest iteration in a long history of political discourses of fathering, these messages mobilized norms of masculinity and fatherhood long associated with white, class-privileged, married men. Race and class have been primary factors of exclusion from hegemonic notions of masculinity predicated on breadwinning abilities. For far too long, marginalized men have fallen outside the ideological boundaries of what constitutes good fathering. Depictions of poor men of color as uninvolved fathers have elevated and valorized notions of white, middle-class fatherhood that normatively value caregiving while still practically prioritizing breadwinning. Ultimately, political narratives of "absentee" fathers, which are most often thinly veiled racist critiques that obscure systemic racial and class inequities, require an ideological counterpart: the always present, egalitarian, emotive man who both provides for and nurtures his children.

The reality is that white, affluent men seen to epitomize responsible fatherhood are still significantly less likely than mothers to directly engage with and perform care labor for children. Yet commentators rarely criticize these men as "absent" from the reproductive labor needed to sustain children's lives. Beyond this, privileged men benefit from the vilification of poor fathers of color as hypermasculine, emotionally restrained, and minimally engaged. This stigma bolsters privileged men's efforts to embrace more sensitive and caring versions of masculinity that fortify a newer and perhaps softer, though no less powerful, form of patriarchy.

"New" fatherhood has never really challenged or questioned the gendered division of parenting labor. It has merely redefined patriarchy at critical historical junctures to be more emotional and inclusive of care without fundamentally altering the material conditions of care work.[34] The current iteration shares many commonalities with previous efforts to make fathering seem more caring, most notably its emphasis on the message that good fathering need only be more relational, memorable, and fun.

This has significant ramifications for the workings of patriarchy and the gendered power dynamics of parenting. To use the words of sociologist Michael Messner, by emphasizing emotional closeness over the performance of care labor, this softening of masculinity transforms patriarchal power by promoting a change in the style of fathering rather than its substance or the social positions of power from which men and women parent.[35] Shifting the style of parenting—from the stoic traditional father to the expressive new one—without fundamentally changing who does the dirtier, less fun labor of child-rearing does not merely fall short of equality. It masks and perpetuates it.

Masculinity scholar Stephen Whitehead concluded, "While being a 'new father' implies a break with increasingly dated ideas of traditional male roles, . . . in practice it can often mean little more than a symbolic attachment to the *idea of being a father* rather than a full, equal, and unmitigated engagement in its harder practices."[36] Similarly, hybrid fatherhood refers not only to the combination of stereotypically masculine and feminine traits in cultural and political constructions of responsible fathering, but also to how messages about men's caretaking can actually fortify patriarchy while appearing to undermine it.

Individual men are not the sole source of patriarchal power. Patriarchy is a larger system of political and social control that favors manhood, demeans femininity, and subjugates women, in large part by tasking them with greater caregiving responsibilities and stigmatizing families without fathers as substantially lacking. Poverty rhetoric in the United States, especially after the passage of the 1996 Personal Responsibility Act, has pathologized single motherhood as the cause of higher poverty rates and other social problems disproportionately experienced by Black and Latinx families. When it comes to fatherhood, patriarchy has an insidiously dual nature: It works in privileged families to protect "new" men from the burdens of equitable caregiving, while it operates in poor families of color to blame insufficient fathering for race and class inequalities.[37] Hybrid political constructions of fatherhood reinforce this dual nature of patriarchy by concealing the power of privileged men and implicitly devaluing women and mothering.

Ultimately, diversifying meanings of acceptable manhood and responsible fatherhood so that more dads fit into the "man box" will only go so far. Dismantling the box entirely requires disentangling meanings of manhood from ideas of good parenting, not starting with the assumption that one must identify as a man before embracing one's role as a parent. As long as the box remains intact, no matter how expansive, there will always be fathers who risk falling outside it, not for reasons of personal choice or lack of individual initiative, but because they lack the social and economic means to "man up" according to dominant definitions of masculinity. As history has repeatedly shown, men marginalized by class and race tend to carry the stigma of being inferior fathers who are lesser parents and failed men for not living up to these definitions. As long as there is a gendered litmus test for responsible fathering and masculinity norms intersect with race, class, and sexuality, some men will always fall short.

How DADS staff and fathers talked about men's emotions also needs to be understood at the intersection of these same race, class, and gender inequalities. DADS did not encourage men to reveal their feelings just for the sake of being expressive or showing affection for children. It was also about giving men a social and emotional escape valve for the psychological effects of childhood trauma, racism, incarceration, and especially living and raising their own children in deep poverty. On the surface, these lessons were about how men are hemmed in by gender stereotypes that dictate how to be stoic fathers whose value to families depends on their earning capacity. Looking deeper, they are really about what happens when men are denied opportunities to stake their masculinity in economic and white privilege.

Characterizations of "new" versus "older" fathers have a pointed meaning for poor men of color, who stereotypically represent everything "new" fathers are not—aggressive, domineering, uninvolved. Encouraging men to cry was an invitation to interrogate meanings of manhood steeped in white, middle-class notions of paternal responsibility and respectability. Privileged men's economic position helps them maintain their status as "real" men who provide for, protect, and play with their children. This privilege has shielded them from criticisms that they need to "man up" as better fathers, despite long-standing gender disparities in parenting. DADS did something quite revolutionary by teaching poor fathers of color that they, too, were socially acceptable fathers who play a unique and valuable role in their children's lives as men. Alas, it did so by relying on old and oppressive ideas of fathering under the guise of "newer" ways to be a man.

6   Teaching the Essential Father

DADS would never have been without Samuel. He beamed as he talked about being an involved father to his sixteen-year-old daughter. Their close relationship inspired him to develop a parenting program specifically for men. Along with several others, he wrote the original grant application that secured federal funding for DADS. The initial idea emerged from conversations with fellow family service organization directors about the disadvantages of not having a positive paternal presence in the home. Samuel shared: "A reoccurring theme that we kept seeing was the young men and young ladies coming into the programs, most of them did not have a father figure. We have an orientation where young people come. I'll never forget when I asked one group to raise their hands if their father had been a positive impact in their lives. Eighty percent of them did not raise their hands." Samuel recalled his surprise and sadness for those who kept their hands down. His own father, a highly respected and longtime community leader, had a profound influence on Samuel, who followed in his father's footsteps by heading up one of the city's most prominent organizations serving those in need.

Through this work, Samuel encountered many people who struggled with poverty, gangs, and crime. He described how he saw these problems as linked to missing fathers: "We have a lot of young men who have been in the system who are gang related, and since they don't have fathers in their lives, they look to other young men to bond with. That's when you get the gangs. And you have the young ladies who don't have that role model of what a man should be, so they kind of latch on to the first man who shows them some attention." According to Samuel, people often find themselves in dangerous circumstances that jeopardize their lives and life chances because they are in search of relationships to compensate for not having close fathers. This feeling of loss and lack, he believed, motivated many to enroll in DADS: "They know the impact that not having that parent in their lives had, and they want to change and give their child something they didn't have. . . . There are better outcomes if the father is present."

A major goal of DADS was to help men break the cycle of missing fathers and their impact on children's opportunities and self-worth. This is why the program offered school and work. It was also the rationale for including fathering classes focused on manhood and teaching men about models of healthy masculinity. Samuel explained:

> They're trying to overcome eighteen to twenty years of bad influence where they may have come from a background of not seeing their father get up every day and go to work because their father's in jail or the mother was the one [parent] or grandma. . . . So how do you in a year teach this young man what it means to be a man when they haven't seen a man function day to day? . . . They're surrounded here by people who can exhibit what it is to be a man. If you don't see that firsthand, it's hard to learn how to be there. . . . The sons look at fathers and see how to become a man. Their role is just as important for daughters because the daughters look at the father as what a real man should be. . . . If she doesn't have a man in her life to model what she should be looking for, it's very easy to get hooked up with men who don't have their best interests in mind.

The crux of Samuel's argument was that boys look to their fathers as their first and primary role models of real manhood, whereas girls learn from fathers what to look for in future romantic partners. According to this logic, missing fathers do not just deprive children of necessary resources; they also leave an emotional and psychological void children seek to fill, often with disastrous consequences.

Samuel's explanation touched on many deeper questions raised by a policy that targets fathering to address inequalities. What specific role, if any, do fathers play in family life as men? Can we explain the higher poverty rates and lower school completion rates among children of color in terms of their relationships (or lack thereof) with their fathers? In trying to prevent the problems that caused so much suffering for the fathers described throughout this book, what do we miss if we focus on parents' gender? What do we miss if we don't? Many major controversies over responsible fatherhood policy come down to a couple basic questions to which Samuel provided definitive, yet questionable, answers: Are fathers essential, and if so, why?

Samuel's remarks also point to dual meanings of "essential" when it comes to views about fathering. Psychologists Louise Silverstein and Carl Auerbach critiqued this idea about the gendered necessity of fathers.[1] They emphasized two fundamental and flawed premises of the "essential father" discourse: (1) that mothers and fathers parent differently due to natural or essential gender differences between women and men; and (2) that men are necessary or essential for children's well-being due to their exclusive ability to role-model healthy masculine behavior.

Silverstein and Auerbach argued that the concept of the essential father is a reaction to growing gender equality and the decline of men's power within families. Paternal essentialism as an ideological justification for fathers' family authority gained political traction just as dual-earner and same-sex families became more common and socially acceptable. Efforts to restore the idea of contrasting and complementary gendered parental roles emerged once men started to lose the privilege attached to being primary family wage earners.[2]

In this chapter, I show how the "essential father" idea has a particular salience for poor men of color who cannot stake their identities as successful fathers in class and race privileges. DADS offered participants a compelling rationale for their unique value to children as responsible fathers who, despite their economic hardships, were committed to being masculine role models of attention and affection—two aspects of involvement that do not depend entirely on money.

This also reveals how participants' relationships with their fathers shaped their experiences with DADS. Studies of other fathering programs found that many men enrolled to develop the parenting skills they believed they lacked due to limited or negative relationships with their own fathers.[3] As detailed earlier, fathers in DADS joined for various reasons, including the ability to combine work and school, better job opportunities, social support, and help navigating coparenting obstacles. Many also mentioned strained or nonexistent relationships with their fathers as another motivation.

Of the fifty fathers I interviewed individually, over half—twenty-seven—would likely not have raised their hands in response to Samuel's question during orientation. They either did not know or have contact with their fathers during childhood, or saw them so rarely that they did not regard them as real parents. Yet another twenty-one fathers described having close positive relationships with their dads, whom they saw as parenting exemplars. These twenty-one men viewed the program as an opportunity not to overcome the effects of missing fathers, but as a second chance to follow in their dads' footsteps and become responsible parents.[4] Thus, some men in DADS attributed their motivation to be good parents to having had an involved father, and others to not having had one present at all. About a third also described learning how to be responsible dads from the mothers and/or grandmothers who raised them. These men wanted to emulate the attention, care, and nurturing parenting behaviors they learned from women.

This chapter reveals that the "essential father" discourse is not merely a backlash against more egalitarian families. Challenging ideas of breadwinning-only fathering, this discourse is also a way of incorporating poor men of color into definitions of responsible fatherhood. Interrogating these messages and their implications for marginalized men's understandings of parenting and poverty goes to the heart of the larger implications of policies on responsible fatherhood. The "essential father" discourse teaches men that they add indispensable and irreplaceable value to children's lives, despite how race and class inequalities undermine their ability to provide. However, the evidence on the crucial ways fathers contribute to their children's lives does not support claims that men's value to families derives from their maleness or masculinity.

WHY FATHERS MATTER

The idea that fathers are important as gender role models emerged during the mid-twentieth century when the rising popularity of sex-role social-ization theories met the growing concern that family life had become too feminized.[5] Sex-role theories presumed that biological sex determines family roles, such that mothers are naturally primed and better suited for caregiving.[6] Around the same time, social learning theorists Bandura and Walters popularized the idea that children develop their gender identi-ties and learn gender norms by observing and imitating the behaviors of parents of the same gender.[7] These theories assumed that learning how to navigate and enact gender difference is beneficial for children and society and that the absence of same-gender parents prevents the development of stable gender identities. Social problems, including poverty and unem-ployment, have been attributed ever since to insecure forms of masculinity among boys who presumably spent too much time with mothers and too little with fathers—and hence never learned how to be "real" men.[8]

Sex-role parenting theories rely on circular reasoning that conflates sex and gender, as they presume that only a father can teach a boy how to be a man because he is male. They are also ahistorical in how they ignore the great variety of fatherhood and masculinity norms across time. Perhaps most problematically, they overlook the wide diversity of parenting behav-iors within and across gender groups; they fail to consider that not all men parent alike and that many men parent more like some women.[9]

Despite these flaws, the idea that parents' sex and gender fundamen-tally shape children's well-being remains strong, with many drawing links between "fatherless" homes and negative outcomes. David Popenoe claimed that boys need fathers to develop a stable sense of masculinity that supports self-control and empathy, while girls need fathers to pro-vide physical and emotional security and to model heterosexual trust and intimacy. He stated: "In a desperate search for substitute forms of male affection, some [women] have inappropriate sexual contacts, become overly dependent on men, and allow men to take advantage of them."[10] Sons and daughters without close fathers, Popenoe and other authors have argued, long for a man to protect, love, and care for them.[11] Many social problems, including poverty, crime, unemployment, and prostitution, purportedly result when a critical mass of children miss the sense of security only fathers can provide. This reasoning has a strange and insidious paradox at its core: It simultaneously paints a very bleak picture of men as naturally violent, rapacious, and selfish, and yet, as parents, essential for children to learn to be healthy people and productive members of society.

Sociologist Philip Cohen has shown how the religiously motivated emphasis on the natural law of "complementarity" in parenting opposes family diversity, as well as gender equality.[12] Gender inequality demands gender differentiation, and policy's insistence on the natural and necessary contributions of fathers is an effort to uphold the gender binary, while simultaneously blaming other inequalities on its decline. Highlighting the importance of parents' gender differences, especially the notion that children benefit from distinctive paternal and maternal styles or contributions, has been the lynchpin of religious, legal, and political arguments against families that deviate from the heterosexual, married, two-parent standard. Insisting that children need both male and female parents is a defense of gender difference that disparages single parents, same-sex couples, and parents who perform nontraditional roles.

Ultimately, essentialist claims about fathers' gendered importance reinforce and reflect gender inequality. Any "benefits" that derive specifically from having a man as a parent are due to how power and privilege accrue more to men. As Popenoe explained: "Daughters learn from their fathers much that will be of value in their work and professional lives, especially the skills they need for coping in a still male-dominated world [including] ... assertiveness, independence, and achievement."[13] Involved fathers, he noted, are necessary to elevate the social status of women because they can ease mothers' workload and model for children how men can share social power and authority.[14] However, the implication that mothers cannot just as effectively model achievement and authority fortifies men's family dominance.[15]

To a point, Popenoe was correct that involved fathers are linked to elevated social status and greater authority for women. Sociologist Scott Coltrane found that in societies where fathers were involved, specifically through routine childcare, women were more active in public decision-making and had a higher status.[16] That is, women had more power in societies where fathers had greater contact and were more affectionate with children. But Popenoe had the causal argument backwards. Women's public participation tends to precede men's involvement in childcare; cooperation in other domains paves the way for task-sharing in families and valuing care work as something both men and women should do. However, as I showed in chapter 5, political promotion of father involvement in the United States has not translated into advocacy for equitable sharing of the more laborious tasks of child-rearing. Nor has it been part of policy efforts to enhance the status of women or caregiving, a missed opportunity if there if ever was one.

Still, there is widespread agreement about and evidence to support the idea that fathers promote children's emotional, social, and economic well-being.[17] Yet why and how they do so is still a matter of debate. Many argue that fathers' gendered parenting style is beneficial for kids.[18] Some claim that different interactions—particularly fathers' tendency to engage in active rough-and-tumble play and mothers' inclination toward more nurturing, expressive activities such as feeding and soothing—provide distinct developmental opportunities for children to learn physical, emotional, and social skills.[19] Others argue that men uniquely promote children's problem-solving abilities, cognitive capacities, self-control, moral sensitivity, and physical development by giving children "an opportunity to explore and interact with the essence of maleness itself and to explore male-female differences."[20]

Other explanations for the value of paternal involvement have little to do with fathers' masculinity or maleness. Fathers can promote secure infant attachment, provide access to beneficial economic connections, and link children to a larger network of extended family.[21] Yet none of these benefits derives specifically from fathers' sex or gender. Some research has found that fathers give children more economic advantages than mothers do.[22] This is because men typically earn more for equal work, face less discrimination in the labor market (especially for being parents), and are less likely to be concentrated in low-paying jobs and perform unpaid care labor. It is not because parenting abilities are dichotomous or exclusive to gender.[23] To the extent that children benefit from fathers beyond what they get from mothers, it is through another kind of patriarchal dividend whereby children capitalize on their fathers' male privileges.

Although women and men exhibit overall differences in parenting behaviors, there is no consensus about why, how flexible these differences are, or the consequences of the distinctions for children.[24] Role modeling is indeed an effective way to convey gender norms to children, but this is a positive outcome only if one assumes that being able to identify, internalize, and enact gender norms is desirable.[25] Parents, some deliberately, others unconsciously, raise children to conform to stereotypes of gendered behavior, often out of fear that children will face social censure if they do not.[26] Fathers overall do tend to be more stimulating and nondirective during play, whereas mothers are inclined to be more responsive and structured.[27] Yet these are general patterns that say nothing of individual differences and the vast diversity of interactions all parents have with children. Time spent with children, rather than gender, seems to explain much of the variation in gender-typed parenting behaviors.[28] Rather than using this information to advocate that children benefit when their caregivers exhibit diverse play and interaction styles, it more often gets translated into the unsubstantiated directive that children should have both a mother and a father.

All told, the "essential father" discourse lacks empirical support. On average, children who live apart from their biological fathers do have lower high school graduation rates and worse childhood emotional and adult mental health.[29] Yet few studies have examined whether the gender of the absent parent in single-parent homes accounts for the different outcomes among single-mother and two-parent heterosexual families. Children in single-mother families are also more likely to grow up in poverty and see their parents break up. Both are associated with children having access to fewer resources that support mental and emotional health and educational success. Number of parents and the quality of parenting, which are also strongly influenced by access to social support and economic resources, seem to matter far more for children's well-being than their parents' marital status or genders. This is likely why there is even

less evidence linking father-child interaction and better childhood outcomes among low-income families.[30] When children miss a father, they
are potentially missing more emotional and financial resources, but this
does not mean they miss an essential part of socialization, love, or care.[31]

Children raised by two parents of the same gender bear this out. Those
from two-mother families and two-parent families that include a resident
mother and father are almost indistinguishable.[32] Alas, the "essential
father" discourse implies that women cannot on their own raise boys into
successful men. It assumes that boys develop their gender identity and a
sense of pro-social masculinity by emulating fathers alone. This is a limited and flawed understanding of how gender identity develops.

Just as research on "othermothering" reveals that many women tend
to share in the work of raising children, otherfathering happens too.[33]
Mothers recruit men—nonresident fathers, intimate partners, members
of extended family and support networks, teachers—as role models for
children.[34] Black single mothers especially rely on older sons as "brother-
mothers" for younger children.[35] Boys specifically look to their mothers
as exemplars of good parenting.[36] These varied models all support men's
efforts to become good parents despite, or in some cases because of,
negative experiences with their own fathers during childhood.[37] Not having a nurturing father can be a primary motivating factor to be a highly
involved parent.[38] Yet the "essential father" discourse denies men's agency
and abilities to become good parents and men after experiences with
paternal absence. It also discredits women's capacities to single-handedly
provide positive parenting role models.

The idea that children need mothers and fathers in the same household
to thrive is taken-for-granted ideology of family and gender, not empirical
fact. Despite this, it is an ideology that powerfully shapes children's and
parents' identities and experiences. Parenting is a highly gendered experience, both structurally and conceptually. Women and men have different
overall social, economic, and political positions that influence their parenting capacities. To the extent that mothering and fathering differ, it is
because there are different behavioral expectations for women and men
in a context where men have more power and resources than women; it
is not because innate or essential differences between females and males
cause them to parent differently.[39]

Adults and children learn to identify, expect, and enact gender differences. That so many believe fathers' masculinity is an important feature of men's parenting reflects how children are taught that "mothering" and "fathering" are distinct rather than substantial differences in how mothers and fathers behave.[40] That is, what it means to be a mother versus a father differs, even when moms and dads do not act differently. Fathers are important *as men* largely because adults and children believe they are.

When Samuel and other staff discussed the importance of fathers, they were often talking about this gendered social essence of parenting more than innate differences. Children look to parents of a certain gender to help them navigate social worlds infused with gender norms and hierarchies. Sociologist Maria Johnson found that Black women's relationships with their fathers influenced how they enacted racialized ideas of femininity within a society still heavily infused with white privilege and male dominance.[41] A fundamental way that fathers tend to differ from mothers is their lived experiences being treated and judged as men with all the attendant privileges and prejudices.

Even if fathers can provide firsthand insight into these experiences, it still begs the question about the developmental value of teaching children to navigate rather than dismantle these inequities. Shifting attention from whether gender differences in parenting exist to why they become salient for children's well-being stands to reveal more about social problems, especially those rooted in the subjugation of women and people of color.

Focusing on the presumed masculine features of fatherhood seems to have more to do with carving out a unique family role for men than any particular gendered benefit of fathering.[42] The tendency to talk about fathers' family contributions as "manly" simply because fathers are male, which not all are, assumes a false equivalency between biological sex and gender identity. It also belies how masculinity is neither monolithic nor unmalleable. Overall gender differences in parenting behaviors between those who identify as mothers and fathers are quite small, and often much smaller than differences across all mothers and all fathers.[43] Any distinctions between two individual mothers or fathers are likely to be greater than overall differences between "mothering" and "fathering." Yet there is a strong tendency to obscure these individual distinctions and magnify group differences when talking about the gendered features of parenting. The preponderance of evidence does indeed suggest that fathers make important contributions to children. But it does not support the fundamental premises of the "essential father" discourse that their contributions are unique or distinct from mothers'.

Why, then, was the "essential father" discourse so compelling for staff like Samuel and men in DADS? Psychologist Joseph Pleck argued that fathers find it inspirational, while fatherhood practitioners see it as a rationale for their work, especially in a cultural context where fathers are devalued as parents compared to mothers: "For many fathers this belief may be the only one available with which to construct a narrative justifying or explaining why they should be involved."[44]

I argue that the salience of this narrative, for DADS specifically and responsible fatherhood policy generally, cannot be understood merely as a gendered rationale justifying men's involvement. It also has profound racial and economic implications. Fatherhood programs work against a deeply engrained set of stereotypes about what marginalized fathers can contribute to their children. As I will show, the idea that they can be positive role models, not due to their earning potential but via their manhood, is more than motivating to men who are made to feel expendable. It provides a compelling explanation for their difficult life paths and promises what fathers wanted most: upward mobility for their children. Alas, in doing so, it faults marginalized men for the very inequalities that compromise their families' life chances.

ROLE-MODELING RESPONSIBILITY

Speaking to five fathers, Manesh began a 24/7 Dad class by explaining that the purpose of DADS was to become "better fathers than we had." One of fathers' primary responsibilities, he continued, was to be "fair, firm, and consistent" in disciplining children and to model positive behaviors by being dads who "walk the talk." For two hours, the group shared memories of their dads, the values they imparted, what they did when they got angry, and how much they told their sons they loved them. Once men opened up, Manesh asked directly: "What did you learn from your fathers and father figures about being good parents? What did they teach you, by word or by action, about being good men?"

Two said that their fathers were "not around" when they were kids. They learned that men leave or get taken away. One of these had no knowledge of who his father was, while the other shared that his father was falsely incarcerated for a robbery he did not commit. The consequences were the same. Both grew up without knowing their fathers and were raised by strong single mothers who did the best they could as solo parents. The other three men simply shared that their fathers "were there." One was a great financial provider, but gave his son little in the way of emotional support. Another was a single father who "did everything." The third could get "mean with a belt or a switch." Altogether, five grown sons with five different experiences gathered on that fall Friday afternoon to talk about fathering. Yet only once in those two hours spent discussing role models did Manesh ask fathers to think about and recount what they learned from mothers and women about being good parents and moral people. The unspoken message was that, for better or worse, men alone teach boys how to parent.

Many exercises from the *24/7 Dad Fathering Handbook* similarly taught men that boys develop masculine traits by modeling fathers and that girls learn to recognize healthy masculinity by relating to them. Session Six on "The Father's Role" asked participants to recall one memory of their fathers and to list the duties and traits of an ideal father. Role modeling, it noted, is "One of the most important ways that parents teach morals and values. . . . Dads who say one thing but do another confuse their children because they don't 'walk the talk.'"[45] One exercise asked fathers to "Write up to 7 traits you would like to pass on to your son(s) or to model for your daughter(s)."[46] The lesson on "Getting Involved" noted that: "Research shows that when dads are more involved their children get better grades, have fewer behavior problems in school, and are less likely to drop out."[47] Only once did the curriculum note that benefits of involved dads can come from having more than one parent to care, provide, and teach valuable life lessons. Other messages about the value of two-parent families, such as that taught in the section on "What It Means to Be a Man," focused on how successful parenting depends on complementary gender roles.

The overarching message was that fathers confer specific benefits to children because of men's uniquely masculine parenting style and that missing fathers compromise children's socialization and life chances. As Samuel explained, the purpose of DADS was not just to offer education and job opportunities. It was to provide positive masculine role models of responsible work, relationship, and parenting behaviors, which many fathers were presumably missing. In trying to impart lasting ideas about the importance of fathers, these lessons implied that men raised without them were damaged and lacking.

Other staff echoed these claims about the repercussions of missing fathers. Amber, a program director, explained that many men in DADS lacked confidence in their parenting abilities because their own fathers were either absent or otherwise left most of the parenting to mothers. This, she reasoned, led men to believe that they were irrelevant:

> In our program, we talk a lot about the statistics and how many outcomes fathers influence that mothers don't necessarily, in terms of being involved in their children's lives. Just being there and having that presence, you bring things to the table that are going to help your kids be more successful in life. We always ask, "How many of you had your father in your life?" At least 70 percent will say, "No, my dad was incarcerated," or "My dad wasn't around" or some negative experience. . . . It also has to do with a large amount of our participants come from households dealing with poverty. . . . If this is all you ever know, then you pass it on to your kids. Unless somebody says, "Hey, was your daddy in your life, or what kind of influence did you have?" they may not really see the importance of being there. Because that was their normal, and they think, "Then your mom can take care of you while I do what I need to do. . . . That's why I don't feel confident as a father because I don't know what that looks like. Or maybe I do, and I don't like what I saw. Or my dad was great but I don't know how I can fulfill that role because I haven't gotten a job yet."

According to Amber and other staff, participants raised in poverty normalized low paternal involvement and saw few examples of men as engaged parents. Teaching about the gendered importance of men's presence was a strategic way of convincing fathers of their value to families.

Melanie, the other program director, likewise described how she talked to parents about the specific benefits of men's involvement for children:

I say [to mothers], "I commend you if you are doing this alone, that you are being even more responsible because it's one instead of two. But if you can communicate with this person, there's no abuse, there's nothing going on that would harm you or the child, and you can work it out, please do because this is what the father brings." . . . This is not what the mom brings. She brings her own set of unique values and qualities, but it's so important to have him involved with the child. What stands out to me most is the confidence and the education. Those stick out because I've worked with a low-income population. . . . I share with dads, "Did you know that if the father is involved, the kids are less likely to be obese? They are more confident, more likely not just to attend college but actually complete college. . . . Fathers, you bring stability, the ability to break cycles and change by your presence and being there for your child."

Staff claimed that, due to being raised primarily by single mothers, men in DADS rarely understood how fathering could halt the intergenerational transmission of disadvantage. To quote Amber and Melanie, they needed men as parenting role models to truly understand "the importance of being there" and to "break cycles" of poverty for children.[48]

Recalling the instructor Darren's comments from chapter 5 about the importance of teaching sons that they are worthy of "male love," fathering was also framed as an antidote to outcomes such as incarceration and prostitution. When fathers care for children, Darren and others reasoned, kids are less likely to look for masculine validation through other men who do not have their best interests at heart. The intention behind the focus on modeling was to teach fathers that they profoundly influence their children's self-worth and social and economic success. Darren reiterated, "I always get their minds thinking about their kids. 'How long are you going to be a father?' A long time. 'When the kid is twenty, will you still be their father? When they call you from a bail bondsman, will you be their father? Can you still be a father when you're in jail? Do you want your kid in jail? How do we avoid that? How do we keep that girl or boy from being unhealthy? We love them. As men, we recognize them.'" Staff views echoed those who argued that boys and girls without fathers fail to develop a strong sense of self-worth because they hunger for role models to teach them that they are worthy of men's love. This perspective did not account for the effects of race, class, and gender inequalities, namely how discrimination and blocked opportunity compel men of color into incarceration and women of color into sex work. It instead presumed that these outcomes result from children's misguided efforts to compensate for absent fathers who deprive them of a necessary masculine influence.

On one hand, program messages about fathers' role modeling were not prescriptive of parenting styles deemed masculine. On the other, staff and participants agreed that fathers uniquely support children's success and are necessary to impart knowledge about manhood. Yet all struggled to explain what about fathers, per se, was essential for children's well-being other than noting that they are men. When respondents did articulate specific reasons for why children benefit from having men as parents, they offered one of two explanations: that men parent differently than women, and that fathers have more authority with children. This idea that they are valuable parents because of some essential, and largely ineffable, masculine quality deeply resonated with fathers.

TEACHING WHAT ONLY A MAN CAN

Participants struggled to articulate what about fathers uniquely qualified them to teach boys how to be healthy real men and girls how to recognize them. Still, they agreed that men were essential for these reasons. Jamal, a twenty-four-year-old Black father of one, had never met his biological father. The person he recognized as his dad was an older brother, whom Jamal spoke with on the phone every other day. Jamal believed that only men could offer children insight about how men think and behave:

> A woman can't teach a girl what a man can. What I mean by that, I don't mean, as far as boys, a female can't really teach her daughter, a girl, about boys because she's not a boy to know the things that boys think about. Maybe they can give them ideas, but can't really necessarily break it down like, "OK, this is what men do. This is how boys are. This is what to expect from boys." Just like a man can't teach a woman how to be a woman. I can't explain that part because I'm a man. . . . My dad wasn't there. Even though my brother, he was there, but not to teach me things like, "OK, you're growing up. As a man you're supposed to be working. You're supposed to be in

school, not slacking and chilling." . . . My mom wasn't able to teach me those things. I learned by going through it. She told me, but her telling me wasn't enough. She worked hard, she paid all the bills, and she did everything. But it's different seeing a dad do it.

Although Jamal credited his mother as being a strong, hardworking provider and his brother as a constant source of love and support, he saw neither as a true role model.

Several men shared with me that they no longer cared about school after their fathers left. Facundo, a nineteen-year-old Latino father of one, had little interest in finishing his education because his father's departure disrupted the "balance" that kept him motivated. His mother encouraged him to focus on his classes, but he stopped heeding her advice when his father was no longer there to back her up:

> Once I didn't have a father figure, I wasn't paying attention. I wasn't going to school. I was ditching. I was smoking marijuana. I didn't give a shit because my dad wasn't there. I didn't have that straight parent to be like, "No, you need to get your butt home." I stopped taking my mom seriously at one point. My mom was the loving one, and my dad was the strict one. When they were together, it blended just perfectly. When they were both there, I would be calm and loved by both. But one goes missing, and it all went bad. The balance went off. After that, I didn't care. I was hardly at home. I was out in the streets with my friends, just doing bad stuff, not giving a shit. Then I got a girl pregnant.

In these men's experiences, their mothers had been just as likely as their fathers to encourage finishing school, but they were less likely to respect a woman's parenting directives without a man's reinforcement.

Not taking mothers as seriously was a common explanation for why participants ended up in jail, struggled to remain employed, and unintentionally became young fathers. Rarely did staff or fathers mention how growing up in impoverished and low-income families as men of color made these outcomes significantly more likely, regardless of family form. Instead, they relied on individualistic explanations of paternal absence to explain the challenges that brought men to the program, thus ignoring the structural effects of race, class, and gender on the outcomes they highlighted. They believed that mothers and fathers complement one another to meet children's needs for affection, discipline, and security, and that without both, sons suffer and their future prospects shrink.

Some fathers specifically discussed how men can give children a sense of security that women simply cannot provide. Randall, a twenty-three-year-old Black father of two, described the affection he felt for his stepfather while recalling a scary childhood memory of facing an armed intruder:

> I feel like a dad is a backbone, that he's supposed to be the protector. When we were little, I heard a knock on the window, looked through it, and there was a dude with a ski mask on and a gun. He said, "Open the door!" I closed them curtains, and I ran and told [my sisters.] Honestly, I feel like if my stepdad wasn't there, I don't know what would have happened. My mom, she did have a gun back then to protect our house, and she had her gun license for it, but I felt like I got much love and respect for my stepdad because he was there. My stepdad had a gun, too, and though my mom had her own gun, she was sitting on the bed outside the closet while we were in it. He said, "If I don't come back, you guys should call the police." He left, and I heard some gunshots go off. My stepdad came back and said, "Call the police, he's in the backyard. I shot him in the ass." Yeah, the dad, he's the protector.

Randall was visibly shaken after telling this story of his seven-year-old self fearing for his life and the lives of his parents and sisters. He remembered how brave he thought his stepfather was for confronting the intruder. When I asked how he felt about his mother sitting outside the closet with a loaded gun, he admitted: "She had a backbone, too, a nurturing one. Before I had my job, when I had my first kid, and I didn't have no diapers, she bought the baby some clothes and stuff I needed. I feel like that's a backbone. You call her, you need her, and she's there." Randall concluded that men provide physical security, while women offer "emotional protection."

Like many of the twenty-seven interviewees who did not have close relationships with their dads, Randall described his biological father as a "reverse role model" who taught him the importance of being there through his absence. These men felt compelled to be highly involved fathers because they knew what it was like to grow up without one. As did Jamal and Randall, many eventually became close to stepfathers, older brothers, uncles, and grandfathers who taught them the masculine norms they believed they needed to survive in school, at work, and on the streets. Randall explained:

> My dad taught me how to be a dad by not being a dad. . . . He was never there. I was coming home from school one time, and there were these grown dudes. I don't know what they were doing. Well, back then I didn't know. I didn't know not to walk in the circles. I walked through the circle. They started chasing me, and they told me that if I ever come back this way, I ain't going to make it home. That was the one time my mom called my dad, and when she called him, he didn't come. But my stepdad was already there.

The story of the circle, a gang code of conduct, epitomized Randall's feelings about how paternal absence negatively influenced him. He attributed this case of life-threatening lack of knowledge to not having a father to teach him about such things.

Other men talked of reverse role models who taught them about the kinds of fathers they did not want to become. Jonathan, twenty-three, Latino, and a father of two young sons, shared: "I grew up without a father, so that makes it all the more important for me to be there for them. . . . Maybe if I had a dad, I wouldn't think it's such a big deal." Jonathan's uncle was a strong, positive father figure to him, but he lamented how neither his uncle nor his mother encouraged him to finish school. Although he was not sure if having his father around would have made a difference, he was convinced that his life "could've been better. But I'm here [at DADS] right now. I never went to high school, and I wish mom would've pressured me a little more." Few people in Jonathan's family had finished high school, which may have better explained the lack of "pressure" or ability to support their son's educational attainment. Nevertheless, Jonathan experienced his limited education as an outcome of not having a father around.

Others had more mixed experiences that revealed important differences between positive and negative role models. Daniel, a twenty-six-year-old Black father of five, was in and out of various foster placements during his youth. He lived with some great men whom he looked up to as masculine models of good parenting: "They were the ones that I felt I could trust and open up to. Those were the ones I just felt like I can take on their actions. But the ones that I felt they were just there for the money, they had no good intentions, like the one foster group that put their hands on me and treated me different than the other kids." Daniel's diverse father figures showed him that having a man in the home was not necessarily a positive thing, and that those with "no good intentions" were models of how not to parent.

It is particularly noteworthy that most men talked about the importance of fathers in terms of gendered forms of protection, love, and role modeling, while few noted their specific role as economic providers. They emphasized that a man's parental value derives from his gendered abilities to model responsible masculine behavior, describe the male body and point of view, and offer masculine forms of security and affection. These were all things fathers could "provide" by being present as men, irrespective of their employment status or earning potential. Monty, a thirty-four-year-old Latino father of six, explained: "They taught us in the [DADS] classes that dads are there to do certain things with the kids, and a boy needs his father in his life, just like the girl needs her father in life. Both need two different parts and a manly type of love." Like almost four in five of the fathers I studied, at no point did Monty mention money in describing the essential contributions of fathers.

When explaining key differences between manly and motherly love, fathers emphasized physicality, protection, play, and presence. Curtis, an eighteen-year-old Latino father of one, told me: "I think the dad's more of the loving protector, the physical one. I don't really know how to explain it, except that he's always playing with or loving the baby. He's there, the one that's sitting there watching television with the baby." Gendered love also came up in discussions of what children lacked without involved fathers. Reuben, a nineteen-year-old multiracial expectant father, described how DADS taught him that a father's love "is not the same as from a mother. The baby needs their dad, the man, to be there, to get safety and protection. It makes them a better person to grow up feeling love and affection from both parents. They're not missing something."

Many dads believed that they had needed strong fathers as role models of responsibility to help them survive as men of color. One was Justin, thirty-four, Black, and a father of three, who praised his dad for being an authoritative disciplinarian. Justin spent his first ten years in and out of various foster homes until his father regained full custody as a single parent. He noted that, "As a young Black man, if Dad's not around, we tend to go the wrong way. I know I did." Justin acknowledged that mothers often do an admirable job raising sons on their own, but that men miss out when they lack fathers. "A lot of single mothers do great, but I think it takes a man to raise a man, to teach him the moral values that my father instilled in me, prayer, respect, manners, physical [skills], athleticism, these types of things. Moms are just softer." Race figured in many fathers' explanations for why mothers alone were insufficient to raise sons of color with the values and skills they needed to thrive. Yet they rarely acknowledged how racial inequities affected their families' abilities to stay together, such as the greater likelihood that children of color like young Justin end up in the foster system.

Fathers instead held fast to the idea that a dad's love and guidance could counteract how racial inequalities shape their children's futures. As Justin concluded:

> I'll have to stay on top of my girls because they can be judged. What's the typical stereotype, Black women are loud and ghetto? This is not true, and it won't hold for my daughters. . . . What fathers like myself give is time and so, so, so much love. When girls have this in childhood, they don't look for that in a man. . . . I know several women who weren't raised by their fathers, and now they're prostitutes, searching for that love they missed in childhood. The pimp becomes what they had been looking for, what they had missed in their upbringing, the love they didn't get, or the love their fathers didn't tell them.

According to Justin and others, Black women could avoid "ghetto" behaviors and becoming prostitutes beholden to abusive pimps as long as they received adequate paternal love. This ideology mistakenly reduced complex systemic problems of poverty, sexual exploitation, and sexist and racist stereotypes simply to whether girls had fathers who loved them enough.

The common belief among staff and participants that paternal love inspires children's confidence to prevent such problems presumed essential differences in parenting styles and abilities. Even more so, it signaled their recognition and acceptance of, or at least acquiescence to, men's dominance and authority. Aaron, a twenty-one-year-old multiracial father of three, explained: "The mother shows them love, but I teach them responsibility. Usually the father is the rough one, gives them that confidence they need in order to survive out there, to deal with a problem instead of running away from it. It's something about being a man. It's in our DNA, I guess." Like Aaron, respondents frequently referenced biological or natural attributes to explain why men had unique parenting abilities and advantages.

Although none talked about this as a reflection of gender inequality, many men implied that mothers' parenting capacities were limited by gender stereotypes. Marcus, a twenty-one-year-old Black father of one, told me that fathers are important for "discipline because it's only so far that a mother can do, right? As [my son] gets older, when [his mother] tells him to do something, he might slack a little. When I tell him, he's going to do it right because he knows Dad don't play. I was raised by a woman, and I came out fine, but I think it means more to have a father there, to see him get up every day and be a role model." Marcus looked up to his aunt because she "taught me manners, my work ethic, to never turn down work, but I'll stay in my son's life to be the male role model I still needed."

The emphasis on role modeling especially resonated with participants who could point to their fathers' absence as a compelling reason for their economic challenges and struggles to remain involved in their own children's lives. Despite explaining social problems in terms of individual rather than structural causes, messages about paternal essentialism reduced self-blame, especially men's tendencies to fault themselves for their poverty, minimal job prospects, and unplanned routes to fatherhood. Udell, a twenty-three-year-old Latino father of two, had a close relationship with his stepfather as a teenager, but he never knew his biological father. He shared with me that, "I always wanted to become a better father than my real dad had never been." Udell wanted to model healthy romantic relationships for his three-year-old daughter. However, for his one-year-old son, Mateo, he was more concerned about how growing up outnumbered by girls would prevent him from developing a strong masculine identity:

> I try to treat my daughter right, wake up in the morning and make heart-shaped pancakes. My daughter is going to see that, and she's going to be like, "I want a guy like Dad was." I'm their first love. . . . My boy, too, being a man, he needs a man role model around him. He's just surrounded by girls, and he's soft right now being around girls a lot. He cries over everything. . . . My son, with me being there, will learn how to play sports and things

physical like. He'll man up on things instead of whining and crying and feeling depressed.

Program messages about the importance of men as role models were powerful for Udell, who attributed his mental health and financial struggles to not having a consistent father figure who taught him to "man up" in the same way. Udell believed that staying around for Mateo would prevent his toddler son from developing a "soft" compromised masculinity of the kind that he believed caused his own personal turmoil.

Fathers spoke almost as much about the importance of role modeling for daughters. Nicholas, a nineteen-year-old Latino father of one, told me that a dad is important "especially if the kid's a girl. If she can't look up to me and see how a man is supposed to be, what is she going to look up to later on. Whatever I represent, that's what she's going to think all guys are supposed to be." David, a twenty-two-year-old Black father of a daughter, Aubrey, wanted "to be the man that I would want her to marry. When she sees someone in the future, I want her to think, 'Oh, he reminds me of my dad.' I just want to teach her what a man is supposed to be like so she won't get confused and get someone who's bad." Beyond showing her what a good man is, David wanted to be a cautionary tale for Aubrey about what can happen when you do not finish school: "I want her to do good in school because I did bad. Hopefully she makes the choice to go to college. I just want to let her know what's out there, introduce her to stuff, even if I didn't have it growing up. . . . I grew up with that mindset, like, 'I grew up without a dad, so it doesn't matter if I'm not there for my kid.' But now I don't think that's right. I really didn't have a father to show me." For fathers like David, giving their children a dad to show them things was as much about modeling healthy masculinity and good life choices as it was about providing the opportunities they believed they missed after their fathers left. As DADS taught, David and others believed that they could prevent their children from going down the same impoverished path if only they stuck around.

Seeing and hearing other men talk about staying around for the sake of their children was, according to Aaron, a twenty-one-year-old multiracial father of three, the biggest revelation for many men enrolled in the program: "They've been raised in an environment where they really didn't see any other fathers around their kids, just dads leaving all the time. Here they will get that experience from one of the dads telling them, 'OK, I've been there for my son and daughter.'" Just as the DADS director Samuel had hoped, Aaron and his fellow participants came to see fathering as a masculine activity that uniquely and directly influenced their children's lives and future opportunities.

THE MYTHS OF MISSING MEN

Although fathers eagerly embraced messages about paternal essentialism, their understandings of how their own caregivers shaped their parenting motivations and abilities were often at odds with these ideas. Participants generally agreed that fathers play a unique role in children's lives for whom no one else can fully compensate. Yet most were also quick to defend their non-father caregivers as having provided for all their needs. What fathers learned about role models therefore did not always align with how they understood their gender identities, parenting abilities, and life chances.

Program messages about role modeling implied that, without involved dads to model paternal responsibility, sons would struggle to develop identities and abilities as committed fathers. Yet these fathers acutely understood what they had missed by not having involved dads, and this inspired them to become the fathers they had longed for. Fathers found it difficult to articulate what uniquely enabled a man to model specific qualities for children. Still, many explained in vivid detail how growing up without consistent paternal contact and support motivated them to be in their children's lives and enroll in DADS. Owen, a twenty-year-old multiracial father of three, explained that he signed up for the program because he did not really know his own father:

> My dad went to prison when I was five or six and didn't get out until I was thirteen. I don't want to be what he is. I look up to him as far as learning from his mistakes. I'm not talking about learning from his mistakes in general. He went to jail, and so did I. I'm talking about as far as being a father. Growing up without a father, my mom was always there for me for my sports events. I'd always see other kids have their dad, and he'd be like, "Good job!"

Walking to the park, you see a dad playing catch with their son. I didn't have that. I was playing catch with my little brothers.

Like Owen, who looked to his father as a role model of what not to do, many participants described how paternal absence galvanized their fathering ambitions.

Several fathers talked about this in terms of not wanting their own children to suffer the same paternal longing they did. Darius, a twenty-three-year-old Black father of one, explained why he enrolled: "It was more not having a father and then telling myself I'm going to be the best. I'm not going to let my daughter go through what I did. Without even trying, he is my motivation and my drive because he didn't motivate nor drive me." Peter, a twenty-three-year-old Black father of two, attributed his sustained involvement to his absent father and to the example set by his paternal grandmother who raised him: "My father did absolutely nothing. I can only say that he saved me from going into the system. He never put me in sports. He never talked to me. . . . I thought about leaving the kids once, but I was only gone for a week because I couldn't do what my dad did to me."

Some described how their fathers explicitly taught them to be better parents than they were. Keegan, a twenty-one-year-old Black father of three, shared: "When I was younger, my dad wasn't around. He was in and out of jail. I grew up with my mom and thought, 'No matter what, I'm going to be different from Dad. I'm going to be there every day for my child.' . . . When my dad was out, he would always tell me, 'Be better than me.'" These men developed their parenting goals vis-à-vis their own fathers' absence.

How missing dads motivated commitment to paternal involvement was a primary theme of several of the focus groups. In one, three of five participants did not grow up with involved fathers. Arturo, a twenty-two-year-old Latino father of one, first learned his father's name only because it was on the transcripts the DADS high school needed to enroll him: "I ain't never seen a picture. I think that played a big part because I grew up without a dad. . . . I don't want my daughter to grow up not knowing her dad or not having her father there because I went through it, and it sucked." Jonathan, a twenty-three-year-old Latino father of two, agreed: "Yeah, my dad was never in my life, and that plays a big part of me being a father towards my sons. I'm really dedicated to being there and want to be a father." Joshua, a forty-one-year-old multiracial father of two, eagerly added:

> I grew up without my dad, too, and it was kind of tough to be self-taught, to just watch everybody else's fathers be the way they are with their kids. I tried to teach myself to become a father figure even though I didn't have my dad around when I tried to coach my friends. . . . Most of us here have not had our father in our lives the whole time, maybe some of the time, but not the full 24/7 dad that we are committed to being to change the cycle we went through growing up. I made the effort to step up because how I grew up. I got in trouble and resorted to drugs to cover up my pain for what I went through as a kid. I needed to change this around, make it right. [DADS] has really changed the way I think.

Program messages about cycles of missing fathers struck deep for the poor men of color the program aimed to change. They learned to think of their economic and social challenges as the faults of fathers who deliberately chose to leave. Despite its emotional resonance as an all-encompassing explanation for fathers' struggles, this rationalization was completely divorced from the larger structural issues that shaped men's lives.

Even though over half of the interviewees did not have involved fathers as positive parenting role models, the other twenty-one men did. Messages about the negative effects of missing fathers did not account for the experiences of these dads who had close father-son relationships and yet still encountered the same social and economic setbacks. Despite having positive paternal role models, they too struggled with poverty, not finishing school, unemployment, and incarceration. Monty said: "I steered away from what my dad taught me. He raised me to have manners, to have respect, don't talk back to people, and do good in school. He was all for school, working hard, and having a good life. That's not what I did. I was doing the exact opposite at one point." Michael, a twenty-four-year-old Latino father of two, similarly described his positive relationship with his dad:

> He gave me everything I wanted. He disciplined me when I needed it. If he wasn't hard on me when I was little, then I don't think I would be the good dad I am to my kids. . . . Ever since I grew up, I've always seen my dad work and come home tired and still try to have a good time with his kids. . . . That

really showed me that he was the man of the house, and he has to protect and provide for his family. Everybody looks to him as a role model.

Having highly involved fathers as masculine role models of responsible parenting did not necessarily protect these men from suffering the effects of inequality.

Fathers invoked varied experiences with their dads—ranging from highly engaged single parents to completely unknown "sperm donors"—to explain strikingly similar motivations for their parenting commitments and abilities. Ricardo, a twenty-two-year-old Latino father of two, was among several participants whose mothers were uninvolved. He credited his single father with his devotion to being there for his children: "My dad could have left us for anything, but he chose to stay. My mom chose a guy over us when I was a baby. [Dad] worked, he did everything he could do for us, put clothes on our back, and got our house. We were never homeless. That's why I'm with my kids."

DADS attracted sons like Owen and Peter who wanted to break cycles and heal emotional wounds by becoming better fathers to their children. It also brought in men like Michael and Ricardo who wanted equally as much to emulate their positive childhood experiences with fathers who provided for them in all the ways they were learning about through the program. Experiences of paternal absence or presence can be the impetus from which fathers develop a sense of themselves as good men and parents. Political narratives that attribute personal troubles and social problems to a scourge of "fatherlessness" obscure these complex roots of men's parenting commitments and the structural barriers to fulfilling them.

Messages about essential fathers also downplayed the contributions of parents and caregivers who were not men. Almost all participants believed they were good fathers, an ability many attributed to mothers, grandmothers, aunts, and older sisters who made them feel loved and valued. That is, many of the dads believed they learned to be good men and fathers *from women*. They explained how one can miss a father without missing a stable gender identity or the motivation and aptitude to parent well. These fathers also noted how men without a consistent paternal presence can develop immense respect for women, especially those who taught them how to be good parents and people.

Even men who felt deep hurt because their fathers left rarely described missing out on caregivers who loved them and prioritized their well-being. Arturo explained:

> My grandmother was the one actually holding everything down in the family. She was my best role model because she actually did what she had to do. Whatever we wanted on Christmas, we'd have like twenty to twenty-five presents under the tree, all from her. She spoiled us a little bit, but at the same time, she was like, "OK, you got to work to earn this stuff. What are you going to do around the house? Are you doing good in school?" Once my grandma passed, my school was over with. I'm working in the fields, bouncing around a lot, and ended up going to the streets. Everything got off track because of her passing.

Arturo believed his life would have unfolded differently if either his mother or father had been around. He predicted that he would not have left high school to become a low-wage farmworker to pay rent and bills for his siblings after his grandmother's death. However, he did not blame his situation on not having a strong role model of parenting, for he did in his grandmother. Arturo experienced the pain associated with losing a father, but also that of losing a mother and a grandmother, signifying that grief over parental loss is not necessarily gendered. Although many men felt a sense of "father hunger,"[49] none developed a self-image of masculinity or parenting at odds with love. Men instead demonstrated how longing for fathers and love from non-father caregivers motivated them to become parents deeply devoted to their children.

Harris, an eighteen-year-old Black father of one, looked up to his mother as his primary parenting role model, despite growing up with his father in the same household. His dad helped pay the bills and was there physically, but not emotionally: "He was never there to talk to me, play sports, none of that stuff. . . . My mom taught me everything. For example, be home before the street lights come on, make sure I always be respectful and be a gentleman toward women." Like Harris, who became a father during his freshman year of high school, his dad was a teen parent who "didn't know how to be a father at the time." Their relationship now was much stronger after having a "heart-to-heart talk" about the stressors of young, unexpected fatherhood that gave Harris "chills" because of the parallels between his and his father's early parenting experiences. A self-described "mama's boy," Harris choked backed tears when he started talking about his mother, the person he really strove to emulate as a parent. Just because a father is around, Harris concluded, does not mean he is worth modeling.

Dustin, a twenty-two-year-old Black father of one, also credited his mother as his main parenting role model. Being in DADS tempered Dustin's fear that he would inherit his father's aggression and become violent and abusive toward his child. It also gave him confidence that he could live up to his mother's example:

> My mom did everything for us. . . . I talk to my father now. Before he was always locked up or something. It was always from my mom for fighting. Kids are sponges. We soak things up when we're little. That was one thing I soaked up. I seen him beat my mom, literally beat her. It really hurt me, seriously hurt me. I told him about it. It got to him as the reason why I think he's trying more to be there for us now. I seen myself one time trying to carry over that trait. I had to really stop myself and look at it like, "Hey, that's not you. You can't carry that over. You got to overcome that."

As Harris and Dustin could attest, not all fathers deserve emulation.

Grandmothers were the strongest role models of responsible parenthood for many men. In one focus group, Gary, a thirty-nine-year-old Black father of two, shared: "When you lose your grandmother in a family the whole house is broke. It never can come back because the foundation is gone. When my grandmother passed, I was sixteen, and everything else fell apart." His classmate, Lawrence, twenty-one, Black, and a father of two, suddenly straightened up, struck by how much Gary's experience resembled his own: "Exactly! My grandmother passed when I was twelve, and that was it for our family. That's what led me to the streets, losing my grandmother. Once she passed, I was out here. It's like some of our grandmothers were our dads. Because she looked on us like a dad was supposed to. I grew up in a house with all my siblings, and it was just my mom raising us. Grandma made sure that everything stayed intact because we were like her kids. No, we were her kids." The group exchanged fond memories of authoritative and loving grandmothers who maintained a stable sense of family and in the process taught them how to be strong men.

Gary's voice slowed and softened as he recalled a particularly sad memory of his grandmother: "I used to sit outside all day waiting on my father, and he never came. Out there all night, and my grandma would tell me to 'Go in the house, Baby, he isn't coming.' I'd say, 'Grandma, yes, he is coming.' She'd let me sit out there a few more minutes and then, 'Go in, Baby, he isn't coming today.'" With that, Lawrence choked up: "I know just what that feels like. Sitting on the porch, twelve, thirteen, all ready for him, suitcase and everything." Gary cleared his throat and with a matter-of-fact tone said:

> I look at this as a positive. When I tell my child that I'm coming to get them, I come to get them. My dad showed me how to be a better father by not being there. That might sound strange, but that's exactly it. My grandma was my dad. My grandma was the one who would keep me out of trouble. . . . After she died, everybody was broken, washed away. I can see myself as that little boy saying, "Daddy's coming, my daddy is coming." Then he doesn't show. That pushes you to be better to your kids. My dad and I had a talk today, and he said, "Son, you've turned out to be a better man than me." I said, "You know why you say that? Because you feel that you could have done better, but you didn't push yourself." But I'm gonna push, and I'm always going to pick up my kids.

After a moment of silence, the group agreed that, although they may not be perfect fathers, at least they would never leave their children sitting devastated on the front porch, packed suitcase in hand, waiting for a father who would never show. They wanted to be like the grandmothers who were there calling them back in the house, waiting with open arms to console them.

Fathers explained how, in cases like these, women taught them to be "real" men by playing all the parenting roles. Randall said of his single mother: "My mom raised me good. She taught me all the little stuff that my dad was supposed to teach me, to respect a woman, how to be a real man. . . . They got to do everything on their own, but an extra strong woman can teach a boy to be a man." Men often spoke of how mothers and grandmothers were "both parents" because they provided for their emotional and material needs. Arthur, twenty-two, Latino, and a father of one, noted that his mom deserved more respect for "being both the father and the mother."

Men's language describing mothers and grandmothers as "like fathers" revealed their beliefs that parental responsibilities are gendered and that "fathering" is distinct from "mothering." In spite of that, few of the men with uninvolved fathers went as far to say that their lives would have been fundamentally different had their fathers been around. The primary reason for this was that the parents, grandparents, and other caregivers they did have loved them fiercely and put everything they had into raising them to be good men. Darius poignantly captured this common theme:

> Mom was the one who never gave up on me. She definitely inflicted morals on us. To be able to take care of four boys on a minimum salary, that was big. She's not rich. She didn't have it like that. . . . None of my brothers have been arrested because of how my mom raised us. The odds that four of us, four Black men, have never been arrested, you don't see that, no run-ins with the law, nothing. . . . You definitely feel certain things would have and could have went better if Dad was in the picture. Maybe basketball would have been better, but he wasn't, so I can't really say. He probably could have pushed me more, . . . but I think it doesn't matter, man, woman, mom, dad. Even if he was there, I don't know if anything would have changed. The way my mom did it, she put fear into me. She seemed like she was a dad. I don't know what he could have added to that. We didn't need anything. I still don't. She'd spend her last dime for what I need.

Darius's view that his mother "seemed like a dad" reflected assumptions that parenting styles and behaviors are gendered and that fathers have more authority to "push" children in the right direction. Yet his experiences, like many others', challenged the central ideology of paternal essentialism that fathers are necessary to raise strong, successful, and masculine men who grow up to be devoted, responsible parents themselves.

REVISITING WHY FATHERS REALLY MATTER

Fathers' motivations for participating in DADS only partially aligned with dominant political ideologies and program messages about why and how children benefit from having men as parenting role models. Their experiences simultaneously challenged fundamental assumptions of the "essential father" discourse and underscored why it is such a compelling justification for paternal involvement among marginalized fathers. DADS taught about role modeling as something that fathers do through their innate masculinity, not their economic standing. Embracing the message that dads are uniquely valuable as role models of healthy masculinity was perhaps the most powerful way of challenging financial definitions of responsible fathering.

Teaching fathers that they are important as men ascribes value to any type and level of paternal involvement, regardless of their other social and economic statuses, including those related to race, education, employment, marriage, housing situations, and incarceration histories. It presents responsible fatherhood as dependent on the physical and emotional presence of men who presumably possess essential masculine qualities that render them valuable parents. This strategically challenges classist and racist assumptions that poor men of color are "deadbeat" dads because they cannot offer their children significant financial or material resources. In essence, it convinces marginalized fathers that they matter—because of who they are, not what they can provide.

Yet teaching men that their children's well-being depends on fathers' involvement as a gendered practice sends messages about paternal essentialism that belie the structural inequalities that negatively shape their and their children's lives. This is another limiting view of responsible fatherhood, one that valorizes fathers for their gender instead of their earning potential. It derives much of its ideological power from discriminatory ideas of family, gender, and sexuality that fail to recognize the diversity of parenting styles and how children raised without men are able to thrive. There are often lasting, negative effects when a parent-child relationship is severed, but not necessarily because of the parent's gender. Messages about essential fathers assume that a father—any father—will have a positive impact on children. But what it means to be a mother or a father, and especially the notion that they are distinct roles beyond procreative processes, is a socially constructed reflection of gender inequality.

The "essential father" discourse relies on a fundamental and faulty assumption that a dichotomous understanding of gender difference is a necessary feature of well-developed children, healthy families, and an orderly society. The emphasis on gender role modeling mischaracterizes the mechanisms that link parent-child relationships and children's success. Instead of claiming that children benefit from diverse interactions and resources another parent might provide, the ideology of paternal essentialism assumes that childhoods are lacking when they do not include parents with a particular combination of gendered identities and behaviors. It attributes to fathers a distinctly valuable role. It also deems families without fathers deficient.

The men in DADS readily embraced these ideas. Despite having had loving caregivers who provided for their needs, most who did not have close relationships with their biological fathers believed their childhoods were lacking. Yet they rarely believed that missing fathers deprived them of valuable socioeconomic opportunities. What they consciously missed most was the powerfully symbolic value of having an involved father, specifically an authoritative head of household who would have presumably structured their lives for greater social and economic success. This symbol of the strong paternal role model served two important purposes for DADS participants: It vindicated their challenging life circumstances and promised upward mobility for their own children. Being in the program was about becoming role models of responsibility that brought this hope of breaking family cycles of suffering and deprivation.

This framework for making sense of why some kids get ahead while others fall far behind individualizes the socioeconomic injustices that shaped men's—and by extension their children's—lives. Most fathers in DADS grew up in deep poverty, went to underfunded schools, and had early entanglements with the criminal justice system. It is hard to say just how much having more engaged fathers would have changed any of this. What can be said is that many in DADS did have highly involved, loving fathers and still didn't take radically different life paths. Perhaps it mattered more that men believed having their dads around would have made a difference. It certainly did for getting them to stay in the program and with their kids. As I discuss next in the final chapter, this has important implications for how to craft effective fatherhood policies and programs.

7 Having It Better

I last spoke with Christopher, the father we met in the introduction, just after he learned that the federal funding for DADS had not been renewed. Staff were working hard to secure alternative sources of support, but the program's status was uncertain. I recalled our conversation a year earlier when Christopher shared with me his optimism: "I was hopeless before I joined the program. I was applying for all these jobs, but nobody was calling me. I was out in the streets trying to figure it out. Then I came here, and it gave me the sense of mind that I could bring home whatever my son needs, that he could grow up to be proud of me. I finally knew that my son could grow up having it better, better than me." *Having it better* had a dual meaning for Christopher. He dreamed of giving his son a better life, that Chris Jr. would never know the struggles of extreme poverty or the fear of having failed as a father and man. It also meant giving his son a better dad, one who could provide for all his needs, someone he could look up to as a responsible role model.

When I asked Christopher what the program's end would mean for him and these dreams, he said with a sigh of resignation, "It's just like throwing me back into the streets. Now this is going to be part of us, but I'm afraid for our brothers, our cousins. My cousin would have been here today if it wasn't shutting down. It helped so many dads. Where can we turn to now?" Christopher's classmates shared these concerns. Gary said: "It's like you've set us up for failure right off the bat. . . . You're not giving us a fair chance. In short, you're going to put us young males, teenagers even, back out there doing something negative because you're taking the foundation out from under us to structure ourselves for our families." Xavier, a twenty-one-year-old Black father of a daughter born just six days earlier, reflected on becoming a parent during his brief time in DADS: "Other people just try to criticize. Here they give you the benefit of the doubt. We're all just here because we want better for our children. They got our backs here. Like if we need Pampers or something, we just ask. They'll give it to you. . . . The first day I didn't want to come, but the next day I didn't care because they were talking about what I was going through. They're my family now." Arturo captured the collective distress of the group when he concluded: "I don't think we'll find another program like this that cares. They've changed our lives. There are so many dads out there who want to do good and just need help, help to step up, to be proactive, to continue the knowledge and power it creates."

Men's worries about what the end of the program would mean for their lives and families revealed a lot about why responsible fatherhood policy and programs matter. Fathers were eventually reassigned to work and school programs within the same organization, but funding for the other support services, including staff counseling and parenting classes, ended when the Pathways to Responsible Fatherhood grant expired. Men were not just worried about losing their jobs and chances to finish high school. They feared the loss of community, structure, and sense of empowerment they had found and come to depend on in DADS.

Yet the program was far from a panacea for men's parenting problems. Many fathers admitted that being in DADS did not allow them to provide as much or see their children as often as they wanted. Their $200 to $600 monthly wages—about what they would have earned in part-time minimum-wage work—were insufficient to meet their families' needs. Some devised strategies to compensate, including getting second jobs, living with friends or relatives who could not accommodate children, or foregoing having a car, all of which limited involvement with their children.

Despite these limitations, fathers described the program as a great success and grieved its impending closure. Like many men, Michael expressed gratitude for what DADS offered: "The money is making a difference. Is it enough? No, it's not, but how could you argue with an opportunity that's being given to you? You get help to raise your child. You get a job. You get to finish school. How could I complain? I'm just grateful for what I have." Michael could not bring himself to criticize DADS, because the $580 he earned each month was a lot more than what he had before. It meant providing something for his kids, making good on a promise to their mother, and feeling more confident about his fathering abilities.

Like Michael, most fathers focused much less on the low pay and more on how DADS was better than the alternatives, especially life-threatening and illegal ways of making money. Men described the opportunities DADS provided—low-wage work that might not lead to longer-term jobs, the chance to complete a minimal education credential, and basic acknowledgment as human beings and committed fathers with worth beyond money—as privileges. Men's overwhelmingly positive descriptions of the program point to the most pressing social problems surrounding fatherhood, and they have little to do with "deadbeat" dads. The things DADS offered should not be considered privileges. They should be the starting point for any society that claims to value children and families. That DADS helped men who were desperate for any income and validation reveals the program's successes. It equally shows how our society frequently fails marginalized fathers.

What does this ultimately teach us about the value of fatherhood programs and how policy should target men's parenting? Taking a narrow view, the short answer is that responsible fatherhood programs have some success as defined by federal outcome measures: increases in level of coparenting support, frequency of child support payments, quality and quantity of paternal involvement, and self-reported parenting abilities.[1] Programs like DADS funded through responsible fatherhood grants have small yet significant effects on fathers' levels of interaction with children and positive parenting skills. They tend to have an even greater impact on coparenting, especially fathers' abilities to cooperate with mothers and, if partnered, father-mother relationship quality. This is all good news, and fathers' stories shared throughout this book help us understand why and how similar programs tend to produce these positive results.

The bad news is that programs do not have significant impacts on fathers' abilities to make higher child support payments and pay off arrears (child support debt), nor do they significantly improve fathers' wages, employment status, or number of hours spent in paid work. Fathers' stories about ongoing obstacles help explain these less positive outcomes and how fatherhood programs are not necessarily at fault. They also reveal other impacts not fully captured by government metrics. Most importantly, their stories suggest how marginalized men can have it better as fathers and that policy has a vital role to play.

As shown in chapter 2, that role begins with taking into account what being involved—or, to use their words, "being there"—really means to marginalized fathers themselves. Chapter 3 revealed how fathers struggled to access the resources necessary for "responsible" involvement as both they and policy defined it. In chapter 4, we saw how these struggles to provide money, time, and care complicated the already complex coparenting arrangements of low-income parents, most of whom were not together as couples and had no plans to marry each other. Chapters 5 and 6 pointed out the paradoxes and pitfalls of gender messages in responsible fatherhood programming that, despite highlighting men's abilities to nurture, risk further marginalizing poor fathers of color. How can we use these findings to inform a more productive set of policies that support marginalized fathers' involvement in their children's lives? How can we more broadly promote egalitarian parenting across lines of race, class, and gender in the process?

Answering those questions requires that we first acknowledge problems with the "responsibility" framing of fatherhood policy. Long-standing stereotypes that low-income fathers of color willingly evade their parenting obligations justify a sanction-based system that is simply not working and is at times counterproductive and harmful. Much of what unfolds in responsible fatherhood programs on the ground directly challenges these stereotypes, as staff assume that fathers want to be involved but lack the means to do so and the confidence that their presence matters.

Although programs like DADS tend to avoid assumptions of irresponsibility, their efforts to convince fathers of their worth using messages about men's gendered contributions to children's well-being are just as problematic. The valorizing image of the "essential father" is in many ways better that the controlling image of the "deadbeat dad." Still, both ultimately fault marginalized fathers for the impacts of inequalities on their children's lives. Therefore, the second major step to envisioning a better fatherhood policy paradigm is to dismantle the "essential father" discourse that dominates public discussions—and fathers' views—of the value men bring to children's lives.

These considerations ultimately point to several policy prescriptions that avoid assumptions of both paternal irresponsibility and essentialism. The best way to address the problems fathers described is to valorize all caregiving as a political and economic activity, regardless of the gender of the person performing it. To challenge masculine breadwinner norms that continue to marginalize poor fathers of color, we must center care in family policy rather than politically endorse "manly" parenting.

WHAT'S WRONG WITH "RESPONSIBLE" FATHERHOOD?

Our society maligns marginalized men's parenting intentions. Of course, some men do willingly abandon their parenting responsibilities or pose a risk of harm that warrants denying them contact with their children. The problem is that our policies assume these failings as the default position, and then we legislate paternal obligations based on the idea that dads who do not pay are deadbeats. We do a huge disservice to marginalized men and their families when we assume irresponsibility as the norm. In many ways, this is what fatherhood policy has done for decades. Since the passage of welfare reform in 1996, the focus of "responsible" fatherhood policy discourses and provisions has been on child support enforcement and increasing fathers' economic "self-sufficiency."

Child support policies are especially punitive when fathers cannot pay—and, paradoxically, in ways that make it even harder for them to support their kids financially. Rescinding a father's driver's license, saddling him with debt, or incarcerating him for lack of payment, as has been done in various states, will likely make it more, rather than less, difficult for fathers to meet support orders. Whose interests do these policies serve? Certainly not fathers', and ultimately not mothers', children's, or the public's.

Given the larger historical and policy context, fatherhood programs are quite radical in their potential to challenge long-standing discourses that prioritize fathers' financial contributions and punish them when they fall short. One could argue that men who willingly sign up for and stay in programs like DADS are the outliers, the fathers who most care about their children and want to be more "responsible." However, evidence does not suggest this to be the case, as most marginalized men express similar commitments to "be there" for their children in a variety of ways.[2] But what if men like Christopher and his classmates are the exceptions and not the rule? Are we not still better off designing policies around the idea that most fathers want to do right by their kids and need support, rather than the notion that they will fail to make responsible choices without a sanction-based system?

That fatherhood programs do not necessarily increase marginalized men's economic stability long term should come as little surprise. As the fathers' stories revealed, their money problems were the results of inter-generational cumulative hardships and deeply entrenched racial and economic inequalities that no one short-term program can fully tackle. Fatherhood programs typically target men who are most disadvantaged in the labor market due to low education, criminal records, and spotty work histories in low-skilled jobs. Men come into these programs having experienced deep poverty and material deprivation, often after growing up in marginalized families and resource-poor communities with weak job markets for men like them. Many fathers in DADS had been working on and off for years, thrust at a young age into the family provider role due to parental incarceration or the early death, disability, or ill health of parents and grandparents. Poor immediate job prospects may have compelled them to walk through the program gates, but the longer paths that led them there were paved with curtailed opportunities going back many generations of families of color.

Like a domino effect, these unfair beginnings begot more problems by pushing men into illegal activities that, when combined with the color of their skin, made it very likely that they would spend some time behind bars, further shrinking their job prospects. Babies entered the picture, often by happenstance, and men became responsible for other young lives when they were already struggling to support themselves. Yet that responsibility gave new meaning to their lives, and they hoped that their children might break the cycle and have it better. Policies must help fathers realize this hope rather than punishing them for perceived irresponsibility connected to intergenerational poverty, racism, and economic and emotional trauma.

The most promising aspect of programs like DADS is how they try to change this perception. U.S. social welfare policy has long framed fathers as financial providers without regard for their caregiving capacities. Low-income fathers frequently struggle to attain a strong sense of paternal self-efficacy, but not only for falling short as breadwinners. It is also because policies reduce their value to money with little regard for the social and economic forces that shape their struggles to provide it. Inequality and ideology collide to obscure how "fatherlessness" is often more about how economic deprivation, incarceration, and early death pull fathers away from their kids than it is about men's personal choices to skip out on hard family situations. Pinning the blame on individual fathers via responsibility discourses renders invisible the ways that policies themselves help create "father-absent" families. A weak U.S. social safety net that severely limits the level of support that poor custodial parents, mostly mothers, receive is the structural and political underpinning of the "pay-to-play" system fathers described. Welfare bureaucracies that prioritize and mandate fathers' financial contributions, while guaranteeing that mothers will continue to need it, are largely responsible for men's sense that the "love don't count without the money."

Although children benefit when their custodial parents receive formal child support payments, most of those advantages also accrue to those who get informal support outside the system.[3] As sociologist Kathryn Edin and colleagues argued, to become a truly family-building institution, child support enforcement should focus more on in-kind support that mimics how noncustodial parents provide. This would require fathers to know things about their children, such as their clothing and diaper sizes and which foods they prefer.[4] Recall Alex from chapter 4, who said that he did not buy his son Fernando new shoes because he did not know his size or even when he would see him next. In-kind support, which currently does not count toward fathers' child support obligations, encourages fathers to identify as both providers and nurturers in ways that automatic wage withholding does not. In-kind support is also especially important for fathers who earn very low or no wages and struggle to pay full support order amounts. As a punitive measure that makes fathers feel powerless, the current system does not encourage stronger father-child bonds or better coparenting relationships. Instead, it becomes just another bill that fathers must struggle to pay.[5]

Rather than demoralizing them, DADS and similar programs seem to have the opposite effect on fathers' identities, sense of agency, and connections to children. They provide crucial situated spaces of fathering in which marginalized men feel supported, safe to be vulnerable, and part of a community of accountability that has their backs. Programs also support meaningful conversations about how anger and fear can be responses to marginalization and how inequalities shape fathering.[6] Fathers need and deserve this kind of support that comes without judgment or stigma. That so many fathers talked about having a supportive space for fathering as a primary benefit of DADS shows just how scarce such spaces are. To echo Xavier, it suggests how rarely low-income fathers of color are given the benefit of the doubt about their parenting intentions.

Unfortunately, programs like DADS are uncommon in the United States, where there are more than five million economically vulnerable fathers who could benefit from the services and support they provide.[7] Federal grants fund fewer than a hundred fatherhood programs a year; DADS served around one hundred fathers during the time of my study. Much of what fatherhood programs do—assistance with school completion, reinstating licenses, and modifying support orders that have accumulated during periods of unemployment or reduced income—entails plugging holes in a larger broken system.

For the small fraction of needy dads able to access fatherhood program services, programs are only successful to the extent that they address what paternal responsibility really means within the context of extreme economic vulnerability and social marginalization. Fathers want to be involved and are willing to pay child support in proportion to their resources and abilities, both of which fatherhood programs can enhance. Courts increasingly refer chronically unemployed fathers to places like

DADS to help them modify support orders in line with their economic realities and create reasonable payment plans for arrears based on their current work situations and earnings. But chronically unemployed and low-income fathers face numerous intersecting challenges that even the best programs cannot overcome, and few fatherhood programs provide services to any individual father beyond a year or two.

Marginalized men try to rewrite fatherhood scripts in line with these economic realities. Alas, the breadwinner ideology still infuses the laws and policies that directly shape their fathering abilities. It also shapes the expectations of those who control access to their children, especially mothers, who are often the ones left to figure out how to be both bread-winners and caregivers for custodial children. Fathers in DADS clearly internalized these expectations and felt like failures when they could not provide money. Nevertheless, there was little evidence from the fathers I studied that this caused them to withdraw from their children. Fathers embraced a broader understanding of paternal responsibility that went beyond breadwinning to include being children's caregivers, friends, teachers, disciplinarians, and especially role models.

Economic vulnerability undermines fathers' abilities to be all these things for their kids. Despite how much fathers and fatherhood programs work to redefine fathers' roles, poor parents, regardless of gender, are prac-tically accountable to breadwinner norms in the context of very little pub-lic support to offset the personal costs of raising children. As long as we see paternal "responsibility" as an individual-level issue, we miss a larger opportunity to fix a flawed system. Messages that low education, unem-ployment, meager wages, and incarceration among men of color—all major social problems connected to low paternal involvement—depend on father-ing as a gendered practice is especially misguided and dangerous. We must therefore reconsider gender-essentialist lessons in parenting programs.

DISMANTLING THE "ESSENTIAL FATHER" DISCOURSE

As I found in DADS, strategies for promoting paternal involvement all too easily slip into essentialist claims that fathers are valuable specifi-cally because they are men, masculine, or male. We will never be able to achieve fully equitable parenting until we dispense with the notion of gendered parenting responsibilities, especially the idea that men provide an essential and uniquely valuable form of care that is somehow distinct from mothering. Research simply does not support claims that, due to their gender, fathers make indispensable or unique contributions to child-rearing beyond what mothers provide. Assertions that they do only perpetuate sexist and heteronormative ideologies of families.

Claiming that fathers are important because they are men actually diminishes their full significance as parents. It ascribes value to fathers' presumed ability to model masculinity, albeit a nurturing version, rather than the numerous ways men meet children's economic, emotional, and relational needs in ways that have nothing to do with gender. There is certainly value in children growing up to see adults of all genders be loving caregivers, but emphasizing the unique value of men's nurturance risks devaluing women's care, which is already politically and economically undervalued. Valorizing care by encouraging men to participate, and in a "helping" capacity" at that, reinforces the idea that unpaid care is less valuable because of its association with women and femininity. Childcare is not something men should do until they can "do better" by bringing home a bigger paycheck. Policies must stop codifying breadwinning over nurturing for fathers.

If we are serious about challenging the idea that responsible fathering happens in special moments—as the "Take Time" ads discussed in chapter 5 suggest—we have to be equally committed to challenging the belief that it happens through money. It is a systemic failure that marginalized fathers so often feel that their most valued contribution to children is a check. Fathers believed that mothers took the attitude that "without the money, the love don't count," and the same attitude can be seen in policies that regulate fatherhood. Many family scholars have argued that nurturance and emotional connection should be central to fathering and fatherhood policy.[8] I strongly concur with this recommendation. Making paternal nurturance a political priority will require ridding policies of any vestiges of the idea that men are less capable or accountable as full-time caregivers.

Legal scholar Nancy Dowd advocated for a political redefinition of fatherhood that centers nurturance as the "psychological, physical, intellectual, and spiritual support of children."[9] Unfortunately, men's socialization still encourages them to avoid qualities of care and emotionality central to this idea of good parenting. We cannot promote nurturing fatherhood without rethinking models of masculinity passed on to boys that attach little value to caregiving and demean it as feminine. As I showed in chapters 5 and 6, DADS promoted a "manly" form of care to signal that fathers' nurturance has great value. In doing so, it defined nurturance as having masculine and feminine components and as being essential to good fathering and mothering with distinct gender-specialized capacities.

Making nurturance central to policy will require a much more comprehensive overhaul of U.S. family policy and ideology. We must first dismantle the political and social structures that still prioritize fathers' financial contributions above all the other ways they can and do provide for children. It will also involve reconsidering taken-for-granted ideas about caregiving, especially assumptions about the gendered dynamics of parental involvement that infuse responsible fatherhood policy and programming. Fathering as a caring act is indeed essential, but not as a gendered attribute; rather, it is part of the necessary reproductive labor children and society require. Truly embracing this will require more than a reenvisioning of fatherhood. It demands a fundamental rethinking of the political role and economic worth of care.

As I have shown throughout this book, responsible fatherhood programs represent an important step forward toward that goal. Yet they also reinforce some of the very ideologies that disparage caregiving. Children learn to identify, expect, and react to gender differences among their caregivers, despite how women and men make important and equivalent contributions to child development. Those children grow into adults who take for granted, based on a lifetime of socialization, that fathers' masculinity innately shapes their parenting. Parents' gender becomes salient only because children and adults learn to see fathering as a gendered practice, one distinct from and not interchangeable with mothering.

Not surprisingly, the more we study how fathers contribute to child development—and the positive qualities such as paternal warmth and responsiveness that make that involvement valuable—the more we learn that their contributions are just as important as any other caregiver's.[10] Claiming that fathers are essential has been an effort to bring men in from the gendered margins of parenting. Nonetheless, after much empirical effort to disentangle the independent influences of mothers and fathers and the variables that moderate those effects, the research record is clear: Fathers are not essential. What is most essential for children is having parents and caregivers who love them, care for them, and have the means and support to provide for their practical, emotional, and relational needs. Saying that fathers are not essential does not mean that they are irrelevant. It simply means that good parenting is not gendered.

On the ground, it is easy to muddle this nuanced message about why fathers are important. A key puzzle fatherhood programs must fundamentally tackle is how to support good parenting among our society's most marginalized men. The "essential father" discourse circulated in DADS characterized participants as worthy fathers—and by implication, worthy men—for "being there" and providing responsible role models of masculinity, instead of money, for their children. These messages cast low-income men of color as fundamental, rather than peripheral, to families. "Essential father" messages serve as a powerful framework for marginalized men to make sense of their difficult childhoods and to hold out hope that their actions and choices can drastically improve their children's lives and life chances.

But, ultimately, this discourse is as limiting as ideologies that fathers are important primarily as economic providers. As the history of U.S. fatherhood policy has shown, reducing a parent's value to any one attribute, role, or responsibility risks stigmatizing them and weakening relationships with children. The more we perpetuate the ideology that their masculinity or maleness is what matters, the more we lose sight of what marginalized men have to offer as parents and how programs and policies can meaningfully support them. Directives to "man up" or be "real men" based on particular ideas of good fathering will always set up marginalized men to feel like failures if they do not meet certain metrics of responsibility that inevitably depend on resources they do not have. Fatherhood programs can provide some of these resources, but they must so do without resorting to messages that fathers are valuable parents because they are men.

So how can policies avoid the trap of paternal essentialism? They can take a cue from the men in DADS. Fathers talked about striving to emulate the variety of positive parental role models in their lives, including many women. These stories cast doubt on claims that fathers have a gendered need for men to teach them about masculinity. They also beg several important questions. How much do narratives of fatherlessness that deem sons without involved dads as lacking contribute to the father hunger many men experience? What are the dangers of teaching marginalized men that missing fathers can account for their poverty, incarceration, and struggles to parent their own children? What are the drawbacks of encouraging men to believe that their children can have it better if only they stick around? Do we set them up for a greater sense of failure if they really start to believe that their fathering—if only "responsible" enough—is the golden ticket to upward mobility for their kids? Knowing that fathers are more likely to be and stay involved if they see themselves as competent, worthy, and valuable parents, these are not hypothetical questions.

We all have a responsibility to consider how the "essential father" discourse is in part responsible for creating the problems policies work to prevent. It resonates as a personal and political narrative because it provides a concise and convenient explanation for many of our worst social problems and inequities. Blaming fathers and "father-absent" families lets those with privilege off the hook. In this framework, poverty is not about systemic inequality, the shrinking social safety net, or economic exploitation; it is about missing fathers not performing their breadwinner roles. The filling of jails with poor men of color is not about the racialization of mass incarceration; it is due to single mothers raising boys of color who commit violent acts to prove their masculinity. Family complexity is not about how economic deprivation makes it much harder to be supportive parents and partners, but about how certain people do not have the right family values.

Despite how the "essential father" discourse resonates with poor men of color because it affirms their sense of value as parents and reduces some personal culpability, promoting it as a matter of policy draws attention away from the structural forces that undermine parenting. Racism and economic marginalization deny poor men of color almost every other opportunity to claim a good provider status. The "essential father" discourse may empower marginalized men to identify as worthy parents based on their gender, but it also blames them for the very social and economic injustices that deny them access to a responsible father identity in the first place.

By providing a space to deconstruct ideologies about what makes a responsible parent, programs like DADS could instead help dismantle the "essential father" discourse and firmly center care in family policy. Even if families prioritize men's nurturance, we cannot address many of the issues fathers talked about if we continue to disregard care as a fundamental political practice and economic activity. Making care central to social provision is necessary to empower all parents and caregivers, especially low-income women and women of color whose association with care work and nurturance as "natural" expressions of maternal love has directly contributed to their subjugation. Preventing mothers' oppression relies in large part on bringing the men with whom they share children more fully into family life and labor.

Fathering scholars William Marsiglio and Kevin Roy argued that nurturance is a "social arrangement," one for which the "gendered realities of everyday life and the institutions and ideologies that structure the expectations, rhythms, and resources associated with family life continue to create an uneven parenting landscape that privileges female, motherly nurturance."[11] I argue that nurturance is also a political arrangement, one for which neither women nor men receive much public support. Caregiving and nurturance are political in that they are implicated not only in policies pertaining to fatherhood, but also in the unequal power relationships that structure all of family life. "Female, motherly nurturance" is a paradoxical "privilege" given how gendered ideologies of women as naturally better-equipped caregivers justify their greater responsibility for unpaid care labor.

Policies and programs that recognize the value of men's caregiving—and hold them responsible for it—indicate progress. But they will only be effective if embedded in larger political and economic investments to valorize and remunerate care work. Welfare reform provisions requiring work in exchange for aid and fathering policies emphasizing men's economic self-sufficiency and monetary child support are part of a larger transition to a work-based safety net in recent decades. The biggest challenge for fatherhood policy is one of family policy more generally, which is that care and nurturance are not politically and economically valued as much as paid work. This has long been true for fathers, but is increasingly true for all parents.

Policies regulating fatherhood have historically emphasized men's bonds with children's mothers. Yet, if fathers were seen as primary caretakers, relationships with and responsibilities to their children would not be defined in terms of coupling or marriage. Responsible fatherhood policy is rooted in legitimate concerns for children's well-being, but the strategies used to promote paternal involvement are the culmination of decades of policies promoting self-sufficiency, work, and individual responsibility. Nurturance as a political goal is at odds with legislating strict self-sufficiency and individualism. The former is about recognizing and supporting our emotional and relational needs for one another, whereas the latter denies that connection. The contradiction comes to the fore in policies that task individual parents with providing for all their children's needs almost entirely on their own without a strong social safety net that acknowledges and offsets the high costs of care.

Many problems encountered by the fathers detailed in this book reflected this contradiction and how it played out in poor parents' family relationships. "Gatekeeping" is not just about mothers trying to maintain their parenting turf or fathers trying to get around a "pay-to-play" arrangement. It also signals how U.S. welfare and child support systems stress individual parental responsibility in ways that pit mothers' and fathers' interests against each other. Parents individually experience these tensions from gendered social positions and perspectives, but many coparenting conflicts are born of systems that do little to help either mothers or fathers meet their children's care needs. The real problem goes beyond policies that prioritize men's wage earning over caregiving; it entails how paid work is given primacy over public support for care in almost all family policies. Making nurturance central to a social change agenda for fatherhood is a good start, but it must be part of a more comprehensive political and economic valorization of care work.

A MORE RESPONSIBLE POLITICAL AGENDA FOR FATHERHOOD

Fatherhood programs in the United States are numerous and diverse, and the findings described throughout this book only capture what happened for a certain group of men in one. However, there is much to be learned from fathers' experiences in DADS about the problems and promise of anti-poverty parenting policies more generally.[12] Programs like DADS allow and encourage participants to engage with similarly disadvantaged men who inspire one another to be nurturing fathers and confront shared structural and relational barriers to paternal involvement.

Other ethnographic studies of fatherhood programs found that they can be springboards of social activism, collective healing, and especially a greater sense of personal and paternal agency and status for economically vulnerable fathers.[13] Using support from another state grant, DADS was starting a social activism component when staff received notification that their federal funding was not renewed. Staff were gearing up to include fathers in initiatives focused on improving community-police relations and parks and urban renewal. These efforts to encourage social engagement among fathers reflected the program's larger mission to support marginalized men in many capacities—as parents as well as members of their communities too often seen as threats rather than contributors to society. Numerous fathering programs across the country incorporate low-income fathers of color in similar community development projects.[14]

There is a growing network of fatherhood scholars and policy experts who have advocated for more systemic efforts to engage fathers directly. One of these, Kirk Harris, coleader of the Fathers, Families, and Healthy Communities program in Chicago, argues that marginalized men's voices are too frequently ignored in policy debates that have direct bearing on their families.[15] This book is an effort to rectify that. What do fathers' stories teach us about how to create a more responsible—and responsive—political agenda for fatherhood? They point to four major policy changes.

Support Fathers as Caregivers and Not Just Paid Workers

First, we should rid our policies of the stigmatizing language of "responsibility" and reform the welfare system that assumes fathers are absent and primarily valuable as a source of monetary child support. Recent changes to U.S. need-based aid policies are at odds with these goals, as the social safety net is quickly transforming from one based on need to one based on work.[16] Since the 1990s, policies have expanded services for working poor families, while rescinding support for the nonworking poor, through work requirements for welfare cash aid and increased eligibility for social services specifically for employed adults. Despite the fact that a very small portion of American families adhere to it, the U.S. welfare state is still based on a patriarchal model that envisions the family as comprised of a married husband as the economic head of household and a caregiving wife and children as his financial dependents.[17] Fatherhood policy must grapple with this patriarchal history of U.S. welfare programs.

The increasing tendency to tie social supports to employment means that many of the most effective anti-poverty programs are either unavailable or only minimally accessible to fathers like the men in DADS, who tend to be noncustodial parents and earn little through official work. For example, the Earned Income Tax Credit (EITC), a refundable tax credit for low- and moderate-income working families, allows individuals and couples to increase their annual income by claiming qualifying children on their federal taxes. As more parents time out on cash assistance due to lifetime limits on welfare receipt, the EITC has become an important part of poor families' safety nets.[18] Although many other countries offer similar tax credits in the form of child subsidies available to anyone raising residential children, the EITC is tied directly to legal employment. A noncustodial parent can receive a small credit, but men most likely to be in fatherhood programs—nonresidential fathers who struggle with unemployment, have been recently incarcerated, work in the informal economy or off-the-book jobs, or are undocumented and therefore ineligible—rarely qualify for tax credits.

In U.S. policy, the care of one's own children, an activity disproportionately performed by women but increasingly by men, is not defined as work. This has huge implications for policies focused on promoting more care and relational involvement among fathers, especially those who have the fewest economic resources to support the individual costs of caregiving. Gender inequality and low paternal involvement will persist as long as policies value reproductive labor within the family less than "productive" work outside it. Being there beyond breadwinning is not just about teaching fathers to be more involved in the nurturance of their children. It must be about not letting work, money, and economic self-sufficiency take precedence in political definitions of responsible parenting. To the extent that "parent" is politically recognized at all, it is treated as a temporary barrier to labor market participation.[19] Single parenting especially is construed as a cultural problem and personal market failure that the government should address through family values campaigns and market-based solutions, such as job training or work-based tax credits.

By failing to recognize or remunerate parenting as both a political and economic activity, these limited policy interventions fail to account for how the unpaid work of caregiving is necessary to produce future workers that sustain a vigorous economy. As sociologist Caitlyn Collins showed, of all industrialized countries, the United States has the least generous benefits for parents and the lowest public commitment to caregiving.[20] The United States is one of only two countries worldwide without federally mandated paid parental leave. We have no minimum standard for sick or vacation days, few employers offer childcare, and rarely do even qualifying parents receive enough public subsidies to offset the majority of their childcare costs. More public support for caregiving by those of all genders must be the cornerstone of any responsible parenting policy.

Provide More Comprehensive and Longer-Term Support for Education, Employment, and Fulfilling Child Support Obligations

Given the abysmally small public supports for child-rearing in the United States, the second recommendation for fatherhood policies is to increase access to employment and educational opportunities, especially more direct connections to jobs that can improve fathers' long-term financial prospects and sense of paternal self-efficacy. Fatherhood programs face many constraints based on federal funding guidelines, including time-limited monetary support. Systematic efforts to engage fathers as involved parents will require more resources and longer-term investment than two- or three-year grant periods. It will also require forging connections across distinct public departments and agencies that tend to operate as silos.[21] More services for fathers are being integrated into other federal agencies, but their reach is still quite limited.[22]

Another huge problem, especially for fathers of color, is that when men become entangled in the net of mass incarceration it cuts off contact, not only with children, but also with relatives and friends who can help them find jobs after release.[23] Mass incarceration has created a crisis of fatherhood, one more often experienced by young children of color.[24] The majority of incarcerated men are fathers, and a quarter of their children are four years old and younger. Children most likely to grow up with their fathers behind bars are those who were already living in conditions of economic insecurity before their parents' incarceration.[25] Much like fatherhood programs generally, reentry programs that target formerly incarcerated dads are tasked with helping men overcome the obstacles put in place by a system that tends to sever, rather than strengthen, father-child connections. This is especially important for fathers who accrue significant child support debt during incarceration.

Some states are pursuing more proactive, holistic strategies that explicitly engage fathers and account for these constraints. These strategies include modifying child support orders based on self-support reserves, reducing what men in poverty owe for arrears, allowing fathers to earn credit against debt for consistent work, and matching "pay-it-off" programs that double-count fathers' child support payments.[26] With the goal of meeting fathers where they are at, more child support agencies are connecting fathers to mediation services, revising documents to have less intimidating legal language, and ensuring that family services reflect a broader definition of "family" that includes mothers and fathers, regardless of parents' relationship status. There is growing recognition that child support does not necessarily strengthen fathers' relationships with their children, and that to be a truly family-building institution, services for parents must take a more integrative approach that incorporates economic support.[27]

Unfortunately, targeted fatherhood services are still a specialized issue in the mother-centric child welfare field, and patchwork funding comes from an inconsistent variety of federal, state, and local sources. The good news is that many fatherhood program staff take a strengths-based perspective that avoids stigma and shame and instead starts with the assumption that fathers want to be involved and require support to do so. Growing interagency collaboration means more support for fathering activities through the wide array of programs serving noncustodial parents, formerly incarcerated individuals, and those with child support plans. This seems to be money well spent. Evaluations reveal that, for every dollar invested in fatherhood programs and services, there is a three- to eight-fold return in terms of child support payments, fathers' earnings, tax revenue, and alternatives to incarceration.[28]

Alas, very little public money is spent on programs like DADS that holistically address father engagement beyond job services, and few programs with this approach do so at the state level. One notable exception is the South Carolina Center for Fathers and Families, a statewide program financed directly using welfare funding through Temporary Assistance for Needy Families. It combines employment and parenting services for noncustodial parents who have fallen behind in child support payments. Like DADS, their service model includes one-on-one case management, job assistance, parenting education delivered in a peer-support format, and help with driver's license reinstatement and state-owed arrears. As of 2019, only four states have legislatively authorized fatherhood initiatives that provide these comprehensive services.[29] We should prioritize similar federal and statewide efforts to include fathers across child welfare, education, public health, corrections, and court systems.

We should also consider the drawbacks of using money earmarked for cash support for single mothers on these other services. In a competitive fiscal environment where the government contributes very little to direct cash aid programs as is, even fatherhood programs that have positive results are hard to justify when they operate at the literal expense of funding for aid to custodial parents. Allowing states to use TANF funding for other purposes, even fatherhood programs, will only perpetuate parents' sense that government services for mothers and fathers are a zero-sum game in which support for one comes at the cost of help for the other. Fully funding TANF *and* innovative projects designed to help noncustodial fathers be more involved is feasible with enough political will, and the only way out of this dilemma.

Prioritize Coparenting over Coupling in Family Strengthening Services

To the extent that fathers are engaged with state-funded family services, it is mostly through agencies tasked with collecting monetary support based on biological paternity and assumptions of current or prior participation in heterosexual relationships. When fathers' child support is mediated by the formal enforcement system, it likely means that more informal arrangements with their children's other parents have already broken down. Fathers tend to find local child support agencies intimidating, and fatherhood programs can help them navigate what often feels like an overwhelming and impersonal system.

This is a primary reason responsible fatherhood programs tend to increase the proportion of participants of who pay something on their support orders, even though participation does not tend to increase the amount of support paid. This can present a problem for coparenting. To ensure that fathers' own basic needs are covered, many states take into account a "self-support reserve" based on a minimal standard of living when calculating fathers' payment amounts. This shifts more of the childcare burden onto mothers, who are now less likely to receive cash assistance. Fathers' payments can be as low as $50 a month, an amount still beyond the means of some men, and yet one that offsets little of the costs associated with raising a child.

Gender norms of who should ultimately be responsible for childcare means that mothers are still viewed as the "experts" on parenting while fathers are seen as voluntary, secondary "helpers." Dominant fatherhood norms reflect the package deal nuclear family model, and marginalized fathers struggle relationally and financially with performing the "good provider" role, especially with more than one coparent and household at a time. Fathers' explanations of how DADS helped them navigate coparenting challenges offers crucial insight into how fathering interventions can provide alternative scripts of good parenting for men whose lives do not readily align with package deal expectations.

Dispensing with family strengthening strategies that assume moms and dads are together—and that families have both moms and dads— allows for broader definitions of responsible parenting that resonate more with fathers' lived experiences. It also avoids assumptions that mothers should be mediators of paternal involvement and that marriage is a desirable or feasible goal for most families. DADS enabled fathers to navigate unsteady family terrain shaped by economic vulnerability and family complexity. Men hoped that mothers would see their participation in DADS as evidence of their parenting commitments. Marriage was indeed a goal for some, and DADS offered indirect support in these cases. More importantly, the program gave fathers a chance to sustain or mend the coparenting relationships on which their connections to children depended.

In addition to asking what policy can do to support coparents' romantic relationships for the sake of children, we should carefully consider how focusing on couple relationships might be a distraction or detriment for some families. Fathers want more support with forging stronger father-child relationships, and they are well aware of how their children's other parents are implicated in that. Setting aside the issue of whether marriage promotion is even effective,[30] it reinforces the primacy of the mother-father couple bond over the relationships with children fathers actually prioritize. As they increasingly reject a package deal understanding of family life, fathers need coparenting scripts that do not assume couple relationships, primary financial provision, or a coresidential living situation. They also need and deserve opportunities to prove their parenting outside the institutional structures that once mediated men's parenting, especially marriage.

This must involve more support for fathers' wider family networks and a reconceptualization of coparenting that is inclusive of others—grandparents, aunts, uncles, older siblings, friends, social parents—who provide much of the care children require. U.S. family policies and programs are not only gendered and heteronormative. They are also still very couple-centric and based on the nuclear family model, which simply does not reflect how many families actually work. Fathering as a social system is embedded in much larger networks of interpersonal relationships, community organizations, and social institutions. If they are to be effective, family policies can no longer focus only on a presumed nuclear family core.

Make Care an Essential Part of More Inclusive Parenting Policies and Support Services

Family services are not always inclusive of fathers and men. Family programs use mostly images of women and language implying that parenting is synonymous with mothering. While it is true that most custodial parents in low-income families are mothers, not all are, and many nonresidential fathers seeking help feel marginalized in parenting programs that mostly serve women and children. Many efforts to present men in parenting roles maintain the very gender norms they seek to subvert. The "Take Time to Be a Dad Today" campaign, for example, does not promote more equitable parenting. It minimizes the parenting contributions of men and obscures how women still perform most care labor for children.

We need more holistic approaches to break down the siloes, typical in family support services, whereby programs target one group or aspect of family life, such as fathers or jobs. Given the gendered dynamics of parenting, there is a place for father-focused services, such as support groups that allow dads to engage with similarly situated men around common obstacles to involvement. As fathers revealed to me, connecting over shared experiences of inequality and desires for their children to have it better is potentially more powerful grounds for the development of a strong parenting identity than one rooted in gender.

Political support for care is the most essential component of a broader, more inclusive family policy agenda, especially as an issue of economic fairness, gender equity, and reproductive justice, whereby parents of all genders have access to the resources for "responsibility." Parents, especially those marginalized by race and class, will struggle to provide and care for their children if we continue to assign little economic and political value to nurturance. A stronger cultural narrative that inspires men to care about their kids misses the point. Most fathers are already committed to caring for their children. In the end, the heart of the issue is not one of missing or irresponsible fathers, but missing political, economic, and social support that all parents need to meet their responsibilities.

After more than five years spent serving around one thousand fathers, the DADS program closed for good in 2018. This was especially unfortunate given that programs like DADS are at the forefront of supporting paternal involvement for our society's most marginalized fathers. If Christopher, his classmates, and their children are ever going to have it better, we must make public support for care central to all policy, which means challenging every attempt to further privatize and feminize caregiving. That will entail recognizing that we are all responsible for creating the conditions for more equitable parenting across lines of race, class, and gender. The men who graciously shared their parenting stories and dreams with me—and the over five million dads in the United States like them—are an essential part of that.

Acknowledgments

The stories in this book belong to the sixty-four men who confided to me about their fathering struggles, successes, and aspirations. To these fathers, thank you for trusting me to relay these stories faithfully and to put them in a larger socio-logical context. Thank you for showing what it means to be there for children in the face of overwhelming inequalities and injustices. The parenting advice really helped.

To the staff of "DADS," thank you for talking with me and granting me access to study the program. You saw men first and foremost as responsible parents who wanted to do right by their children. A special note of gratitude goes to those in the book whom I refer to as "Melanie" and "Samuel." You worked hard to keep DADS going despite funding challenges. You also went out of your way to help me understand how it all worked. We need more visionary people like you on the frontlines of family support programs who truly understand what it means to meet struggling parents "where they're at."

To my wide and generous academic community, thank you for your friend-ship, collegiality, and the ongoing conversations that shaped the book's core ideas. To Orit Avishai, I am very glad you convinced me that this project was the next logical step after studying marriage programs. To Sarah Whitley and Amber Crowell, I value the connections forged from all the times I popped across the hall to Social Science 218 to talk about this project and its many phases and turns. The manuscript benefitted immensely from conversations and feedback from the following: Tristan Bridges, Megan Carroll, Philip Cohen, Dawn Dow,

Kathryn Edin, Daniel Friend, Lynne Gerber, Kirk Harris, Melanie Heath, Casey Scheibling, and Scott Stanley.

A special note of appreciation goes to four incredible scholars and qualitative writing group partners who read almost every word of this book: Daisy Rooks, Jennifer Sherman, Jennifer Utrata, and Kerry Woodward. I'm grateful we're still going strong after almost a decade of lifting up one another through writing and reading together.

To Laurel Westbrook, my dear friend and confidante, you perhaps more than anyone saw the inner workings of how this manuscript came together. For the close reading of each chapter, and especially for supporting me through every insecurity and celebrating every success no matter how small, I am truly grateful.

To the editorial team at the University of California Press—Naomi Schneider, Summer Farah, and Benjy Mailings—thank you for recognizing the value of the book and seeing it into print. The watercolor artwork on the cover is but one reflection of the beautifully artistic mind and talent of Kara Anderson Contreras; thank you for taking my vision and turning it into something so beautiful that captures how fathers felt about their children. The research and writing for this book were generously funded by the American Sociological Association Community Action Research Initiative, the Family Process Institute, and the College of Social Sciences of California State University, Fresno.

To my given and chosen family, thank you for the love, support, and constant reminders of why programs like DADS matter. Christine Bailey and Bill Becker, your commitments to social justice inspire me. Thank you for every time you asked about this book—and my well-being as I was writing it. Bridget and Bennie Randles, words cannot capture the gratitude I feel for all the ways you've nurtured me and my sociological imagination. You raised me to know the value of strong parent-child bonds and that love for a child has no gender. To Craig Bailey, you are still awesome; one of the great joys and privileges of my life is having a front-row seat to your relationship with our daughter. It is an honor to share this life and coparent with you. Christine, thank you for raising this man almost entirely on your own to be an egalitarian partner and essential dad.

To Bridget Christine Randles Bailey, in so many ways, you came into being at the same time as this book. I will be forever grateful to know that many of the first voices you ever heard were those of the sixty-four men who graciously shared their fathering stories and dreams of their children's futures with me (us). Thank you for being my most important reminder that all parents and caregivers deserve the same recognition, resources, and support that nurture our relationship.

Portions of this manuscript have been adapted, with permission, from the following previously published works:

Randles, Jennifer. 2018. "'Manning Up' to Be a Good Father: Hybrid Fatherhood, Masculinity, and U.S. Responsible Fatherhood Policy." *Gender & Society* 32(4): 516–539.

Randles, Jennifer. 2019. "Pregnant Embodiment and Field Research." *Oxford Body and Embodiment Handbook*, edited by Natalie Boero and Katherine Mason, New York: Oxford University Press. Available at: https://www.oxfordhandbooks.com/view/10.1093/oxfordhb/9780190842475.001.0001/oxfordhb-9780190842475-e-3.

Randles, Jennifer. 2020. "Role Modeling Responsibility: The Essential Father Discourse in Responsible Fatherhood Programming and Policy." *Social Problems* 67(1): 96–112.

Randles, Jennifer. 2020. "The Means to and Meaning of 'Being There' in Responsible Fatherhood Programming with Low-Income Fathers." *Family Relations* 69(1): 7–20.

Randles, Jennifer. 2020. "'Harder Being without the Baby': Fathers' Coparenting Perspectives in Responsible Fatherhood Programming." *Journal of Marriage and Family* 82(2): 550–565.

Pregnancy and Parenthood
in the Field

I observed only one 24/7 Dad class during this two-year project. Staff were concerned that a woman might inhibit fathers' candor and comfort. I, too, was anxious about being there, a rare place where marginalized men felt supported, encouraged even, to share about their parenting challenges and insecurities. I read the participant's manual cover to cover before the class. With lessons titled "What It Means to Be a Man" and "The Father's Role," it had me worried that, being neither a man nor a parent, I would raise suspicions about my interest in the DADS program. Still, I knew that seeing actual classes was crucial for understanding how fathers talked and interacted in these spaces.

That early fall Friday afternoon class brought together five fathers—two Black, two Latino, and one Native American, all in their late twenties and thirties—in a small meeting room that was part of a housing services agency. As we waited on Manesh, the instructor, to lead us to the class, two dads, Orlando and David, reluctantly made small talk with me. Sitting on narrow benches attached to tables, reminiscent of elementary school lunch rooms, Orlando asked me why I wanted to "hang out with a bunch of down and out dads" on such a nice sunny day. I told him that I was a professor interested in programs for fathers. Orlando nervously mentioned his five kids and showed me their pictures from his wallet. In a search of something to talk about, he asked if I "had any little ones at home" of my own. I did not, at least not yet. What Orlando did not know, or knew but was too polite to mention, was that I was almost five months pregnant. Apparently I was starting to show, because David, pointing to my belly, playfully said, "I think she's got a little something, something going on there though."

Once in the classroom, we all sat at the single rectangular table while waiting for Manesh to get some materials. The fathers chatted, clearly familiar with each another from previous classes. I sat between Caleb and Orlando with Tomas, David, and Hank sitting on the other side facing us. The table bumped up softly against my protruding belly. Although Manesh had sought fathers' consent for me to sit in on the class, Tomas asked if I was a new instructor. I shared that I was a professor studying fatherhood programs and asked everyone again if it was OK if I joined them. They responded with affirmative nods and resumed catching up with one another while saying nothing to me. There was a palpable awkwardness as we anticipated Manesh's return. I feared that the men were anxiously waiting for me, this strange white woman professor, to leave and let them get on with their class.

Manesh began by asking everyone to answer three questions about their children—how many they had, their names, and their favorite things to do. Manesh gestured to Caleb, who was sitting on my right, to begin. Caleb shared that his two older children were grown and out of the house and that he was trying to regain custody of his youngest child. I was next. I assumed Manesh would introduce me as a researcher and move on to Orlando, but he asked me about the three questions. I briefly considered saying that I did not have any children, but recalling David's "little something, something" remark, I responded with a hesitant smile that I was expecting my first the following spring. All five fathers immediately perked up, leaned toward me, and offered a collective enthusiastic "Congratulations!" Hank excitedly exclaimed, "Good for you! It's the best thing you could ever do. To just be starting out on this journey, you're so lucky." Tomas offered a light-hearted, prescient warning: "Get you some sleep now, 'cause you ain't ever sleeping once that baby comes." With that, the men accepted me in the group. All they wanted to talk about was my due date, if I knew the baby's sex, what names I had in mind, and especially how I was feeling about becoming a parent.

Socially and economically, those five fathers and I were about as different as people can be. Other than age—I was thirty-three at the time, around the average for the group—we shared few personal characteristics and life circumstances. They were all men of color; I am a white woman. Few had graduated from high school and lived above the poverty line; I have a PhD and am comfortably middle class. They all shared children with women in conflicted or otherwise complicated coparenting relationships; I was happily married, and neither my husband nor I had children with previous partners. All of the men had grown up in low-income neighborhoods or spent time in prison or jail, experiences from which my class and race privileges protected me.

Before I revealed my pregnancy, fathers astutely sensed that we had few shared experiences to draw upon as a basis for connecting and generating rapport. After, they eagerly accepted me into the group as a fellow, albeit relatively inexperienced, parent in need of advice and support. Not only was this shared parenting status crucial for bridging my outsider position, it provided critical insight into men's experiences in DADS. I quickly learned that how fathers responded to my pregnancy revealed as much about how they saw me as it did about how they viewed themselves, especially as parents.

THE BELLY EFFECT: PREGNANCY
AND EMBODIED REFLEXIVITY

I conducted the first of the fifty individual interviews with fathers when I was four months pregnant, and the last took place ten days before my daughter was born. Given this coincidental convergence of my pregnancy and fieldwork, I feared that being pregnant might undermine my credibility as a researcher. After all, pregnant people still face workplace and other forms of discrimination, and many professional women prefer to remain unmarked by the feminine and motherly status that pregnancy connotes. Few scholars had written previously about doing research while visibly pregnant.[1] One was sociologist Jennifer Reich who studied the U.S. child welfare system and discovered that being publicly pregnant meant having her body become an integral part of the research experience. It gave her unique access to data about the social expectations of parenthood and mothering. But it also meant that her body—and her life—were on display in ways not usually experienced by researchers. She wrote: "While I was in the field to study other people's reproduction and families, my own were equally present and observable. . . . I was particularly aware of how my body invoked awareness of my gender, my sexuality, and my marital status."[2]

Pregnant bodies are subject to a strong public gaze. People often touch, discuss, and offer unsolicited advice about them.[3] This tendency to talk openly about pregnancy can be a rich, if invasive, source of data. Political theorist Iris Marion Young described the pregnant body as "decentered, split, or doubled in several ways" and the pregnant person as "experienc[ing] her body as herself and not herself" through a set of shifting corporeal boundaries.[4] Likewise, the pregnant researcher can experience the self as a set of shifting analytic boundaries—a splitting into both observer and participant—through a body at once doing analysis and a body under investigation revealing meanings central to that analysis.

After Caleb, Orlando, Tomas, David, and Hank reacted to my pregnancy announcement in that class with so much joy and enthusiasm, I decided to be more open about it during interviews. Rather than undermining my credibility as a researcher, as I feared, my pregnancy lent me greater authority and trustworthiness. I soon realized that my pregnant belly was more than just a part of my body during interviews. It was an analytic text onto which fathers projected their own parenting successes, challenges, and aspirations. Throughout the interviews and fieldwork, I took detailed notes about men's commentary on and nonverbal responses to my pregnancy. As I analyzed those notes and reflected on what my body signaled to men in DADS, I strove to be personally reflexive about the consequences of this fortuitous merging of pregnancy and fieldwork. This risked being merely a case of naval gazing, figuratively and literally. I quickly discovered that fathers' tendencies to talk about my pregnancy became one of the most important grounds for connection, empathy, and answering the central research questions about responsible fatherhood policy and programs that inspired this book.

They also presented an opportunity to engage in what psychologist Maree Burns called embodied reflexivity, or understanding "the impact of the body on the knowledge and meanings produced" through research.[5] Connections with respondents depend on how readily the researcher establishes reciprocity and rapport, which in turn depend on the behavioral and relational expectations respondents bring to fieldwork encounters. Researchers are usually attentive to their presentation of self—how they speak, dress, and move—and how their embodied social characteristics, namely gender, race, and age, can facilitate or impede trust and comfort.[6] Otherwise, researchers' bodies are rarely considered analytically noteworthy. Feminist standpoint theorists have long attended to how researchers' social identities shape ethnographic encounters, data, and analysis.[7] Yet reflexivity in qualitative research tends to be limited to researchers taking account of themselves with only limited attention to how those selves are embodied.[8] Bodies and the meanings attached to them materialize through relationships of power. They therefore exist as lenses through which to see and make sense of the power relations researchers want to understand.[9] This is particularly evident with a pregnant body, which, like all bodies, is both a site of lived experience and a surface upon which others impose meanings and expectations.[10]

As sociologist Elana Neiterman argued, just as all people are held accountable to gendered behavioral expectations—what sociologists Candace West and Don Zimmerman called "doing gender"—pregnant people are expected to "'do' pregnancy [by] actively performing socially established practices that signify the status of the body as pregnant."[11] I gained fathers' trust in part by "doing" pregnancy well. As researchers, we expect answers to our questions about the intimate details of respondents' lives. Rarely are we willing to share as much of ourselves in the same interactions. Being pregnant put my personal life on display in ways that reduced this imbalance.

My pregnancy also evoked powerful memories of men's transitions to parenthood and the meanings they attached to parental responsibility. It was an important window into how marginalized fathers thought about their roles and identities as parents. The belly made me seem less intimidating and more familiar and relatable, like a fellow parent who would understand what drove them to DADS. It helped generate a special rapport, allowing me to negotiate a key kind of insider status with otherwise dissimilar individuals. As my belly grew, so too did fathers' interest in my pregnancy and their tendencies to lay bare their vulnerabilities. Perhaps this was a consequence of taking classes that encouraged fathers to show emotions and be open about their parenting insecurities. Though I suspect it was more than this. My pregnancy was an opportunity, one more obvious than most, to relate to respondents as an insider to the world of parenting. Most importantly, I think, it was because this dynamic encouraged me to acknowledge them foremost *as fathers*.

A shared "master status" fundamentally shaped our interactions in these research encounters. A master status is a characteristic that is most influential for someone's identity and behavior and for how others perceive and treat that person.[12] The fathers and I were so unalike according to the demographic characteristics that shape one's life chances and experiences of parenting. Yet we related to each other as parents equally committed to our children's success and happiness. For these men struggling to claim the valued status of a good parent while casting off the stigmatizing labels of ex-convict, dropout, loafer, gang member, and especially deadbeat, the fact that I could look beyond these other externally imposed identities straight to "father" was decisive. As I listened to and observed the men, I came to realize that this was the very reason they were in the program—to see themselves and have others see them essentially as hardworking, responsible dads who defied the deadbeat dad stereotype.

Even before my daughter's birth, I knew that their parenting struggles were far removed from any I would experience. I fretted about which expensive baby lotion would work best for her delicate skin. They worried about how they could afford everything their children needed and what impossible choices they would have to make when they couldn't. I was anxious about how to manage family leave from my stable, well-paying job. They agonized about having any job at all and were grateful for one that would allow them to provide something—anything—for their kids. I stocked my daughter's nursery with diapers in three sizes. Fathers scrounged for change to buy small packs of diapers so as not to show up empty-handed to see their kids. I embodied all the traits stereotypically associated with "good" parenting—femininity, whiteness, affluence—while their bodies bore the gendered, racialized, and classed marks of "absentee" parenthood. In a society that vilifies poor men of color as those most likely to shun their parenting responsibilities, recognizing them as equally capable and committed parents was the vital link in our connection. This recognition also became core to my analysis of the powerful potential of fatherhood policies.

Our shared parent status prompted fathers to offer me advice for how to be a good mother, which was particularly telling about fathers' identities and goals for their time in DADS. I interviewed Marcus, twenty-one, Black, and father to Brayden, when I was five months pregnant. He shared with me:

You've got something in store for you. With the crying, you should nurture and rub the head. I like that part, cuddling my son. But the late nights and mornings trying to figure out what's wrong, and you don't know if he's hungry. That took a lot of learning. After a while, you get to know your child. I could sit there, and when [Brayden] was eight months, I could tell when he was about to wake up. He would wake up, look around, and be looking for me. . . . Noticing all that is about being there because my dad, he wouldn't have noticed stuff like that. You don't unless you're there. I spend a lot of time with my son. It's why I'm here.

Marcus's advice better captured how he thought about "being there" for his son and his relationship with his own father than his responses to my direct questions about these topics. In relating to me as a future parent, Marcus revealed himself as a responsible father. His narrative captured how he was a highly involved dad, so much so that he watched Brayden even while he slept, knew within seconds when he would wake, and got up with him during the late-night hours. After our interview, as we were about to leave the DADS building, Marcus gently gestured to my belly and said: "Remember, both of you need to be parents who know their baby like I know [Brayden]. Know her. Be there when she wakes up. Be the people she looks for."

In this and other ways, my pregnant belly was a welcoming third entity in research encounters, one that allowed me to negotiate the liminal space I occupied between insider and outsider status. Fathers showed me pictures on their cell phones of pregnant girlfriends before their children were born, and we compared the sizes of our bumps around the same point in the pregnancies. The belly also provided much-needed comic relief when interviews veered into hard-to-talk-about topics, such as violence, childhood trauma, and deprivation. I interviewed Elias, a twenty-one-year-old Latino father of one, when I was eight months pregnant. As Elias described his grief over the loss of his father, who died by suicide in the family garage the day before Elias's fourteenth birthday, the baby's hands and feet made noticeable movements under my snug-fitting maternity shirt. Elias was noticeably shaken, both due to reflecting on his father's passing and his concern that something might be wrong with the baby. I assured him everything was fine, that it just tickled a bit, and joked that she liked his voice. Elias grinned, said that made him feel better, and asked that we go to the next question. The visible movements happened again during the next interview with an expectant father who excitedly showed me a video on his phone of how his girlfriend's belly made similar wave-like movements as his baby "danced."

I strategically presented myself as a future parent in these moments of empathy and connection.[13] It brought to mind psychologists Sonya Corbin Dwyer and Jennifer Buckle's discussion of how we are never fully insiders nor outsiders to our respondents' worlds, regardless of how many social characteristics we share.[14] We must therefore approach fieldwork with the recognition of how we are both fundamentally like and unlike those we seek to understand. Through embodied reflexivity, I came to see my pregnancy as a valuable resource that allowed me to bridge that gap.

POSITIONING DADS AS PARENTING EXPERTS

Being pregnant gave me a unique opportunity to establish an empathic connection with fathers. It also meant I had an obligation to relate to them without ignoring how race, class, gender, and other distinctions shaped our parenting experiences. This was especially important for understanding what sociologists Michael Schwalbe and Michelle Wolkomir called "masculinity displays," or how men perform gender by "signify[ing], in culturally prescribed ways, a credible masculine self" during interviews.[15] Interviews are a vulnerable situation and challenge two core ideas of normative masculinity in U.S. culture: being authoritative and in control. This can be worse for low-income men of color who lack other social characteristics associated with dominant ideas of manliness.

To decrease the perceived threat to men's masculinity, Schwalbe and Wolkomir recommended encouraging them to take charge as experts of the research topic and their own experiences. I channeled fathers' desires to talk about my pregnancy in the service of that goal. It was particularly important for fathers in DADS to present themselves as successful providers, broadly defined, who were committed to "being there" for their children as strong parental role models of manhood. Understanding fathers' investments in this particular masculinity display helped me grasp why they enrolled in the program and what they got out of it.

Following Schwalbe and Wolkomir's advice, I asked fathers what recommendations they had for me as someone on the verge of becoming a parent. They eagerly offered guidance about everything from sleep and diapering to coparenting and finances. Rightly so, they came to see me as someone in need of parenting advice they felt qualified to give. That advice reflected what they thought responsible parents feel, think, do, and say. Justin, a thirty-four-year-old Black father of three, told me: "Just be open and teachable. New parents, we think we're ready and we're going to know what to do, but parenting is a learning experience. You learn as you go." In a fitting turn, Harris, an eighteen-year-old Black father of one, recommended DADS to me, noting that, "This is a nice program. They teach you a lot. They taught me a lot, and I'm pretty sure it could teach you a lot, too." Fathers offered nutritional advice, tips for websites and phone applications I could use to track the pregnancy, and endorsements for toys their babies loved. Mostly they assured me that it was stressful for everyone and that I should be confident in my parenting instincts and abilities.

My pregnancy also evoked responses that allowed fathers to position themselves as masculine caregivers. Many asked during interviews how the pregnancy was going, whether I was comfortable or tired, and if I needed a break when I fidgeted. They made sure I had water, ample bathroom breaks, and moments to stretch and adjust my body. These masculinity displays were evident from the first interview when I spoke with Jonathan, a twenty-three-year-old Latino father of two. Jonathan spoke at length about his commitment to being a financial provider and emotional caregiver for his two sons and especially his desire to pass on to them his love for gardening. Sensing that Jonathan was curious about my bump, but reluctant to ask, I inquired if he had any questions for me. "Do you have any kids?" he asked. I shared that I was almost four months pregnant. "Congratulations! Your first? Are you feeling OK? Have you seen a sonogram of the baby yet? As a man, it was kind of weird to see the baby on the screen with all its little fingers and toes." After noting that I had an ultrasound scheduled for the following week, he couldn't help but ask: "Are you ready for your child? Have you finished decorating the nursery? I know how women really get into all that stuff. I let my girlfriend take care of all that." We parted after he proudly shared a final story of making a wooden nameplate with his eldest child for his youngest son's nursery. Woodworking and gardening were two ways he wanted to model being a good man for his sons.

Like Jonathan, men eagerly assumed the roles of more experienced parent, masculine authority, and caring father during interviews. They were especially forthcoming with advice about caring for a newborn, how my life would change after becoming a parent, and what I should do differently depending on whether the baby was a girl or boy. They also challenged what they believed were common misperceptions about having a baby, offered health advice, and shared tips for sleep training and discipline. Many assured me that any anxieties I had about being a parent would fade once I held the baby in my arms. They assuaged my fears about being good enough and promised that everything would be fine once I saw her face. This, I reasoned, must have been what others told them when they were about to become fathers. It was also crucial data. I learned a lot about their parenting experiences by listening to and understanding what they anticipated for mine.

The pregnancy also revealed fathers' beliefs about parenting and gender that might not have come up otherwise. Many inquired about whether I knew the baby's sex, which always prompted fathers to share their beliefs about essential differences between boys and girls and how fathers and mothers must parent differently to account for those distinctions. Fathers often asked about how my husband and I would split parenting responsibilities—who would be the "strict" or "softer" parent, if and when I would go back to work, and who would "really take care of the baby." Fathers' questions about what I planned to name my daughter inspired them to share how they chose their children's names. These conversations were telling about how naming practices signaled questionable paternity, the meanings of "real" fatherhood, and the much greater likelihood for men to be their children's namesakes.[16]

Many fathers were reluctant to compare their parenting experiences with mine because I was a woman. Tanner, a thirty-seven-year-old multiracial father of two, told me to practice patience, wished me luck, and offered to introduce me to his "significant other" so that she could tell me "what it was really like because men only know so much." I sensed that not only was this because she did more of the childcare, but because Tanner believed our gender differences limited how much we could empathize with one another's parenting experiences and expectations.

Fathers' relationship advice to me was also particularly illustrative about their coparenting challenges. Men frequently asked if I was with the baby's father and if we got along. Understandably, given the strained relationships many fathers were in, the most common parenting advice they gave was to do whatever I could, if not to stay together, at least to be peaceful and cooperative in front of the child. Udell, a twenty-three-year-old Latino father of two, told me: "Don't let the other person's problems drag you down. What would you want your kids to see from you? Always give *them* attention, and don't get stressed out or mad. Whatever you do, don't let it out on them. . . . That will damage them. They'll get confused and be like, 'What am I getting in trouble for?'" Udell was speaking both from his own childhood memories of his parents' fighting and the coparenting knowledge he learned from DADS. Cayden, a twenty-four-year-old Black father of two, similarly shared: "Stick through it with your man. There's going to be a lot of ups and downs. . . . You have to be way more family oriented. You've got to change. You've got to leave some friends alone. You've got to cut your time short, and sometimes it's just the scheduling of it all. You know you love each other, but it's the schedule. That's the hardest part. Changing diapers and stuff like that, it's pretty simple." I imagined this was the advice he would have given himself as a younger, less experienced father.

For many of the men, my situation recalled their unstable relationships with their children's other parents during pregnancy and how they wished it had been otherwise. Jamal, a twenty-four-year-old Black father of one, advised me: "Stay loyal and support each other, be a good mother, and make sure you have a good baby's father that loves you for who you are, not because of your job, not because of your income. None of that." These remarks poignantly touched on fathers' common fears that coparents and others valued them only for the money they could provide.

In most cases, my pregnancy was a positive aspect of the interviews. Fathers proudly showed me sonogram pictures on their phones and asked to see mine, recommended baby names, and got genuinely excited each time I startled when the baby kicked or hiccupped. Yet for some, the pregnancy triggered painful memories, regrets, and grief. The most challenging interview I conducted was with Emmett, twenty-four and Black, who described through tears the trauma of losing his only child, Shannon, when she was four weeks old due to Sudden

Infant Death Syndrome. Emmett repeatedly congratulated me on the pregnancy while looking at my large belly, an obvious reminder that his baby was gone. As described in chapter 2, Emmett questioned if he "still counted as a father" and decided to stay in DADS for his future children. Although I asked several times if he wanted to stop the interview, he urged me to continue, noting that he was finding healing in finally opening up about her brief life and tragic death. As the interview ended, he gestured toward my belly and implored me not to forget how precious this baby was and to treasure each day we had together. Never has an interview so emotionally affected me. I went back to my car and wept as my baby kicked and turned, almost as though she knew I needed a reminder in that moment that she was still very much there. I cried harder when I remembered Shannon was not.

Most of all, men offered me kindness and encouragement. Dustin, twenty-two, Black, and a father of one, said to me: "You will have moments of so much joy where it's just a beautiful thing. You got me thinking about when I first looked at [my daughter]. Just be a good mother. I know you are, but continue to push yourself to be the best mother you can be. I know you can do it." I wondered how many people told Dustin the same when his child was born. How much did he still need to hear it? I sensed that reassurance was part of what kept him in the program. I cannot say for sure if my study would have yielded different data had I not been pregnant. What I do know is that it gave me a level of insight and rapport I would not have had otherwise and that connections with these men were gifts that graced me with a much richer and more compassionate transition to parenthood.

PARENTING ACROSS LINES OF RACE, CLASS, AND GENDER

These connections revealed how parenting experiences across lines of race, class, and gender share fundamental attributes, including love for one's children, aspirations for their futures, and the strains of caregiving. They showed just as clearly how those lines demarcate distinct parenting challenges that differ both in kind and degree. Cayden, the father who shared with me that changing diapers was simple, stressed that affording diapers was not. As a man, he felt responsible for getting diapers at any cost, and as a young Black man, he knew that the costs could be quite high if he made any perceived misstep. Now four years into my own parenting journey, I viscerally understand what Cayden meant when he told me that the "scheduling of it all" is one of the hardest parts of being a parent. Still, I will never fully empathize with what he sacrificed and risked to get those diapers before he found DADS.

My pregnancy was an opportunity to relate to fathers as fellow parents equally invested in our children's well-being. It also came with the obligation to recognize how the costs of being good parents were much higher for them. No one questioned my parenting. Few outside DADS gave fathers the benefit of the doubt about theirs. As I have shown throughout, this was why they were in the program, to prove their parenting commitments and give their children more.

Critically reflecting on how fathers responded to my pregnancy during the interviews primed me to think of the similarities and differences in our parenting experiences long after the interviews were complete. My daughter, Bridget, was born a little over a week after I finished the final interview with Alec, a twenty-one-year-old Black father of six-month-old Felicity.[17] Alec and his girlfriend chose a name to represent what they hoped the baby would bring to their lives and experience in hers—peace, calm, and happiness. Alec had been his five younger siblings' primary provider since he was sixteen, a role he was thrust into after his grandmother passed, his father became disabled, and his mother and older brother were incarcerated. A fieldworker with an eleventh-grade education, Alec was trying to "get his life on track" and "do better for [Felicity]."

The day I had Bridget, I remembered Felicity's delighted face from the picture Alec showed me during our interview. As I held my daughter, I wondered how her and Felicity's lives would likely unfold along distinct paths through no fault or responsibility of their own. Most fundamentally, the goal of responsible fatherhood policies and programs is to equalize the life chances of children like Bridget and Felicity, born only a few months and mere miles apart but in drastically different life circumstances that will shape divergent futures.

After Bridget was born, I took a six-month break from the project. My views and experiences of parenting changed radically in that half year. I was no longer the pregnant person who conducted the interviews. I was the deeply contented and stressed parent of an infant; in some ways I empathized more, but in others ways much less, with the fathers who shared their stories with me. I could relate with the identity and relational shifts fathers described as part of their entry to parenthood. As I went back through the interviews in audio recordings and written transcripts a second and third time, my analysis was refracted through this transformation. Their descriptions of the drive to become better fathers had a different resonance, and I felt closer to them as an insider to the world of parenting.

At the same time, I became even more of an outsider to their social worlds as marginalized men struggling to become and have others see them as responsible parents. While changing my daughter, I recalled men's stories of scrounging for diaper money. I thought of Keegan from chapter 2, who spent three months in jail after writing a hot check to buy diapers. While feeding Bridget, I remembered Facundo from chapter 3, who was committed to doing whatever it took to stay in

DADS so he could make sure his son had food. When my husband and I fought, deep in the sleep-deprived abyss of learning to coparent, it evoked memories of Alex from chapter 4, who cried himself to sleep at night over missing his son when the child's mother had to move away. The day Bridget turned a month old, I thought of Emmett from chapter 5 and how he was coping now that Shannon had been gone for over a year. Every day since, I wonder what I am modeling for my daughter, and I think of Darius from chapter 6, who credited his mother, his primary role model of responsibility, with raising four strong Black sons all on her own.

As I write this final section of the book on the eve of my daughter's fourth birthday, I understand more why these fathers were in DADS. I also empathize less with what they went through to prove their parenting. Marginalized fathers need resources and spaces to develop a sense of themselves as responsible parents. Rather than teaching them to be "manly" fathers who take time to be dads, we must address the real and varied obstacles that men confront in breaking out of the breadwinner box and providing the money, time, and care children need. Equalizing opportunities for the likes of Felicity and Bridget depends on it. Policies must reflect that Keegan, Cayden, Facundo, Emmett, Darius, and the millions of fathers like them are essential, not because they are men, but because they are parents whose prospects shape the paths their children's lives will take.

I do not mean to suggest that researchers without children would have struggled to sympathize with these fathers and their experiences. Those unlike me in terms of gender, race, and class would likely embody social statuses that would have allowed them to connect with the men I studied in other fundamental ways. What I am saying is that embodied reflexivity necessitated reflecting on how my pregnancy shaped the data I was able to collect and ultimately how I analyzed it.

Most of all, it demanded deep gratitude to the men who shared their fathering challenges and aspirations with me. They neither knew me nor had any reason to trust that I would tell their stories faithfully. Still, they saw and treated me as a parent and gave me the benefit of any doubts that I wanted to be a responsible one. In the end, the DADS program's greatest success was doing the same for them.

Notes

1. To protect respondent confidentiality, all names, including "DADS," are pseudonyms.

2. Obama White House Archives (2012: 1).

3. Edin and Nelson (2013); Hamer (2001); Mincy, Jethwani, and Klempin (2015); Waller (2002).

4. Office of Family Assistance (2018a).

5. For a notable exception, see Marsiglio and Roy (2012).

6. Men who participated in the Supporting Father Involvement study (Cowan et al. 2009) became more engaged with their children and more satisfied in relationships with their children's mothers. The Parents and Children Together evaluation found that participating in a responsible fatherhood program increased how nurturing fathers believed they were, including how often they encouraged children to discuss feelings and how much they ate or played together (Avellar et al. 2018; Holcomb et al. 2019). However, there was no effect on how much contact fathers had with children or the amount of financial support fathers contributed, and although they were employed for longer, participating fathers did not end up making more money. Earlier studies of the Parents' Fair Share (Miller and Knox 2001) and the Non-Custodial Parent Choices PEER (Schroeder et al. 2011) programs similarly found that participating fathers neither contributed more overall child support nor experienced greater financial stability.

7. Gavanas (2004); Mincy and Pouncy (2002).

8. Cott (2000); Fineman (1995).

9. Mead (1986); Murray (1984).

10. Abramovitz (1996); Roberts (1999).

11. Freud ([1905] 2011).

12. See Griswold (1993) and Pleck (1987) for an overview.

13. Cherlin (2009); Coontz (1997).

14. Moynihan (1965). See Alexander (2010) and Rainwater and Yancy (1967) for analyses of the impact of the Moynihan report.

15. Garfinkel, Meyer, and McLanahan (1998).

16. Collins (2000: 69).

17. Battle (2018); Haney (2018).

18. U.S. Congress, Personal Responsibility and Work Opportunity Reconciliation Act (1996: 6).

19. Soss, Fording, and Schram (2011) described how, along with "welfare queens" and "unwed teens," "deadbeat dad" was one of three major categories of "welfare miscreants" discussed during debates over welfare reform legislation. Senator Byron Dorgan of North Dakota noted: "There is an army of deadbeat dads in America, men who have babies and leave. . . . Guess who pays for that child? The American taxpayer." Former Secretary of Education William Bennett specifically criticized young men who "think it is a show of macho maleness to impregnate five women" they are too poor to support (both quoted in Soss, Fording, and Schram 2011: 181).

20. Connell (2005); Hearn (1998); Messner (2000); Williams (1998).

21. Popenoe (1996: 111).

22. Gavanas (2004).

23. Blankenhorn (1995: 31).

24. Gallagher (1998: 165).

25. In describing other authors' arguments, I use *male* and *man* interchangeably when they do, even though the former typically refers to sex and the latter to gender. I critically analyze this tendency to conflate the concepts of "male," "man," and "masculine" in chapter 6.

26. Parke (2013); Pruett (2000).

27. Coltrane (2001); Heath (2012).

28. Gavanas (2004).

29. Cohen (2018).

30. Office of Planning, Research & Evaluation (n.d.).

31. See Heath (2012) and Randles (2017) for an overview of marriage promotion policy during the George W. Bush administration. Also see Obama (1995), a memoir describing President Barack Obama's relationship with his own father.

32. Obama White House Archives (2012: 1).

33. Amato and Gilbreth (1999); Cabrera, Shannon, and Tamis-LeMonda (2007); Carlson (2006); Choi and Pyun (2014); Coley and Medeiros (2007); King and Sobolewski (2006); McLanahan, Tach, and Schneider (2013); Menning (2006).

34. Townsend (2002).

35. Danziger and Ratner (2010); Sinkewicz and Garfinkel (2009); Smeeding, Garfinkel, and Mincy (2011); Sum et al. (2011).

36. Manning, Stewart, and Smock (2003); Tach and Edin (2011); Tach et al. (2014).

37. Carlson et al. (2011); Cowan et al. (2009); Friend et al. (2016); Gibson-Davis (2008); Holcomb et al. (2015); Ryan, Kalil, and Ziol-Guest (2008).

38. Friend et al. (2016); Martinson and Nightingale (2008).

39. Edin and Kefalas (2005).

40. Carroll (2018).

41. Obama White House Archives (2012).

42. Badgett, Durso, and Schneebaum (2013); Gates (2015).

43. Goldberg, Gartrell, and Gates (2014).

44. Amato (1998); Doherty, Kouneski, and Erickson (1998); Hawkins and Palkovitz (1999); Lamb (2000); Lamb et al. (1985); Levine and Pitt (1995).

45. Gerson (1993); Pleck (1987); Waller (2002).

46. Coley and Chase-Lansdale (1999); King, Harris, and Heard (2004).

47. Allen and Connor (1997); Edin and Nelson (2013); Forste et al. (2009); Hamer (2001); Jarret, Roy, and Burton (2002); Lupton and Barclay (1997); Marsiglio and Roy (2012); Newman (1999); Roy (2004); Summers et al. (2006); Waller (2002).

48. Nelson, Clampet-Lundquist, and Edin (2002); Roy (2004).

49. Orloff and Monson (2002); Smeeding, Garfinkel, and Mincy (2011); Williams (1998).

50. Holcomb et al. (2015); Knox et al. (2011); Martinson et al. (2007); Martinson and Nightingale (2008).

51. Office of Family Assistance (2019).

52. Office of Family Assistance (2018a). See also Knox et al. (2011); Mincy and Pouncy (2004).

53. Anderson et al. (2002); Gerson (1997); Hawkins and Dollahite (1997).

54. Small, Harding, and Lamont (2010).

55. Edin and Nelson (2013); Waller (2002); Young (2004).

56. Lamont (2000).

57. Waller (2010).

58. Collins (2015).

59. Gavanas (2004).

60. Messner (1993). Also see Bridges and Kimmel (2011) for a discussion of how this is a case of "soft essentialism."

61. Gavanas (2004); Gillis (1996); Griswold (1993); LaRossa (1997); Townsend (2002).

62. Kimmel (1994).

63. Hondagneu-Sotelo and Messner (1994).

64. Griswold (1993); LaRossa (1997).

65. Gillis (1996); Griswold (1993); Kimmel (1996); LaRossa (1997).

66. LaRossa (1997); Lazar (2005).

67. Dush, Yavorsky, and Schoppe-Sullivan (2018); Wall and Arnold (2007).

68. Thiede, Kim, and Slack (2017).

69. Biblarz and Stacey (2010).

70. Silverstein and Auerbach (1999).

71. Gavanas (2004).

72. Badgett, Durso, and Schneebaum (2013).

73. Cabrera et al. (2011); Fagan et al. (2014); Pleck (2010).

74. Doucet (2009); Doucet and Lee (2014); Fagan et al. (2014); Palkovitz, Trask, and Adamsons (2014).

75. Carlson and Magnuson (2011).

76. Clarke and Kitzinger (2005); Goldberg and Allen (2007); Roy and Burton (2007).

77. Forste et al. (2009); Masciadrelli, Pleck, and Stueve (2006).

78. Jorja Leap (2015: 70) found that men in a program called Project Fatherhood gained a greater sense of control over their lives by engaging one another in collective healing around experiences of poverty, incarceration, and "father wound"—"a deep and abiding sense of sadness" from not having grown up with fathers. See also Holcomb et al. (2015).

79. Bos et al. (2012).

80. Patterson (2006); Wainright, Russell, and Patterson (2004).

81. Henley and Pasley (2005).

82. Marsiglio and Roy (2012).

83. Five fathers were attending community colleges or training programs outside DADS. The other fifteen men were not enrolled in any formal education at the time of the research.

84. Mincy et al. (2015).

85. Seven staff persons were men, while three, including both program managers, were women. Their ages ranged from twenty-six to eighty-five. Six staff identified as Black or African American, three as white, and one as Asian Indian. All staff were college educated, and two had graduate degrees. Nine staff were married, and nine were parents.

CHAPTER 2. BEING THERE BEYOND BREADWINNING

1. Edin and Nelson (2013); Tach and Edin (2011); Waller (2010).

2. Henley and Pasley (2005); Pasley et al. (2014).

3. Fox and Bruce (2001); Stryker and Serpe (1994).

4. Pleck (1987).

5. Diemer (2002); Fraser (1994); Walby (1991).

6. Myers and Demantas (2016).

7. Schrock and Schwalbe (2009).

8. Edin and Nelson (2013); Jarret, Roy, and Burton (2002); Lane (2011); Myers and Demantas (2016); Sherman (2009).

9. Sociologist Jennifer Sherman (2009) found that some unemployed fathers were "gender-rigid" and did little at home to compensate, while others were "gender-flexible" and redefined childcare as something valuable that men should do. See also Allen and Conner (1997); Edin and Nelson (2013); Forste et al. (2009); Hamer (2001); Jarret, Roy, and Burton (2002); Newman (1999); Roy (2004); Summers et al. (2006); Waller (2002).

10. Edin and Nelson (2013); Jarret, Roy, and Burton (2002); Roy (2004); Summers et al. (2006); Waller (2002; 2010).

11. Waller (2002).

12. Edin and Nelson (2013).

13. Marsiglio and Roy (2012).

14. Carlson, VanOrman, and Turner (2017).

15. Collins (2000).

16. Swidler (1986).

17. Brown (2010: 64).

18. Sociologists Kathryn Edin and Maria Kefalas (2005) found that this was a prominent theme in poor mothers' descriptions of how becoming parents enriched and altered their lives.

19. Edin and Nelson (2013).

20. Curran and Abrams (2000); Roy and Dyson (2010). Fatherhood scholars Kevin Roy and Omari Dyson found that responsible fatherhood programs helped marginalized men construct alternative versions of good fathering and manhood by deemphasizing the provider role and redefining caregiving as the core of a responsible fatherhood identity. Similarly, social welfare scholars Laura Curran and Laura Abrams argue that fatherhood programs construe fathers as both financial providers and caregivers.

21. Anderson and Letiecq (2005).

22. Anderson and Letiecq (2005); Roy and Dyson (2010).

23. Hawkins and Palkovitz (1999).

24. See Waller (2010) for a discussion of the importance of culturally resonant fatherhood policies.

25. Edin and Kefalas (2013); Johnson and Young (2019); Townsend (2002); Waller (2002).

26. Edin and Nelson (2003); Waller (2002); Young (2004).

CHAPTER 3. RESOURCES FOR RESPONSIBILITY

1. Mead (1997).

2. Haney (2018); Orloff and Monson (2002).

3. Blankenhorn (1995); Popenoe (1996).

4. Gerson (1997).

5. Marsiglio, Roy, and Fox (2005).

6. Anderson and Letiecq (2005).

7. Anderson et al. (2002); Anderson and Letiecq (2005); Curran and Abrams (2000); Leap (2015); Roy and Dyson (2010).

8. Curran and Abrams (2000: 670).

9. Curran and Abrams (2000: 671).

10. Roy and Dyson (2010: 153).

11. This reflects what scholars call ecological or family systems theories, which highlight how systemic factors shape men's parenting motivations, identities, and abilities. See Belsky (1984); Bronfenbrenner (1979); Cowan et al. (2009); and Hawkins and Dollahite (1997).

12. The Parents and Children Together study of federally funded responsible fatherhood grantees found that men voluntarily enrolled because they wanted to "be there" for their children and become better fathers who were stably employed (Holcomb et al. 2015). Participants positively appraised the programs because they allowed fathers to develop parenting skills, access resources, and create emotionally supportive social networks (Valdovinos D'Angelo et al. 2016).

13. Knox et al. (2011); Smeeding et al. (2011); Tach and Edin (2011).

14. Holcomb et al. (2015); Martinson et al. (2007).

15. Curran and Abrams (2000); Roy and Dyson (2010). This aligns with research on subsidized employment programs, which have been found to reduce recidivism and receipt of public benefits but rarely lead to long-term unsubsidized employment because they tend to target hard-to-employ populations (Dutta-Gupta et al. 2016).

16. Pasley, Petren, and Fish (2014).

17. Collins (2000).

18. In this context, "cupcaking" meant being flirtatious, engaging in public displays of affection, and spending significant time with a romantic/sexual partner while ignoring other friends and family members.

19. Kane, Nelson, and Edin (2015).

20. Tach, Mincy, and Edin (2010).

21. Kane, Nelson, and Edin (2015) found similar themes among fathers in their research on low-income fathers' in-kind support.

22. See Marsiglio and Roy (2012) for a detailed overview of this perspective.

23. See Waller (2010) for a more extensive discussion of this potential.

24. Halpern-Meekin et al. (2015).

25. For an analysis of the stigma poor mothers have experienced as welfare recipients, see Edin and Lein (1997). See Collins and Mayer (2010) and Morgen, Acker, and Weigt (2010) about the hardships single mothers faced after the implementation of welfare-to-work requirements in 1996.

CHAPTER 4. MAKING A CASE TO MOTHERS

1. Hays (2003); Randles (2017).

2. Office of Family Assistance (2019).

3. Additional Responsible Fatherhood program activities as specified in the Claims Resolution Act of 2010 included: "Disseminating information on the causes of domestic violence and child abuse; Marriage preparation programs and premarital counseling; Skills-based marriage education; Financial planning seminars; [and] Divorce education and reduction programs, including mediation and counseling." See Office of Family Assistance (2019).

4. Carlson et al. (2011); Coates and Phares (2014); Cowan et al. (2009); Gibson-Davis (2008); Ryan, Kalil, and Ziol-Guest (2008); Sobolewski and King (2005).

5. Friend et al. (2016); Mollborn and Jacobs (2015).

6. Doherty, Kouneski, and Erickson (1998).

7. Sinkewicz and Garfinkel (2009); Tach and Edin (2011).

8. Friend et al. (2016); Martinson et al. (2007).

9. Edin and Nelson (2013: 17).

10. Martinson and Nightingale (2008).

11. Townsend (2002); Edin, Nelson, and Reed (2011).

12. Randles (2013).

13. Edin and Nelson (2013).

14. McBride et al. (2005).

15. McLanahan and Beck (2010).

16. Tach and Edin (2011).

17. Edin and Nelson (2013); Goldberg (2015); Turner and Waller (2017); Waller and Emory (2018).

18. Goldberg (2015); Nepomnyaschy (2007).

19. Lin and McLanahan (2007).

20. Fagan and Barnett (2003).

21. Friend et al. (2016); Holcomb et al. (2015); Tach and Edin (2011).

22. Allen and Hawkins (1999: 205). Family scholars Allen and Hawkins found that one-fifth of mothers in dual-earner families were "gate closers" who had high childcare and housework standards, believed that women and men should perform distinct family roles, and felt that childcare was central to their identities as wives and parents.

23. Puhlman and Pasley (2013); Schoppe-Sullivan et al. (2008). These more recent studies addressed how gatekeeping takes less tangible forms. Mothers can keep fathers from seeing and spending time with their children, but they can also restrict how much fathers have a say in decisions about their children and how confident dads feel about their fathering abilities.

24. Trinder (2008).

25. Fagan and Barnett (2003); Schoppe-Sullivan et al. (2015).

26. Fagan and Kaufman (2015).

27. Friend et al. (2016); Holmes et al. (2018).

28. Cannon et al. (2008)

29. Edin and Kefalas (2005).

30. Edin and Nelson (2013: 169).

31. Edin and Nelson (2013).

32. Adamsons (2010).

33. Edin and Nelson (2013: 216).

34. Edin and Nelson (2013).

35. Tach et al. (2014).

36. Edin and Nelson (2013).

37. There is more evidence for how programs help committed couples improve their relationships than there is for how programs help nonresidential fathers become more engaged with children. Couple-focused fathering programs that intervene early when men are still connected to their children and children's mothers, such as the Supporting Father Involvement Project, have proven most effective. See Knox et al. (2011) and Pruett et al. (2017).

38. McHale, Waller, and Pearson (2012).

39. Holcomb et al. (2015).

40. Friend et al. (2016).

41. Given that I was able to collect more detailed data from individual interviewees than focus group participants, I report coparenting statistics on interviewees only throughout this chapter.

42. This was similar to what Friend et al. (2016) found in the Parents and Children Together (PACT) evaluation of fatherhood programs. A third of fathers in PACT had cooperative coparenting relationships; another third described their relationships as conflicted; and the other 40 percent reported disengaged, low-cooperation, low-conflict coparenting.

43. See Edin and Kefalas (2005); Randles (2017); and Smock, Manning, and Porter (2005) for discussions of how low-income parents' economic situations cause them to delay or forgo marriage.

44. Fathers for whom marriage is desired and appropriate would still find support for their longer-term family formation goals, especially given how commitment through cooperative coparenting is associated with couples staying together and greater father involvement (Hohmann-Marriott 2011; McClain 2011).

45. Edin and Kefalas (2005).

46. Schoppe-Sullivan et al. (2008).

CHAPTER 5. NEW FATHERS AND OLD IDEAS

1. Gavanas (2004); Hearn (1998); Williams (1998).

2. Curran and Abrams (2000); Orloff and Monson (2002).

3. Connell (2005); Connell and Messerschmidt (2005); Messerschmidt (2016).

4. Curran and Abrams (2000); Gavanas (2004); Kim and Pyke (2015); Randles (2013).

5. Gramsci (1971).

6. Connell (2005); Demetriou (2001); Messerschmidt (2010); Messner (1993); Pascoe and Bridges (2016).

7. Bridges and Pascoe (2014). Also see Aboim (2010); Connell and Messerschmidt (2005); and Demetriou (2001).

8. Coltrane (2001); Gavanas (2004); Marsiglio and Roy (2012); Randles (2013, 2017).

9. Anderson and Letiecq (2005); Roy and Dyson (2010).

10. In partnership with the Administration for Children and Families, the Office of Family Assistance, and the National Responsible Fatherhood Clearinghouse, the Advertising Council launched this media campaign featuring fathers with their children in 2008. See the National Responsible Fatherhood Clearinghouse, https://www.fatherhood.gov/multimedia.

11. Wall and Arnold (2007). Among highly educated, white, heterosexual dual-earner couples with children, women do significantly more childcare and housework than men (Dush, Yavorsky, and Schoppe-Sullivan 2018), and low-paid women of color do much of the outsourced childcare labor for privileged families (Vogtman 2017).

12. Townsend (2002); Wall and Arnold (2007).

13. Jones and Mosher (2013).

14. Jones and Mosher (2013).

15. LaRossa (1997). See also Messner (1993, 2000) and Lazar (2005).

16. Gavanas (2004); Gillis (1996); Griswold (1993); LaRossa (1997). As one indication that this understanding of fatherhood focused on play and school involvement is quite old, see Griswold (1993: 117): "Evidence from the 1920s and 1930s certainly belies any great male commitment to domestic work. Fathers' involvement with children was not about work but play, hobbies, and excursions, about listening to radio programs, reading child-care articles, and attending PTA meetings and child study groups."

17. LaRossa (1997)

18. Hondagneu-Sotelo and Messner (1994).

19. Gillis (1996); Griswold (1993); LaRossa (1997).

20. Kimmel (1994).

21. Aboim (2010); Doucet (2006).

22. Bridges and Kimmel (2011).

23. Cornell (2000: 184).

24. Brown (2010: 1).

25. Brown (2010: 2).

26. Brown (2010: 2).

27. Brown (2010: 64).

28. Hondagneu-Sotelo and Messner (1994); Roberts (1993).

29. Connell (2005).

30. Brown (2010: 50).

31. Brown (2010: 69).

32. Brown (2010: 2).

33. Brown (2010:11).

34. Griswold (1993); LaRossa (1997).

35. Messner (1993).

36. Whitehead (2002: 154).

37. Roberts (1993).

CHAPTER 6. TEACHING THE ESSENTIAL FATHER

1. Silverstein and Auerbach (1999).

2. Silverstein and Auerbach (1999).

3. Holcomb et al. (2015); Leap (2015).

4. The other two interviewees reported that their fathers died when they were very young, leaving them without any recollection of their father-son relationship.

5. Griswold (1993).

6. Parsons (1954); Parsons and Bales (1953).

7. Bandura and Walters (1963).

8. LaRossa (1997).

9. Connell (1985); Pascoe and Bridges (2016); Stacey and Thorne (1985).

10. Popenoe (1996: 159).

11. Gallagher (1998).

12. Cohen (2018).

13. Popenoe (1996: 143).

14. Popenoe (1996: 163).

15. Sociologist Nancy Chodorow (1978) argued that the tendency for women to perform the bulk of childcare shapes gendered personalities that reproduce inequality and patriarchy.

16. Coltrane (1988).

17. Rohner and Veneziano's (2001) meta-analysis found that "fathers' love" powerfully influences children's social, emotional, and cognitive development. However, most of the research they reviewed was based on middle-class white families.

18. Blankenhorn (1995); Doherty, Kouneski, and Erickson (1998); Parke (1996, 2013); Pruett and Pruett (2009).

19. Parke (2013). Actually, both mothers and fathers engage in rough-and-tumble play; mothers do absolutely more, while fathers do relatively more compared to other styles of play. See Lamb (2013).

20. Pruett (2000: 57). See Bornstein (2013) for an overview of how parents contribute to children's gender development in four ways: socialization (gendered differential treatment of children); modeling (shaping children's impressions of what it means to be a man or a woman); scaffolding (encouraging children to participate in different activities based on gender); and reinforcement (validating children's conformity to gendered behavioral norms).

21. On infant attachment, see Bretherton (1985); on economic connections, see Coleman (1988); on extended family, see Bronfenbrenner (1979).

22. Eggebeen (2013).

23. Biblarz and Stacey (2010).

24. As family scholars Fagan, Day, Lamb, and Cabrera (2014) argue, this is largely a measurement issue. In an effort to identify separate dimensions of fathering and mothering, most studies have not compared the effects of similar parenting behaviors among women and men.

25. Bornstein (2013); Palkovitz (2013).

26. Kane (2012).

27. Palkovitz (2013); Paquette (2004).

28. Fields (1978); Risman (1987). Mothers' parenting behaviors seem to exert a greater influence on children because women spend more time with children than men do. See Raley, Bianchi, and Wang (2012).

29. McLanahan, Tach, and Schneider (2013). There is weaker evidence for the effect of father absence on children's cognitive ability and little consistent evidence of negative effects on adult family structure, income, and college educational attainment.

30. Carlson and Magnuson (2011).

31. Many make similar claims about the importance of having teachers of the same gender for boys' educational success. Although there is some evidence that girls benefit academically from having women teachers (Helbig 2012), research does not support the idea that the "boy crisis" in education is due to the feminization of the teaching profession (Maylor 2009; Neugebauer, Helbig, and Landmann 2010; Oeur 2017).

32. Golombok (2000); Patterson (2006); Wainright, Russell, and Patterson (2004). One way they do differ is that sons raised by gay and lesbian couples and single heterosexual mothers tend to behave in less gender-stereotypical ways and express more gender-flexible attitudes (Drexler and Gross 2005).

33. Collins (2000); Gerstel (2011); Roy (2004); Sarksian and Gerstel (2004); Stack and Burton (1993).

34. Stack and Burton (1993).

35. Elliott, Brenton, and Powell (2018).

36. Forste et al. (2009).

37. Floyd and Morman (2000); Masciadrelli, Pleck, and Stueve (2006).

38. Coles (2002).

39. Doucet and Lee (2014); Fagan, Lamb, and Cabrera (2014); Palkovitz, Trask, and Adamsons (2014); Pleck (2010).

40. Bussey and Bandura (1999).

41. Johnson (2013). Johnson found that daughters with minimally involved fathers still developed a solid sense of self and personal strength.

42. Lamb (2010).

43. Pleck (2010).

44. Pleck (2010: 51).

45. Brown (2010: 33).

46. Brown (2010: 7).

47. Brown (2010: 48).

48. Father involvement is associated with higher academic achievement (Jeynes 2015). However, the effect size of paternal engagement is less than half that of parental engagement generally, suggesting that fathers support children's educational success *as parents* but not as men independently of the contributions that mothers make.

49. Gallagher (1998).

CHAPTER 7. HAVING IT BETTER

1. Holmes et al. (2018).

2. Edin and Nelson (2013).

3. Argys et al. (1998); Nepomnyasky, Magnunson, and Berger (2012).

4. Edin et al. (2019).

5. Edin et al. (2019). Many punitive measures for lack of child support payment—driver's license suspensions, financial penalties such as frozen bank accounts and damaged credit, and jail time—have direct negative impacts on fathers' economic security and job options, further undercutting their ability to pay support.

6. Leap (2015) similarly found that men used a fatherhood program as a forum to discuss their shared challenges and traumatic experiences of poverty, homelessness, violence, and not growing up with their own fathers.

7. Mincy et al. (2015).

8. Dowd (2000); Marsiglio and Roy (2012).

9. Dowd (2000: 157).

10. Prior to the 1970s, most studies did not include variables linking fathers' behaviors to children's developmental trajectories (Cowan and Cowan 2019). Correcting this oversight was a primary goal of much of the early fatherhood involvement research cited as empirical support for claims about fathers' importance.

11. Marsiglio and Roy (2012: 16).

12. Most fatherhood programs address similar themes, although there is likely variation in how and how much they address gender issues. Of the fourteen responsible fatherhood curricula listed by the federal Administration for Children and Families, many cover the same topics as 24/7 Dad, including developing parenting and relationship skills, coparenting, and the importance of identifying as men and fathers (see Administration for Children and Families n.d.). Evaluations of other fatherhood programs using 24/7 Dad have found significant positive impacts, including fathers' self-reported increases in parenting skills and confidence and more father-child interaction and paternal involvement (Lewin-Bizan 2015; Osborne, Michelsen, and Bobbitt 2017).

13. Leap (2015); Roy and Dyson (2010).

14. Harris and Metler (2014).

15. Harris (2018).

16. Tach and Edin (2017).

17. Eichler (1997).

18. Halpern-Meekin et al. (2015).

19. O'Connor, Orloff, and Shaver (1999).

20. Collins (2019).

21. Cowan and Cowan (2019).

22. In 2019, federal initiatives included: "Fatherhood Buzz," a Department of Health and Human Services program that reached dads through barbershops with information about positive paternal involvement; the Reconnecting Homeless Veterans with Their Children Program coordinated through the Department of Veterans Affairs; the Department of Labor's Transitional Jobs for Non-Custodial Parents Program; the Building Assets for Fathers and Families financial education and savings program; and the Fathers Supporting Breastfeeding program offered through the Special Supplemental Nutrition Program for Women, Infants, and Children (National Fatherhood Initiative 2019).

23. Alexander (2010); Western (2018).

24. Glaze and Maruschak (2010).

25. Turney and Schneider (2016).

26. Pearson (2018).

27. Cowan and Cowan (2019).

28. Pearson (2018).

29. Office of Family Assistance (2018b).

30. Randles (2017).

APPENDIX

1. Reich (2003); Salisbury (1994); Schrijvers (1993).

2. Reich (2003: 356, 362).

3. Nash (2012).

4. Young (2014: 46–47).

5. Burns (2003: 1643).

6. Coffey (1999); Schwalbe and Wolkomir (2002); Warren and Karner (2015).

7. Collins (2000); Harding (1991); Smith (1991).

8. Sandelowski (2002).

9. Hartsock (2006).

10. Grosz (1994).

11. West and Zimmerman (1987); Neiterman (2012: 372–373).

12. Hughes (1945).

13. Mazzei and O'Brien (2009) defined "active positioning" as the strategic deployment of shared characteristics in fieldwork.

14. Dwyer and Buckle (2009).

15. Schwalbe and Wolkomir (2002: 203).

16. I used the "Jr." form of fathers' names for children's pseudonyms when relevant.

17. The pseudonym "Felicity" is a synonym for the child's actual name.

References

Aboim, Sofia. 2010. *Plural Masculinities: The Remaking of the Self in Private Life*. Burlington, VT: Ashgate.

Abramovitz, Mimi. 1996. *Regulating the Lives of Women: Social Welfare from Colonial Times to the Present*. Boston, MA: South End Press.

Adamsons, Kari. 2010. "Using Identity Theory to Develop a Midrange Model of Parental Gatekeeping and Parenting Behavior." *Journal of Family Theory & Review* 2(2): 137–148.

Administration for Children and Families. N.d. "Strengthening Families Curriculum Resource Guide." https://hmrfcurriculum.acf.hhs.gov/Curricula.

Alexander, Michelle. 2010. *The New Jim Crow: Mass Incarceration in the Age of Colorblindness*. New York, NY: New Press.

Allen, Sarah M., and Alan J. Hawkins. 1999. "Maternal Gatekeeping: Mothers' Beliefs that Inhibit Greater Father Involvement in Family Work." *Journal of Marriage and Family* 61(1): 199–212.

Allen, William D., and Michael Connor. 1997. "An African American Perspective on Generative Fathering." In *Generative Fathering: Beyond Deficit Perspectives*, edited by Alan J. Hawkins and David C. Dollahite, 52–70. Thousand Oaks, CA: Sage.

Amato, Paul R. 1998. "More Than Money? Men's Contributions to Their Children's Lives." In *Men in Families: When Do They Get Involved?*, edited by Alan Booth and Ann C. Crouter, 241–278. Mahwah, NJ: Erlbaum.

Amato, Paul R., and Joan G. Gilbreth. 1999. "Nonresident Fathers and Children's Well-Being: A Meta-Analysis." *Journal of Marriage and Family* 61(3): 557–573.

Anderson, Elaine A., Julie K. Kohler, and Bethany L. Letiecq. 2002. "Low-Income Fathers and 'Responsible Fatherhood' Programs: A Qualitative Investigation of Participants' Experiences." *Family Relations* 51(2): 148–155.

Anderson, Elaine A., and Bethany L. Letiecq. 2005. "Situating Fatherhood in Responsible Fatherhood Programs: A Place to Explore Father Identity." In *Situated Fathering: A Focus on Physical and Social Spaces*, edited by William Marsiglio, Kevin Roy, and Greer L. Fox, 187–208. Lanham, MD: Rowman & Littlefield.

Argys, Laura M., H. Elizabeth Peters, Jeanne Brooks-Gunn, and Judith R. Smith. 1998. "The Impact of Child Support on Cognitive Outcomes of Young Children." *Demography* 35(2): 159–173.

Avellar, Sarah, Reginald Covington, Quinn Moore, Ankita Patnaik, and April Wu. 2018. *Parents and Children Together: Effects of Four Responsible Fatherhood Programs for Low-Income Fathers*. OPRE Report #2018-50. Washington, DC: Office of Planning, Research and Evaluation, Administration for Children and Families, U.S. Department of Health and Human Services.

Badgett, M. V. Lee, Laura E. Durso, and Alyssa Schneebaum. 2013. *New Patterns of Poverty in the Lesbian, Gay, and Bisexual Community*. Los Angeles, CA: The Williams Institute, UCLA School of Law. Available at: https://williamsinstitute. law.ucla.edu/wp-content/uploads/LGB-Poverty -Update-Jun-2013.pdf.

Bandura, Albert, and Richard H. Walters. 1963. *Social Learning and Personality Development*. New York, NY: Holt, Rinehart & Winston.

Battle, Brittany Pearl. 2018. "Deservingness, Deadbeat Dads, and Responsible Fatherhood: Child Support Policy and Rhetorical Conceptualizations of Poverty, Welfare, and the Family." *Symbolic Interaction* 41(4): 443–464.

Belsky, Jay. 1984. "The Determinants of Parenting: A Process Model." *Child Development* 55: 83–96.

Biblarz, Timothy J., and Judith Stacey. 2010. "How Does the Gender of Parents Matter?" *Journal of Marriage and Family* 72(1): 3–22.

Blankenhorn, David. 1995. *Fatherless America: Confronting Our Most Urgent Social Problem*. New York, NY: Harper Perennial.

Bornstein, Marc H. 2013. "Parenting x Gender x Culture x Time." In *Gender and Parenthood: Biological and Social Scientific Perspectives*, edited by W. Bradford Wilcox and Kathleen Kovner Kline, 91–119. New York, NY: Columbia University Press.

Bos, Henny, Naomi Goldberg, Loes Van Gelderen, and Nanette Gartrell. 2012. "Adolescents of the U.S. National Longitudinal Family Study: Male Role

Models, Gender Role Traits, and Psychological Adjustment." *Gender & Society* 26(4): 603–638.

Bretherton, Inge. 1985. "Attachment Theory: Retrospect and Prospect." In *Growing Points of Attachment Theory and Research*, edited by Inge Bretherton and Everette E. Waters, 3–35. Chicago, IL: University of Chicago Press.

Bridges, Tristan, and Michael Kimmel. 2011. "Engaging Men in the United States: Soft Essentialism and the Obstacles to Coherent Initiatives in Education and Family Policy." In *Men and Masculinities around the World: Transforming Men's Practices*, edited by Elisabetta Ruspini, Jeff Hearn, Bob Pease, and Keith Pringle, 159–173. New York, NY: Palgrave Macmillan.

Bridges, Tristan, and C. J. Pascoe. 2014. "Hybrid Masculinities: New Directions in the Sociology of Men and Masculinities." *Sociology Compass* 8(3): 246–258.

Bronfenbrenner, Urie. 1979. *The Ecology of Human Development: Experiments by Nature and Design.* Cambridge, MA: Harvard University Press.

Brown, Christopher. 2010. *24/7 Dad Fathering Handbook*, 2nd edition. Germantown, MD: National Fatherhood Initiative.

Burns, Maree. 2003. "Interviewing: Embodied Communication." *Feminism & Psychology* 13(2): 229–236.

Bussey, Kay, and Albert Bandura. 1999. "Social Cognitive Theory of Gender Development and Differentiation." *Psychological Review* 106(4): 676–713.

Cabrera, Natasha J., Jay Fagan, Vanessa Wight, and Cornelia Schadler. 2011. "Influence of Mother, Father, and Child Risk on Parenting and Children's Cognitive and Social Behaviors." *Child Development* 82(6): 1985–2005.

Cabrera, Natasha J., Jacqueline D. Shannon, and Catherine Tamis-LeMonda. 2007. "Fathers' Influence on Their Children's Cognitive and Emotional Development: From Toddlers to Pre-K." *Developmental Science* 11(4): 208–213.

Cannon, Elizabeth A., Sarah J. Schoppe-Sullivan, Sarah C. Mangelsdorf, Geoffrey L. Brown, and Margaret Szewczyk Sokolowski. 2008. "Parent Characteristics as Antecedents of Maternal Gatekeeping and Fathering Behavior." *Family Process* 47(4): 501–519.

Carlson, Marcia J. 2006. "Family Structure, Father Involvement, and Adolescent Behavior Outcomes." *Journal of Marriage and Family* 68(1): 137–154.

Carlson, Marcia J., and Katherine A. Magnuson. 2011. "Low-Income Men and Fathers' Influences on Children?" *Annals of the American Academy of Political and Social Science* 635(1): 95–116.

Carlson, Marcia J., Natasha V. Pilkauskas, Sara S. McLanahan, and Jeanne Brooks-Gunn. 2011. "Couples as Partners and Parents over Children's Early Years." *Journal of Marriage and Family* 73(2): 317–334.

Carlson, Marcia J., Alicia G. VanOrman, and Kimberly J. Turner. 2017. "Fathers' Investments of Money and Time across Residential Contexts." *Journal of Marriage and Family* 79(1): 10–23.

Carroll, Megan. 2018. "Gay Fathers on the Margins: Race, Class, Marital Status, and Pathway to Parenthood." *Family Relations* 67(1): 104–117.

Cherlin, Andrew J. 2009. *The Marriage-Go-Round: The State of Marriage and the Family in America Today.* New York, NY: Random House.

Chodorow, Nancy. 1978. *The Reproduction of Mothering: Psychoanalysis and the Sociology of Gender.* Berkeley, CA: University of California Press.

Choi, Jeong-Kyun, and Ho-Soon Pyun. 2014. "Nonresident Fathers' Financial Support, Informal Instrumental Support, Mothers' Parenting, and Child Development in Single-Mother Families with Low Income." *Journal of Family Issues* 35(4): 526–546.

Clarke, Victoria, and Celia Kitzinger. 2005. "'We're Not Living on Planet Lesbian': Constructions of Male Role Models in Debates about Lesbian Families." *Sexualities* 8(2): 137–152.

Coates, Erica E., and Vicky Phares. 2014. "Predictors of Paternal Involvement among Nonresidential, Black Fathers from Low-Income Neighborhoods." *Psychology of Men & Masculinity* 15(2): 138–151.

Coffey, Amanda. 1999. *The Ethnographic Self: Fieldwork and the Representation of Identity.* Thousand Oaks, CA: Sage.

Cohen, Philip N. 2018. *Enduring Bonds: Inequality, Marriage, Parenting, and Everything Else that Makes Families Great and Terrible.* Oakland, CA: University of California Press.

Coleman, James S. 1988. "Social Capital in the Creation of Human Capital." *American Journal of Sociology* 94(Supplement): 95–120.

Coles, Roberta L. 2002. "Black Single Fathers: Choosing to Parent Full-Time." *Journal of Contemporary Ethnography* 31(4): 411–439.

Coley, Rebekah Levine, and Lindsay P. Chase-Lansdale. 1999. "Stability and Change in Paternal Involvement among Urban African American Fathers." *Journal of Family Psychology* 13(3): 416–435.

Coley, Rebekah Levine, and Bethany L. Medeiros. 2007. "Reciprocal Longitudinal Relations between Nonresident Father Involvement and Adolescent Delinquency." *Child Development* 78(1): 132–147.

Collins, Caitlyn. 2019. *Making Motherhood Work: How Women Manage Careers and Caregiving.* Princeton, NJ: Princeton University Press.

Collins, Jane L., and Victoria Mayer. 2010. *Both Hands Tied: Welfare Reform and the Race to the Bottom of the Low-Wage Labor Market.* Chicago, IL: Chicago University Press.

Collins, Patricia Hill. 2000. *Black Feminist Thought: Knowledge, Consciousness, and the Politics of Empowerment,* 2nd edition. New York, NY: Routledge.

——. 2015. "Intersectionality's Definitional Dilemmas." *Annual Review of Sociology* 41: 1–20.

Coltrane, Scott. 1988. "Father-Child Relationships and the Status of Women: A Cross-Cultural Study." *American Journal of Sociology* 93(5): 1060–1095.

———. 2001. "Marketing the Marriage 'Solution': Misplaced Simplicity in the Politics of Fatherhood." *Sociological Perspectives* 44(4): 387–418.

Connell, R. W. 1985. "Theorising Gender." *Sociology* 19(2): 260–272.

———. 2005. *Masculinities*, 2nd edition. Berkeley, CA: University of California Press.

Connell, R. W., and James Messerschmidt. 2005. "Hegemonic Masculinity: Rethinking the Concept." *Gender & Society* 19(6): 829–859.

Coontz, Stephanie. 1997. *The Way We Really Are: Coming to Terms with America's Changing Families*. New York, NY: Basic Books.

Cornell, Drucilla. 1998. "Fatherhood and Its Discontents: Men, Patriarchy and Freedom." In *Lost Fathers: The Politics of Fatherlessness in America*, edited by Cynthia R. Daniels, 183–202. New York, NY: St. Martin's Press.

Cott, Nancy. 2000. *Public Vows: A History of Marriage and the Nation*. Cambridge, MA: Harvard University Press.

Cowan, Carolyn Pape, and Philip A. Cowan. 2019. "Enhancing Parenting Effectiveness: Father's Involvement, Couple Relationship Quality, and Children's Development: Breaking Down Silos in Family Policy Making and Service Delivery." *Journal of Family Theory & Review* 11(2): 92–111.

Cowan, Philip A., Carolyn Pape Cowan, Marsha Kline Pruett, Kyle Pruett, and Jessie J. Wong. 2009. "Promoting Fathers' Engagement with Children: Preventative Interventions for Low-Income Families." *Journal of Marriage and Family* 71(3): 663–679.

Curran, Laura, and Laura S. Abrams. 2000. "Making Men into Dads: Fatherhood, the State, and Welfare Reform." *Gender & Society* 14(5): 662–678.

Danziger, Sheldon, and David Ratner. 2010. "Labor Market Outcomes and the Transition to Adulthood." *Future of Children* 20(1): 133–158.

Demetriou, Demetrakis. 2001. "Connell's Concept of Hegemonic Masculinity: A Critique." *Theory and Society* 30(3): 337–361.

Diemer, Matthew A. 2002. "Constructions of Provider Role Identity among African American Men: An Exploratory Study." *Cultural Diversity & Ethnic Minority Psychology* 8(1): 30–40.

Doherty, William J., Edward F. Kouneski, and Martha F. Erickson. 1998. "Responsible Fathering: An Overview and Conceptual Framework." *Journal of Marriage and Family* 60(2): 277–292.

Doucet, Andrea. 2006. *Do Men Mother?* Toronto, ON: University of Toronto Press.

———. 2009. "Dad and Baby in the First Year: Gendered Responsibilities and Embodiment." *Annals of the American Academy of Political and Social Science* 624(1): 78–98.

Doucet, Andrea, and Robyn Lee. 2014. "Fathering, Feminism(s), Gender, and Sexualities: Connections, Tensions, and New Pathways." *Journal of Family Theory & Review* 6(4): 355–373.

Dowd, Nancy E. 2000. *Redefining Fatherhood*. New York, NY: New York University Press.

Drexler, Peggy, with Linden Gross. 2005. *Raising Boys without Men: How Maverick Moms Are Creating the Next Generation of Exceptional Men*. Emmaus, PA: Rodale.

Dush, Claire M. Kamp, Jill E. Yavorsky, and Sarah J. Schoppe-Sullivan. 2018. "What Are Men Doing while Women Perform Extra Unpaid Labor? Leisure and Specialization at the Transition to Parenthood." *Sex Roles* 78(11–12): 715–730.

Dutta-Gupta, Indivar, Kali Grant, Matthew Eckel, and Peter Edelman. 2016. *Lessons Learned from 40 Years of Subsidized Employment Programs*. Georgetown Center on Poverty and Inequality. Washington, DC: Georgetown University Law Center.

Dwyer, Sonya Corbin, and Jennifer L. Buckle. 2009. "The Space Between: On Being an Insider-Outsider in Qualitative Research." *International Journal of Qualitative Methods* 8(1): 54–63.

Edin, Kathryn, and Maria Kefalas. 2005. *Promises I Can Keep: Why Poor Women Put Motherhood before Marriage*. Berkeley, CA: University of California Press.

Edin, Kathryn, and Laura Lein. 1997. *Making Ends Meet: How Single Mothers Survive Welfare and Low-Wage Work*. New York, NY: Russell Sage.

Edin, Kathryn, and Timothy J. Nelson. 2013. *Doing the Best I Can: Fatherhood in the Inner City*. Berkeley, CA: University of California Press.

Edin, Kathryn, Timothy J. Nelson, Rachel Butler, and Robert Francis. 2019. "Taking Care of Mine: Can Child Support Become a Family-Building Institution?" *Journal of Family Theory & Review* 11(1): 79–91.

Edin, Kathryn, Timothy Nelson, and Joanna Reed. 2011. "Daddy, Baby; Momma Maybe: Low Income Urban Fathers and the 'Package Deal' of Family Life." In *Social Class and Changing Families in an Unequal America*, edited by Paula England and Marcia Carlson, 85–107. Palo Alto, CA: Stanford University Press.

Eggebeen, David J. 2013. "Do Fathers Uniquely Matter for Adolescent Well-Being?" In *Gender and Parenthood: Biological and Social Scientific Perspectives*, edited by W. Bradford Wilcox and Kathleen Kovner Kline, 249–270. New York, NY: Columbia University Press.

Eichler, Margrit. 1997. *Family Shifts: Families, Policies, and Gender Equality*. New York, NY: Oxford University Press.

Elliott, Sinikka, Joslyn Brenton, and Rachel Powell. 2018. "Brothermothering: Gender, Power, and the Parenting Strategies of Low-Income Black Single Mothers of Teenagers." *Social Problems* 65(4): 439–455.

Fagan, Jay, and Marina Barnett. 2003. "The Relationship between Maternal Gatekeeping, Paternal Competence, Mothers' Attitudes about the Father Role, and Father Involvement." *Journal of Family Issues* 24(8): 1020–1043.

Fagan, Jay, Randal Day, Michael E. Lamb, and Natasha J. Cabrera. 2014. "Should Researchers Conceptualize Differently the Dimensions of Parenting for Fathers and Mothers?" *Journal of Family Theory & Review* 6(4): 390–405.

Fagan, Jay, and Rebecca Kaufman. 2015. "Co-Parenting Relationships among Low-Income, Unmarried Parents: Perspectives of Fathers in Fatherhood Programs." *Family Court Review* 53(2): 304–316.

Fields, Tiffany. 1978. "Interaction Behaviors of Primary Versus Secondary Caretaker Fathers." *Developmental Psychology* 14(2): 183–184.

Fineman, Martha Albertson. 1995. *The Neutered Mother, the Sexual Family, and Other Twentieth Century Tragedies*. New York, NY: Routledge.

Floyd, Kory, and Mark T. Morman. 2000. "Affection Received from Fathers as a Predictor of Men's Affection with Their Own Sons: Tests of the Modeling and Compensation Hypotheses." *Communication Monographs* 67(4): 347–361.

Forste, Renata, John P. Bartkowski, and Rebecca Allen Jackson. 2009. "'Just Be There for Them': Perceptions of Fathering Among Single, Low-Income Men." *Fathering* 7(1): 49–69.

Fox, Greer L., and Carol Bruce. 2001. "Conditional Fatherhood: Identity Theory and Parental Investment Theory as Alternative Sources of Explanation of Fathering." *Journal of Marriage and Family* 63(2): 394–403.

Fraser, Nancy. 1994. "After the Family Wage: Gender Equity and the Welfare State." *Political Theory* 22(4): 591–618.

Freud, Sigmund. (1905) 2011. *Three Essays on the Theory of Sexuality*. Eastford, CT: Martino.

Friend, Daniel, Jeffrey Max, Pamela Holcomb, Kathryn Edin, and Robin Dion. 2016. *Fathers' Views of Co-Parenting Relationships: Findings from the PACT Evaluation*. OPRE Report Number 2016-60. Washington, DC: Office of Planning, Research and Evaluation, Administration for Children and Families, U.S. Department of Health and Human Services.

Gallagher, Maggie. 1998. "Father Hunger." In *Lost Fathers: The Politics of Fatherlessness in America*, edited by Cynthia R. Daniels, 163–182. New York, NY: St. Martin's Press.

Garfinkel, Irwin, Daniel R. Meyer, and Sara S. McLanahan. 1998. "A Brief History of Child Support Policies in the United States." In *Fathers under Fire:*

The Revolution in Child Support Enforcement, edited by Irwin Garfinkel, Sara S. McLanahan, Daniel R. Meyer, and Judith A. Seltzer, 14–30. New York, NY: Russell Sage.

Gates, Gary J. 2015. "Marriage and Family: LGBT Individuals and Same-Sex Couples." *The Future of Children* 25(2): 67–87.

Gavanas, Anna. 2004. *Fatherhood Politics in the United States: Masculinity, Sexuality, Race, and Marriage*. Urbana, IL: Illinois University Press.

Gerson, Kathleen. 1993. *No Man's Land: Men's Changing Commitments to Family and Work*. New York, NY: Basic Books.

———. 1997. "An Institutional Perspective on Generative Fathering: Creating Social Supports for Parenting Equality." In *Generative Fathering: Beyond Deficit Perspectives*, edited by Alan J. Hawkins and David C. Dollahite, 36–51. Newbury Park, CA: Sage.

Gerstel, Naomi. 2011. "Rethinking Families and Community: The Color, Class, and Centrality of Extended Kin Ties." *Sociological Forum* 26(1): 1–19.

Gibson-Davis, Christina. 2008. "Family Structure Effects on Maternal and Paternal Parenting in Low-Income Families." *Journal of Marriage and Family* 70(2): 452–465.

Gillis, John. 1996. *A World of Their Own Making: Myth, Ritual, and the Quest for Family Values*. Cambridge, MA: Harvard University Press.

Glaze, Lauren, and Laura Maruschak. 2010. "Parents in Prison and Their Minor Children." Washington, DC: Bureau of Justice Statistics. Available at: https://www.bjs.gov/content/pub/pdf/pptmc.pdf.

Goldberg, Abbie E., and Katherine R. Allen. 2007. "Imagining Men: Lesbian Mothers' Perceptions of Male Involvement during the Transition to Parenthood." *Journal of Marriage and Family* 69(2): 352–365.

Goldberg, Abbie E., Nannette K. Gartrell, and Gary Gates. 2014. *Research Report on LBG-Parent Families*. Los Angeles, CA: The Williams Institute, UCLA School of Law. Available at: https://williamsinstitute.law.ucla.edu /research/parenting/lgb-parent-families-jul-2014/.

Goldberg, Julia S. 2015. "Coparenting and Nonresident Fathers' Monetary Contributions to Their Children." *Journal of Marriage and Family* 77(3): 612–627.

Golombok, Susan. 2000. *Parenting: What Really Counts?* London, UK: Routledge.

Gramsci, Antonio. 1971. *Selections from the Prison Notebooks of Antonio Gramsci*. New York, NY: International Publishers.

Griswold, Robert L. 1993. *Fatherhood in America: A History*. New York, NY: Basic Books.

Grosz, Elizabeth. 1994. *Volatile Bodies: Towards a Corporeal Feminism*. Indianapolis, IN: Indiana University Press.

Halpern-Meekin, Sarah, Kathryn Edin, Laura Tach, and Jennifer Sykes. 2015. *It's Not Like I'm Poor: How Working Families Make Ends Meet in a Post-Welfare World*. Oakland, CA: University of California Press.

Hamer, Jennifer. 2001. *What It Means to Be Daddy: Fatherhood for Black Men Living Away from Their Children*. New York, NY: Columbia University Press.

Haney, Lynne. 2018. "Incarcerated Fatherhood: The Entanglements of Child Support Debt and Mass Imprisonment." *American Journal of Sociology* 124(1): 1–48.

Harding, Sandra. 1991. *Whose Science? Whose Knowledge? Thinking from Women's Lives*. Ithaca, NY: Cornell University Press.

Harris, Kirk E. 2018. "Low-Income Black Fathers Want to Be Good Dads, the System Won't Let Them." *The Guardian*, June 17, 2018.

Harris, Kirk E., and David Metler. 2014. "Transforming Responsible Fatherhood Practice and Policy: Bringing Scalability, Sustainability, and Measurability to Father Involvement and Family Strengthening." *Children's Voices* 23(1). Available at: https://www.cwla.org/responsible-fatherhood/.

Hartsock, Nancy C. M. 2006. "Experience, Embodiment, and Epistemology." *Hypatia* 21(2): 178–183.

Hawkins, Alan J., and David C. Dollahite (eds.) 1997. *Generative Fathering: Beyond Deficit Perspectives* Thousand Oaks, CA: Sage.

Hawkins, Alan J., and Rob Palkovitz. 1999. "Beyond Ticks and Clicks: The Need for More Diverse and Broader Conceptualizations and Measures of Father Involvement." *Journal of Men's Studies* 8(1): 11–32.

Hays, Sharon. 2003. *Flat Broke with Children: Women in the Age of Welfare Reform*. New York, NY: Oxford University Press.

Hearn, Jeff. 1998. "Troubled Masculinities in Social Policy Discourses: Young Men." In *Men, Gender Division, and Welfare*, edited by Jennie Popay, Jeff Hearn, and Jeanette Edwards, 37–62. New York, NY: Routledge.

Heath, Melanie. 2012. *One Marriage under God: The Campaign to Promote Marriage in America*. New York, NY: New York University Press.

Helbig, Marcel. 2012. "Boys Do Not Benefit from Male Teachers in Their Reading and Mathematics Skills: Empirical Evidence from 21 European Union and OECD Countries." *British Journal of Sociology of Education* 33(5): 661–677.

Henley, Kari, and Kay Pasley. 2005. "Conditions Affecting the Association between Father Identity and Father Involvement." *Fathering* 3(1): 59–80.

Hohmann-Marriott, Bryndl. 2011. "Coparenting and Father Involvement in Married and Unmarried Coresident Couples." *Journal of Marriage and Family* 73(1): 296–309.

Holcomb, Pamela, Kathryn Edin, Jeffrey Max, Alford Young, Jr., Angela Valdovinos D'Angelo, Daniel Friend, Elizabeth Clary, and Waldo E.

Johnson Jr. 2015. *In Their Own Voices: The Hopes and Struggles of Responsible Fatherhood Program Participants in the Parents and Children Together Evaluation.* OPRE Report Number 2015-67. Washington, DC: Office of Planning, Research and Evaluation, Administration for Children and Families, U.S. Department of Health and Human Services.

Holcomb, Pamela, Heather Zaveri, Daniel Friend, Robin Dion, Scott Baumgartner, Liz Clary, Angela Valdovinos D'Angelo, and Sarah Avellar. 2019. *Supporting the Fatherhood Journey: Findings from the Parents and Children Together Evaluation (PACT).* OPRE Report Number 2019-50. Washington, DC: Office of Planning, Research and Evaluation, Administration for Children and Families, U.S. Department of Health and Human Services.

Holmes, Erin K., Alan J. Hawkins, Braquel M. Egginton, Nathan Robbins, and Kevin Shafer. 2018. "Final Evaluation Report: Do Responsible Fatherhood Programs Work?" Fatherhood Research & Practice Network. Available at: https://www. frpn.org/asset/frpn-grantee-report-do-responsible-fatherhood -programs-work-comprehensive-meta-analytic-study.pdf.

Hondagneu-Sotelo, Pierrette, and Michael A. Messner. 1994. "Gender Displays and Men's Power: The 'New Man' and the Mexican Immigrant Man." In *Theorizing Masculinities*, edited by Harry Brod and Michael Kaufman, 200–218. Thousand Oaks, CA: Sage.

Hughes, Everett Cherrington. 1945. "Dilemmas and Contradictions of Status." *American Journal of Sociology* 50(5): 353–359.

Jarret, Robin L., Kevin M. Roy, and Linda M. Burton 2002. "Fathers in the 'Hood': Insights from Qualitative Research on Low-Income African-American Men." In *Handbook of Father Involvement: Multidisciplinary Perspectives*, edited by Catherine S. Tamis-LeMonda and Natasha Cabrera, 211–248. Mahwah, NJ: Elrbaum.

Jeynes, William H. 2015. "A Meta-Analysis: The Relationship between Father Involvement and Student Academic Achievement." *Urban Education* 50(4): 387–423.

Johnson, Maria S. 2013. "Black Women's Negotiation of Racialized Gender Ideals and the Role of Daughter-Father Relationships." *Gender & Society* 27(6): 889–912.

Johnson, Maria S., and Alford A. Young, Jr. 2019. "Diversity and Meaning in the Study of Black Fatherhood." In *Shifting the Center: Understanding Contemporary Families*, 5th edition, edited by Susan J. Ferguson, 291–307. Thousand Oaks, CA: Sage.

Jones, Jo, and William D. Mosher. 2013. "Fathers' Involvement with Their Children: United States: 2006–2010." *National Health Statistics Reports, No. 71.* Hyattsville, MD: National Center for Health Statistics.

Kane, Emily W. 2012. *The Gender Trap: Parents and the Pitfalls of Raising Boys and Girls*. New York, NY: New York University Press.

Kane, Jennifer B., Timothy J. Nelson, and Kathryn Edin. 2015. "How Much In-Kind Support Do Low-Income Nonresident Fathers Provide? A Mixed-Method Analysis." *Journal of Marriage and Family* 77(3): 591–611.

Kim, Allen, and Karen Pyke. 2015. "Taming Tiger Dads: Hegemonic American Masculinity and South Korea's Father School." *Gender & Society* 29(4): 509–533.

Kimmel, Michael. 1994. "Masculinity as Homophobia: Fear, Shame, and Silence in the Construction of Gender Identity." In *Theorizing Masculinities*, edited by Harry Brod and Michael Kauffman, 119–141. Thousand Oaks, CA: Sage.

———. 1996. *Manhood in America: A Cultural History*. New York, NY: Free Press.

King, Valarie, Kathleen Mullan Harris, and Holly E. Heard. 2004. "Racial and Ethnic Diversity in Nonresident Father Involvement." *Journal of Marriage and Family* 66(1): 1–21.

King, Valarie, and Juliana M. Sobolewski. 2006. "Nonresident Fathers' Contributions to Adolescent Well-Being." *Journal of Marriage and Family* 68(3): 537–557.

Knox, Virginia, Philip A. Cowan, Carolyn Pape Cowan, and Elana Bildner. 2011. "Policies That Strengthen Fatherhood and Family Relationships: What Do We Know and What Do We Need to Know?" *Annals of the American Academy of Political and Social Science* 635(1): 216–239.

Lamb, Michael E. 2000. "The History of Research on Father Involvement: An Overview." *Marriage and Family Review* 29(2–3): 23–42.

———. 2010. "How Do Fathers Influence Children's Development? Let Me Count the Ways." In *The Role of the Father in Child Development*, 5th edition, edited by Michael E. Lamb, 1–26. Hoboken, NJ: Wiley.

———. 2013. "The Changing Faces of Fatherhood and Father-Child Relationships: From Fatherhood as Status to Father as Dad." In *Handbook of Family Theories: A Content-Based Approach*, edited by Mark Fine and Frank Fincham, 87–102. New York, NY: Routledge.

Lamb, Michael E., Joseph H. Pleck, Eric L. Charnov, and James A. Levine. 1985. "Paternal Behavior in Humans." *American Zoologist* 25(3): 883–894.

Lamont, Michèle. 2000. *The Dignity of Working Men: Morality and the Boundaries of Race, Class, and Immigration*. New York, NY: Russell Sage.

Lane, Carrie M. 2011. *A Company of One: Insecurity, Independence, and the New World of White-Collar Unemployment*. Ithaca, NY: Cornell University Press.

LaRossa, Ralph. 1997. *The Modernization of Fatherhood: A Social and Political History*. Chicago, IL: University of Chicago Press.

Lazar, Michelle. 2005. "Performing State Fatherhood: The Remaking of Hegemony." In *Feminist Critical Discourse Analysis: Gender, Power, and Ideology in Discourse*, edited by Michelle Lazar, 139–163. New York, NY: Palgrave Macmillan.

Leap, Jorja. 2015. *Project Fatherhood: A Story of Courage and Healing in One of America's Toughest Communities*. Boston, MA: Beacon Press.

Levine, James A., and Edward W. Pitt. 1995. *New Expectations: Community Strategies for Responsible Fatherhood*. New York, NY: Families and Work Institute.

Lewin-Bizan, Selva. 2015. *24/7 Dad Program in Hawai'i: Sample, Design, and Preliminary Results*. Center on the Family, University of Hawai'i at Mānoa. Available at: https://cdn2.hubspot.net/hubfs/135704/Program%20Assets/24 -7%20Dad/247-Dad-Evaluation-Lewin-Bizan-06102015.pdf.

Lin, I-Fen, and Sara S. McLanahan. 2007. "Parental Beliefs about Nonresident Fathers' Obligations and Rights." *Journal of Marriage and Family* 69(2): 382–398.

Lupton, Deborah, and Lesley Barclay. 1997. *Constructing Fatherhood: Discourses and Experiences*. Newbury Park, CA: Sage.

Manning, Wendy, Susan Stewart, and Pamela Smock. 2003. "The Complexity of Fathers' Parenting Responsibilities and Involvement with Nonresident Children." *Journal of Family Issues* 24(5): 645–667.

Marsiglio, William, and Kevin Roy. 2012. *Nurturing Dads: Social Initiatives for Contemporary Fatherhood*. New York, NY: Russell Sage.

Marsiglio, William, Kevin Roy, and Greer L. Fox (eds.) 2005. *Situated Fathering: A Focus on Physical and Social Spaces*. Lanham, MD: Rowman & Littlefield.

Martinson, Karin, and Demetra Smith Nightingale. 2008. *Ten Key Findings from Responsible Fatherhood Initiatives*. Washington, DC: Urban Institute.

Martinson, Karin, John Trutko, Demetra S. Nightingale, Pamela Holcomb, and Burt Barnow. 2007. *The Implementation of the Partners for Fragile Families Demonstration Projects*. Washington, DC: Urban Institute Press.

Masciadrelli, Brian P., Joseph H. Pleck, and Jeffrey L. Stueve. 2006. "Fathers' Role Model Perceptions." *Men and Masculinities* 9(1): 23–34.

Maylor, Uvanney. 2009. "'They Do Not Relate to Black People Like Us': Black Teachers as Role Models for Black Pupils." *Journal of Education Policy* 24(1): 1–21.

Mazzei, Julie, and Erin E. O'Brien. 2009. "'You Got It, So When Do You Flaunt It?' Building Rapport, Intersectionality, and the Strategic Deployment of Gender in the Field." *Journal of Contemporary Ethnography* 38(3): 358–383.

McBride, Brent A., Geoffrey L. Brown, Kelly K. Bost, Nana Shin, Brian Vaughn, and Byran Korth. 2005. "Paternal Identity, Maternal Gatekeeping, and Father Involvement." *Family Relations* 54(3): 360–372.

McClain, Lauren Rinelli. 2011. "Better Parents, More Stable Partners: Union Transitions among Cohabiting Parents." *Journal of Marriage and Family* 73(5): 889–901.

McHale, James, Maureen R. Waller, and Jessica Pearson. 2012. "Coparenting Interventions for Fragile Families: What Do We Know and Where Do We Need to Go Next?" *Family Process* 51(3): 284–306.

McLanahan, Sara, and Audrey N. Beck. 2010. "Parental Relationships in Fragile Families." *The Future of Children* 20(2): 17–37.

McLanahan, Sara, Laura Tach, and Daniel Schneider. 2013. "The Causal Effects of Father Absence." *Annual Review of Sociology* 39: 399–427.

Mead, Lawrence. 1986. *Beyond Entitlement: The Social Obligations of Citizenship.* New York, NY: Free Press.

———. 1997. *The New Paternalism: Supervisory Approaches to Poverty.* Washington, DC: Brookings Institute.

Menning, Chadwick L. 2006. "Nonresident Fathering and School Failure." *Journal of Family Issues* 27(10): 1356–1382.

Messerschmidt, James. 2010. *Hegemonic Masculinities and Camouflaged Politics.* Boulder, CO: Paradigm Publishers.

———. 2016. *Masculinities in the Making: From the Local to the Global.* Lanham, MD: Rowman & Littlefield.

Messner, Michael. 1993. "'Changing Men' and Feminist Politics in the United States." *Theory and Society* 22(5): 723–737.

———. 2000. *Politics of Masculinities: Men in Movements.* Walnut Creek, CA: AltaMira Press.

Miller, Cynthia, and Virginia W. Knox. 2001. *The Challenge of Helping Low-Income Fathers Support Their Children: Final Lessons from Parents' Fair Share.* New York, NY: MDRC.

Mincy, Ronald B., Monique Jethwani, and Serena Klempin. 2015. *Failing Our Fathers: Confronting the Crisis of Economically Vulnerable Nonresident Fathers.* New York, NY: Oxford University Press.

Mincy, Ronald B., and Hillard W. Pouncy. 2002. "The Responsible Fatherhood Field: Evolution and Goals." In *Handbook of Father Involvement: Multidisciplinary Perspectives*, edited by Catherine S. Tamis-LeMonda and Natasha Cabrera, 555–597. Mahwah, NJ: Erlbaum.

Mollborn, Stephanie, and Janet Jacobs. 2015. "'I'll Be There for You': Teen Parents' Coparenting Relationships. *Journal of Marriage and Family* 77(2): 373–387.

Morgen, Sandra, Joan Acker, and Jill Weigt. 2010. *Stretched Thin: Poor Families, Welfare Work, and Welfare Reform.* Ithaca, NY: Cornell University Press.

Moynihan, Daniel Patrick. (1965) 2003. "The Negro Family: The Case for National Action." In *Welfare: A Documentary History of the United States,* edited by Gwendolyn Mink and Rickie Solinger, 226–238. New York, NY: New York University Press.

Murray, Charles. 1984. *Losing Ground: American Social Welfare Policy, 1950–1980*. New York, NY: Basic Books.

Myers, Kristen, and Ilana Demantas. 2016. "Breadwinning and Bread-Losing: Exploring Opportunities to Rework Manhood." *Sociology Compass* 10: 1119–1130.

Nash, Meredith. 2012. *Making "Postmodern" Mothers: Pregnant Embodiment, Baby Bumps and Body Image*. New York, NY: Palgrave Macmillan.

National Fatherhood Initiative. 2019. *Responsible Fatherhood Toolkit: Resources from the Field*. Fathers Incorporated. Available at: https://www .fatherhood.gov/toolkit/ home.

Neiterman, Elena. 2012. "Doing Pregnancy: Pregnant Embodiment as Performance." *Women's Studies International Forum* 35: 372–383.

Nelson, Timothy J., Susan Clampet-Lundquist, and Kathryn Edin. 2002. "Sustaining Fragile Fatherhood: Father Involvement among Low-Income, Noncustodial African-American Fathers in Philadelphia." In *Handbook of Father Involvement: Multidisciplinary Perspectives*, edited by Catherine S. Tamis-LeMonda and Natasha Cabrera, 525–553. Mahwah, NJ: Erlbaum.

Nepomnyaschy, Lenna. 2007. "Child Support and Father-Child Contact: Testing the Reciprocal Pathways." *Demography* 44(1): 93–112.

Nepomnyaschy, Lenna, Katherine A. Magnunson, and Lawrence M. Berger. 2012. "Child Support and Young Children's Development." *Social Service Review* 86(1): 3-35.

Neugebauer, Martin, Marcel Helbig, and Andreas Landmann. 2010. "Unmasking the Myth of the Same-Sex Teacher Advantage." *European Sociological Review* 27(5): 669–689.

Newman, Katherine S. 1999. *No Shame in My Game: The Working Poor in the Inner-City*. New York, NY: Russell Sage.

Obama, Barack. 1995. *Dreams from My Father: A Story of Race and Inheritance*. New York, NY: Crown Publishers.

Obama White House Archives. 2012. *Promoting Responsible Fatherhood*. Available at: https://obamawhitehouse.archives.gov/sites/default/files/docs /fatherhood_report_6.13.12_final.pdf.

O'Connor, Julia S., Ann Shola Orloff, and Sheila Shaver. 1999. *States, Markets, Families: Gender, Liberalism and Social Policy in Australia, Canada, Great Britain and the United States*. Cambridge, UK: Cambridge University Press.

Oeur, Freeden. 2017. "The Respectable Brotherhood: Young Black Men in an All-Boys Charter High School." *Sociological Perspectives* 60(6): 1063–1081.

Office of Family Assistance. 2018a. Healthy Marriage and Responsible Fatherhood. Available at: https://www.acf.hhs.gov/ofa/programs/healthy-marriage.

———. 2018b. "TANF and MOE Spending and Transfers by Activity, FY 2016." Available at: https://www.acf.hhs.gov/sites/default/files/ofa/fy2016_tanf _and_moe_state_piechart_.pdf.

———. 2019. "Responsible Fatherhood: New Pathways for Fathers and Families Demonstration Grants." Available at: https://www.acf.hhs.gov/ofa/programs /healthy-marriage/responsible-fatherhood.

Office of Planning, Research and Evaluation. N.d. "Strengthening Families, Healthy Marriage & Responsible Fatherhood." https://www.acf.hhs.gov/opre /research/topic/overview/strengthening-families-healthy-marriage -responsible-fatherhood.

Orloff, Ann Shola, and Renee Monson. 2002. "Citizens, Workers or Fathers?: Men in the History of US Social Policy." In *Making Men into Fathers: Men, Masculinities and the Social Politics of Fatherhood*, edited by Barbara Hobson, 61–91. New York, NY: Cambridge University Press.

Osborne, Cynthia, Andrea Michelsen, and Kaeley Bobbitt. 2017. *Fatherhood EFFECT Evaluation Final Report: A Comprehensive Plan for Supporting Texas Fathers and Families*. Child & Family Research Partnership, University of Texas at Austin. Available at: https://childandfamilyresearch.utexas .edu/sites/default/ files/CFRPReport_R0140817_FatherhoodEFFECT.pdf.

Palkovitz, Rob. 2013. "Gendered Parenting's Implications for Children's Well-Being." In *Gender and Parenthood: Biological and Social Scientific Perspectives*, edited by W. Bradford Wilcox and Kathleen Kovner Kline, 215–248. New York, NY: Columbia University Press.

Palkovitz, Rob, Bahira Sherif Trask, and Kari Adamsons. 2014. "Essential Differences in the Meaning and Processes of Mothering and Fathering: Family Systems, Feminist and Qualitative Perspectives." *Journal of Family Theory & Review* 6(4): 406–420.

Paquette, Daniel. 2004. "Theorizing the Father-Child Relationship: Mechanisms and Developmental Outcomes." *Human Development* 47(4): 193–219.

Parke, Ross D. 1996. *Fatherhood*. Cambridge, MA: Harvard University Press.

———. 2013. "Gender Differences and Similarities in Parental Behavior." In *Gender and Parenthood: Biological and Social Scientific Perspectives*, edited by W. Bradford Wilcox and Kathleen Kovner Kline, 120–163. New York, NY: Columbia University Press.

Parsons, Talcott. 1954. *Essays in Sociological Theory*. New York, NY: Free Press.

Parsons, Talcott, and Robert Bales. 1953. *Family, Socialization, and Interaction Process*. London, UK: Routledge.

Pascoe, C. J., and Tristan Bridges. 2016. "Exploring Masculinities: History, Reproduction, Hegemony, and Dislocation." In *Exploring Masculinities: Identity, Inequality, Continuity, and Change*, edited by C. J. Pascoe and Tristan Bridges, 1–34. New York, NY: Oxford University Press.

Pasley, Kay, Raymond E. Petren, and Jessica N. Fish. 2014. "Use of Identity Theory to Inform Fathering Scholarship." *Journal of Family Theory & Review* 6(4): 298–318.

Patterson, Charlotte J. 2006. "Children of Lesbian and Gay Parents." *Current Directions in Psychological Sciences* 15(5): 241–244.

Pearson, Jessica. 2018. "State Approaches to Including Fathers in Programs and Policies Dealing with Children and Families." Fatherhood Research and Practice Network. Available at: https://www.frpn.org/asset/frpn-research -brief-state-approaches-including-fathers-in-programs-and-policies-dealing.

Pleck, Joseph H. 1987. "American Fathering in Historical Perspective." In *Changing Men: New Directions in Research on Men and Masculinity*, edited by Michael S. Kimmel, 83–97. Beverly Hills, CA: Sage.

———. 2010. "Fatherhood and Masculinity." In *The Role of the Father in Child Development*, 5th edition, edited by Michael E. Lamb, 27–57. Hoboken, NJ: Wiley.

Popenoe, David. 1996. *Life without Father: Compelling New Evidence That Fatherhood and Marriage Are Indispensable for the Good of Children and Society*. New York, NY: Free Press.

Pruett, Kyle D. 2000. *Fatherneed: Why Father Care Is as Essential as Mother Care for Your Child*. New York, NY: Broadway.

Pruett, Kyle D., and Marsha Kline Pruett. 2009. *Partnership Parenting: How Men and Women Parent Differently—Why It Helps Your Kids and Can Strengthen Your Marriage*. Cambridge, MA: Da Capo Press.

Pruett, Marsha Kline, Kyle D. Pruett, Carolyn Pape Cowan, and Philip A. Cowan. 2017. "Enhancing Father Involvement in Low-Income Families: A Couples Group Approach to Preventative Intervention." *Child Development* 88(2): 398–407.

Puhlman, Daniel J., and Kay Pasley. 2013. "Rethinking Maternal Gatekeeping." *Journal of Family Theory & Review* 5(3): 176–193.

Rainwater, Lee, and William L. Yancy. 1967. *The Moynihan Report and the Politics of Controversy*. Cambridge, MA: MIT Press.

Raley, Sara, Suzanne M. Bianchi, and Wendy Wang. 2012. "When Do Fathers Care? Mothers' Economic Contribution and Fathers' Involvement in Child Care." *American Journal of Sociology* 117(5): 1422–1459.

Randles, Jennifer M. 2013. "Repackaging the 'Package Deal': Promoting Marriage for Low-Income Families by Targeting Paternal Identity and Reframing Marital Masculinity." *Gender & Society* 27(6): 864–888.

———. 2017. *Proposing Prosperity: Marriage Education Policy and Inequality in America*. New York, NY: Columbia University Press.

Reich, Jennifer A. 2003. "Pregnant with Possibility: Reflections on Embodiment, Access, and Inclusion in Field Research." *Qualitative Sociology* 6(3): 351–367.

Risman, Barbara J. 1987. "Intimate Relationships from a Microstructural Perspective: Men Who Mother." *Gender and Society* 1(1): 6–32.

Roberts, Dorothy E. 1993. "Racism and Patriarchy in the Meaning of Mother-hood." *American University Journal of Gender, Social Policy & the Law* 1(1): 1–38.

———. 1999. "Welfare's Ban on Poor Motherhood." In *Whose Welfare?*, edited by Gwendolyn Mink, 152–167. Ithaca, NY: Cornell University Press.

Rohner, Ronald Preston, and Robert A. Veneziano. 2001. "The Importance of Father Love: History and Contemporary Evidence." *Review of General Psychology* 5(4): 382–405.

Roy, Kevin M. 2004. "You Can't Eat Love: Constructing Provider Role Expectations for Low-Income and Working-Class Fathers." *Fathering* 2(3): 253–276.

Roy, Kevin M., and Linda Burton. 2007. "Mothering through Recruitment: Kinscription of Nonresidential Fathers and Father Figures in Low-Income Families." *Family Relations* 56(1): 24–39.

Roy, Kevin M., and Omari Dyson. 2010. "Making Daddies into Fathers: Community-Based Fatherhood Programs and the Construction of Masculinities for Low-Income African American Men." *American Journal of Community Psychology* 45(1/2): 139–154.

Ryan, Rebecca M., Ariel Kalil, and Kathleen M. Ziol-Guest. 2008. "Longitudinal Patterns of Nonresident Fathers' Involvement: The Role of Resources and Relations." *Journal of Marriage and Family* 70(4): 962–977.

Salisbury, Jane. 1994. "Becoming Qualified: An Ethnography of a Post-Experience Teacher Training Course." PhD dissertation, University of Wales, Cardiff.

Sandelowski, Margarete. 2002. "Reembodying Qualitative Inquiry." *Qualitative Health Research* 12(1): 104–115.

Sarkisian, Natalia, and Naomi Gerstel. 2004. "Kin Support among Blacks and Whites: Race and Family Organization." *American Sociological Review* 69(6): 812–837.

Schoppe-Sullivan, Sarah J., Lauren E. Altenburger, Meghan A. Lee, Daniel J. Bower, and Claire M. Kamp Dush. 2015. "Who Are the Gatekeepers? Predictors of Maternal Gatekeeping." *Parenting: Science and Practice* 15(3): 166–186.

Schoppe-Sullivan, Sarah J., Geoffrey L. Brown, Elizabeth A. Cannon, Sarah C. Mangelsdorf, and Margaret Szewczyk Sokolowski. 2008. "Maternal Gate-keeping, Coparental Quality, and Fathering Behavior in Families with Infants." *Journal of Family Psychology* 22(3): 389–398.

Schrijvers, Joke. 1993. "Motherhood Experienced and Conceptualized: Changing Images in Sri Lanka and the Netherlands." In *Gendered Fields: Women, Men and Ethnography*, edited by Diane Bell, Pat Caplan, and Wazir Jahan Karim, 143–158. New York, NY: Routledge.

Schrock, Douglas, and Michael Schwalbe. 2009. "Men, Masculinity, and Manhood Acts." *Annual Review of Sociology* 35: 277–295.

Schroeder, Daniel, Kimberly Walker, and Amna Khan. 2011. "Non-Custodial Parent Choices PEER Pilot: Impact Report." University of Texas, Austin. Available at: https://repositories.lib.utexas.edu/bitstream/handle/2152 /20412/Non-Custodial %20Parent%20Choices%20PEER%20Pilot%20 Impact%20Report.pdf?sequence=3&isAllowed=y.

Schwalbe, Michael L., and Michelle Wolkomir. 2002. "Interviewing Men." In *Handbook of Interview Research: Context and Method*, edited by Jaber F. Gubrium and James A. Holstein, 203–219. Thousand Oaks, CA: Sage.

Sherman, Jennifer. 2009. "Bend to Avoid Breaking: Job Loss, Gender Norms, and Family Stability in Rural America." *Social Problems* 56(4): 599–620.

Silverstein, Louise B., and Carl F. Auerbach. 1999. "Deconstructing the Essential Father." *American Psychologist* 54(6): 397–407.

Sinkewicz, Marilyn, and Irwin Garfinkel. 2009. "Unwed Fathers' Ability to Pay Child Support: New Estimates Accounting for Multiple-Partner Fertility." *Demography* 46(2): 247–263.

Small, Mario Luis, David J. Harding, and Michèle Lamont. 2010. "Reconsidering Culture and Poverty." *Annals of the American Academy of Political and Social Science* 629(1): 6–27.

Smeeding, Timothy M., Irwin Garfinkel, and Ronald B. Mincy. 2011. "Young Disadvantaged Men: Fathers, Families, Poverty, and Policy." *Annals of the American Academy of Political and Social Science* 635(1): 6–21.

Smith, Dorothy E. 1991. *The Conceptual Practices of Power: A Feminist Sociology of Knowledge*. Boston, MA: Northeastern University Press.

Smock, Pamela, Wendy Manning, and Meredith Porter. 2005. "'Everything's There Except the Money': How Money Shapes Decisions to Marry among Cohabitors." *Journal of Marriage and Family* 67(3): 680–697.

Sobolewski, Juliana M., and Valarie King. 2005. "The Importance of the Coparental Relationship for Nonresident Fathers' Ties to Children." *Journal of Marriage and Family* 67(5): 1196–1212.

Soss, Joe, Richard C. Fording, and Sanford Schram. 2011. *Disciplining the Poor: Neoliberal Paternalism and the Persistent Power of Race*. Chicago, IL: University of Chicago Press.

Stacey, Judith, and Barrie Thorne. 1985. "The Missing Feminist Revolution in Sociology." *Social Problems* 32(4): 301–316.

Stack, Carol B., and Linda M. Burton. 1993. "Kinscripts." *Journal of Comparative Family Studies* 24(2): 157–170.

Stryker, Sheldon, and Richard T. Serpe. 1994. "Identity Salience and Psychological Centrality: Equivalent, Overlapping, or Complementary Concepts?" *Social Psychological Quarterly* 57(1): 16–35.

Sum, Andrew, Ishwar Khatiwada, Joseph McLaughlin, and Sheila Palma. 2011. "No Country for Young Men: Deteriorating Labor Market Prospects for Low-Skilled Men in the United States." *Annals of the American Academy of Political and Social Science* 635(1): 24–55.

Summers, Jean Ann, Kimberly Boller, Rachel F. Schiffman, and Helen J. Raiskes. 2006. "The Meaning of 'Good Fatherhood': Low-Income Fathers' Social Constructions of Their Roles." *Parenting: Science and Practice* 6(2–3): 145–165.

Swidler, Ann. 1986. "Culture in Action: Symbols and Strategies." *American Sociological Review* 51(2): 273–286.

Tach, Laura, and Kathryn Edin. 2011. "The Relationship Contexts of Young Disadvantaged Men." *Annals of the American Academy of Political and Social Science* 635(1): 76–94.

——. 2017. "The Social Safety Net after Welfare Reform: Recent Developments and Consequences for Household Dynamics." *Annual Review of Sociology* 43(4): 541–561.

Tach, Laura, Kathryn Edin, Hope Harvey, and Brielle Bryan. 2014. "The Family-Go-Round: Family Complexity and Father Involvement from a Father's Perspective." *Annals of the American Academy of Political and Social Science* 654(1): 169–184.

Tach, Laura, Ronald Mincy, and Kathryn Edin. 2010. "Parenting as a 'Package Deal': Relationships, Fertility, and Nonresident Father Involvement among Unmarried Parents." *Demography* 47(1): 181–204.

Thiede, Brian C., Hyojung Kim, and Tim Slack. 2017. "Marriage, Work, and Racial Inequalities in Poverty: Evidence from the United States." *Journal of Marriage and Family* 79(5): 1241–1257.

Townsend, Nicholas W. 2002. *The Package Deal: Marriage, Work and Fatherhood in Men's Lives*. Philadelphia, PA: Temple University Press.

Trinder, Liz. 2008. "Maternal Gate Closing and Gate Opening in Postdivorce Families." *Journal of Family Issues* 29(10): 1298–1324.

Turner, Kimberly J., and Maureen R. Waller. 2017. "Indebted Relationships: Child Support Arrears and Nonresident Fathers' Involvement with Children." *Journal of Marriage and Family* 79(1): 24–43.

Turney, Kristin, and Daniel Schneider. 2016. "Incarceration and Household Asset Ownership." *Demography* 53(6): 2075–2103.

U.S. Congress. 1996. The Personal Responsibility and Work Opportunity Reconciliation Act (Public Law 104-193). Washington, DC: Government Printing Office. Available at: https://www.congress.gov/104/plaws/publ193/PLAW-104publ193.pdf.

Valdovinos D'Angelo, Angela, Emily Knas, Pamela Holcomb, and Kathryn Edin. 2016. *The Role of Social Networks among Low-Income Fathers:*

Findings from the PACT Evaluation. OPRE Report #2016-60. Washington, DC: Office of Planning, Research and Evaluation, Administration for Children and Families, U.S. Department of Health and Human Services.

Vogtman, Julie. 2017. "Undervalued: A Brief History of Women's Carework and Child Care Policy in the United States." National Women's Law Center. Available at: https://nwlc.org/wp-content/uploads/2017/12/final_nwlc _Undervalued2017.pdf.

Wainright, Jennifer L., Stephen T. Russell, and Charlotte J. Patterson. 2004. "Psychosocial Adjustment, School Outcomes, and Romantic Relationships of Adolescents with Same-Sex Parents." *Child Development* 75(6): 1886–1898.

Walby, Sylvia. 1991. *Theorizing Patriarchy*. New York, NY: Wiley-Blackwell.

Wall, Glenda, and Stephanie Arnold. 2007. "How Involved Is Involved Fathering? An Exploration of the Contemporary Culture of Fatherhood." *Gender & Society* 21(4): 508–527.

Waller, Maureen R. 2002. *My Baby's Father: Unmarried Parents and Paternal Responsibility*. Ithaca, NY: Cornell University Press.

———. 2010. "Viewing Low-Income Fathers' Ties to Families through a Cultural Lens: Insights for Research and Policy." *Annals of the American Academy of Political and Social Science* 629(1): 102–124.

Waller, Maureen R., and Allison Dwyer Emory. 2018. "Visitation Orders, Family Courts, and Fragile Families." *Journal of Marriage and Family* 80(3): 653–670.

Warren, Carol A. B., and Tracy Xavia Karner. 2015. *Discovering Qualitative Methods: Ethnography, Interviews, Documents, and Images*, New York, NY: Oxford University Press.

West, Candace, and Don H. Zimmerman. 1987. "Doing Gender." *Gender & Society* 1(2): 125–151.

Western, Bruce. 2018. *Homeward: Life in the Year after Prison*. New York, NY: Russell Sage.

Whitehead, Stephen M. 2002. *Men and Masculinities*. Malden, MA: Polity.

Williams, Fiona. 1998. "Troubled Masculinities in Social Policy Discourses: Fatherhood." In *Men, Gender Division, and Welfare*, edited by Jennie Popay, Jeff Hearn, and Jeanette Edwards, 63–97. New York, NY: Routledge.

Young, Alford A., Jr. 2004. *The Minds of Marginalized Black Men: Making Sense of Mobility, Opportunity, and Future Life Chances*. Princeton, NJ: Princeton University Press.

Young, Iris Marion. 2014. *On Female Body Experience: "Throwing Like a Girl" and Other Essays*. New York, NY: Oxford University Press.

Index

Founded in 1893,
UNIVERSITY OF CALIFORNIA PRESS
publishes bold, progressive books and journals
on topics in the arts, humanities, social sciences,
and natural sciences—with a focus on social
justice issues—that inspire thought and action
among readers worldwide.

The UC PRESS FOUNDATION
raises funds to uphold the press's vital role
as an independent, nonprofit publisher, and
receives philanthropic support from a wide
range of individuals and institutions—and from
committed readers like you. To learn more, visit
ucpress.edu/supportus.